Adobe
Muse CC
Second Edition

W9-BON-783

CLASSROOM IN A BOOK®
The official training workbook from Adobe

Brian Wood

Adobe® Muse™ CC Classroom in a Book®, Second Edition

Brian Wood

Adobe Press books are published by Peachpit. Peachpit is a registered trademark owned by Pearson Education, Inc. or its affiliates in the United States and/or other countries. For the latest on Adobe Press books, go to www.adobepress.com. To report errors, please send a note to errata@peachpit.com. For information on getting permission for reprints and excerpts, contact permissions@peachpit.com.

ISBN-13: 978-0-13-454727-5

ISBN-10: 0-13-454727-6

WHERE ARE THE LESSON FILES?

Purchase of this Classroom in a Book in any format gives you access to the lesson files you'll need to complete the exercises in the book.

You'll find the files you need on your **Account** page at peachpit.com on the **Registered Products** tab.

1 Go to www.peachpit.com/register.

2 Sign in or create a new account.

3 Enter the ISBN: 9780134547275.

4 Answer the questions as proof of purchase.

5 Access the lesson files through the Registered Products tab on your Account page.

6 Click the Access Bonus Content link below the title of your product to proceed to the download page. Click the lesson file links to download them to your computer.

CONTENTS

Contributor

 Brian Wood is a web developer and the author of twelve books and numerous training titles covering Adobe products such as Muse, Dreamweaver, InDesign, Illustrator, and more. In addition to training many clients, including Nordstrom, REI, Boeing, Starbucks, Nintendo, and many others, Brian speaks regularly at national conferences, such as Adobe MAX, HOW Design, and HOW Interactive, as well as events hosted by AIGA and other industry organizations. He has also written articles for SmashingMagazine.com, Peachpit.com, CreativePro.com, Adobe Inspire magazine, and more. Brian has a YouTube channel at youtube.com/askbrianwood.com and a corporate training site at BrianWoodTraining.com.

Production Notes

The *Adobe Muse CC Classroom in a Book* was created electronically using Adobe InDesign. Art was produced using Adobe Muse, Adobe Illustrator, and Adobe Photoshop. The Myriad Pro and Warnock Pro OpenType families of typefaces were used throughout this book.

References to company names in the lessons are for demonstration purposes only and are not intended to refer to any actual organization or person.

Images

Photographic images and illustrations are intended for use with the tutorials.

Typefaces used

Adobe Myriad Pro and Adobe Warnock Pro are used throughout the lessons. For more information about OpenType and Adobe fonts, visit www.adobe.com/products/type/opentype.html.

Team credits

The following individuals contributed to the development of this edition of the *Adobe Muse CC Classroom in a Book*:

Writer: Brian Wood
Senior Project Editor: Tracey Croom
Project Editor: Wyndham Wood
Production Editor/ Compositor: Brian Wood
Keystroking: Megan Ahearn
Keystroking: Caleb Lowery / Designer, Doodler, Rock Climber / www.lcandd.com
Keystroking: Michael D. Banks / @4MikeBanks / MichaelBanks.org
Proofreader: Wyndham Wood
Indexer: J&J Indexing
Cover Designer: Eddie Yuen
Cover Image: Anastasios Veloudis
Interior Designer: Mimi Heft

GETTING STARTED

If you are a graphic designer, business owner, or anyone who wants to design and create professional, original responsive websites without ever touching code, Adobe Muse CC is the program you've been waiting for.

With Muse, you can quickly and easily design and create user-friendly, interactive responsive websites without the help of a developer. You just design your site in Muse using design-savvy graphic tools that leverage the same skills as Adobe InDesign and Adobe Photoshop. Then, after creating your site in Muse, you can take your site live using Adobe hosting or export to a provider of your choice, publishing your site as original HTML pages that conform to the latest web standards.

Muse really is that easy and that powerful, and *Adobe Muse CC Classroom in a Book* will help you make the most of it.

About Classroom in a Book

Adobe Muse CC Classroom in a Book is part of the official training series for Adobe graphics and publishing software developed with the support of Adobe product experts. The lessons are designed so you can learn at your own pace. If you're new to Adobe Muse, you'll learn the fundamentals you need to master to put the application to work. If you are an experienced user, you'll find that Classroom in a Book teaches many advanced features, including tips and techniques for using the latest version of Adobe Muse.

Although each lesson provides step-by-step instructions for creating a specific project, there's room for exploration and experimentation. You can follow the book from start to finish, or do only the lessons that correspond to your interests and needs. Each lesson concludes with a review section summarizing what you've covered.

Mac OS vs. Windows

When instructions differ by platform, Mac OS commands appear first and then Windows commands. For example, you might see "press Option (Alt) and click away from the artwork."

Prerequisites

Before beginning to use *Adobe Muse CC Classroom in a Book*, you should have a working knowledge of your computer and its operating system. Make sure that you know how to use the mouse and standard menus and commands, and also how to open, save, and close files. If you need to review these techniques, see the printed or online documentation included with your Microsoft Windows or Mac OS software.

Installing Muse

Before you begin using *Adobe Muse CC Classroom in a Book*, make sure that your system is set up correctly and that you've installed the required software and hardware.

The Adobe Muse software is not included with *Adobe Muse CC Classroom in a Book*; you must purchase the software separately. You can purchase Muse as a single-app membership or with a Creative Cloud complete membership, which also includes Photoshop, InDesign, and more.

Web Edition

Your purchase of this book in any format includes access to the corresponding Web Edition hosted on peachpit.com. Your Web Edition can be accessed from any device with a connection to the Internet and it contains:

- The complete text of the book
- Hours of instructional video keyed to the text (plus bonus videos)
- Interactive quizzes

Accessing the free Web Edition

To access your free copy of *Adobe Muse CC Classroom in a Book* Web Edition:

- If you purchased an ebook from adobepress.com or peachpit.com, the Web Edition will automatically appear on the Digital Purchases tab on your Account page. Click Launch to access the Web Edition. Continue reading to learn how to register your product to get access to the lesson files.

1   Go to www.peachpit.com/register.

2   Sign in or create a new account.

3   Enter ISBN: **9780134547275**.

4   Answer the questions as proof of purchase.

5   The Web Edition will appear under the Digital Purchases tab on your Account page. Click Launch to access your product.

Lesson Files

To work through the exercises in this book, you will first need to download the lesson files from peachpit.com. You can download the files for individual lessons or download them all in a single file.

Accessing the Classroom in a Book lesson files

The lesson files can be accessed through the Registered Products tab on your Account page. Click the Access Bonus Content link below the title of your product to proceed to the download page. Click the lesson file links to download them to your computer. For step-by-step instructions on how to access the files, see the "Where are the Lesson Files" page at the beginning of the book.

Content Update Program

This book is part of the Adobe Press Content Update Program, which provides automatic content updates for major technology improvements.

• As Adobe makes significant updates to Muse CC, sections of this book will be updated or new sections will be added to match the updates to the software.

• The updates will be delivered to you via a free Web Edition of this book, which can be accessed with any Internet connection.

• This means your purchase is protected from immediately outdated information!

Restoring default program preferences

The preference files control how command settings appear on your screen when you open Adobe Muse. Each time you quit Adobe Muse, the position of the panels and certain command settings are recorded in different preference files. If you want to restore the tools and settings to their original default settings, you can delete the current Adobe Muse preference files. Adobe Muse creates new preference files, if they don't already exist, the next time you start the program and save a file.

Note: In certain versions of Mac OS, the Library folder will be hidden. You can show the Library folder by opening the Finder, selecting the Go menu, and holding down the Option key to reveal the Library folder menu item. Click the Library folder menu item to open the folder.

Tip: To quickly locate and delete the Adobe Muse CC preferences folder each time you begin a new lesson, create a shortcut (Windows) or an alias (Mac OS) to the Adobe Muse CC folder.

Note: If you cannot locate the preferences folder, use your operating system's Find command and try searching for "Adobe Muse CC."

To save current Muse preferences

If you want to restore the current preferences for Muse after completing the lessons, you can do so by following these steps.

1   Exit Adobe Muse.

2   Locate the Adobe Muse CC preferences folder as follows:

- (Windows) The Adobe Muse CC folder is located in the folder [*startup drive*]\Users\[*username*]\AppData\Roaming\Adobe\Adobe Muse CC.

- (Mac OS X) The Adobe Muse CC folder is located in the folder [*startup drive*]/Users/[*username*]/Library/Preferences/Adobe/Adobe Muse CC.

Keep in mind that your folder name may be different depending on the language version you have installed. If you can't find the file, you either haven't started Adobe Muse yet or you have moved the preferences folder. The preferences folder is created after you open Muse the first time and is updated thereafter.

3   Copy the folder, and save it to another folder on your hard drive.

4   Start Adobe Muse CC.

To delete current Muse preferences

If you are entering the lessons using Jumpstart, you should delete the current preference files for Muse by following these steps.

1   Exit Adobe Muse.

2   Locate the Adobe Muse CC folder as follows:

- (Windows) The Adobe Muse CC folder is located in the folder [*startup drive*]\Users\[*username*]\AppData\Roaming\Adobe\Adobe Muse CC.

- (Mac OS X) The Adobe Muse CC folder is located in the folder [*startup drive*]/Users/[*username*]/Library/Preferences/Adobe/Adobe Muse CC.

Remember that the folder name may be different depending on the language version you have installed.

3 Delete the preferences folder.

4 Start Adobe Muse CC.

To restore saved preferences

After completing the lessons you can restore your personalized preferences you saved in the "To save current Muse preferences" section, in two steps.

1 Exit Adobe Muse.

2 Find the original Adobe Muse CC preferences folder that you saved and replace the Adobe Muse CC folder found here:

- (Windows) The Adobe Muse CC folder is located in the folder [*startup drive*]\Users\[*username*]\AppData\Roaming\Adobe\Adobe Muse CC.

- (Mac OS X) The Adobe Muse CC folder is located in the folder [*startup drive*]/Users/[*username*]/Library/Preferences/Adobe/Adobe Muse CC.

Again, the folder name may be different depending on the language version you have installed.

Recommended lesson order

Adobe Muse CC Classroom in a Book is designed to take you from A to Z in basic to intermediate website design and creation. Each new lesson builds on previous exercises, using the files and assets you create to develop an entire website. To achieve the most complete understanding of all aspects of web design using Adobe Muse, the ideal training scenario is to start in Lesson 1 and perform each lesson in sequential order through the entire book to Lesson 11. Because each lesson builds essential files and content for the next, you shouldn't skip any lessons or even individual exercises. Although ideal, this method may not be a practicable scenario for everyone. In that case, refer to the "Jumpstart" section next.

Jumpstart

If you don't have the time or inclination to perform each lesson in the book in order, or if you're having difficulty with a particular lesson, you can work through individual lessons using the jumpstart method with the files supplied on your Account page at www.peachpit.com. Each lesson folder includes finished files and staged files (files that are completed to that point in the lessons).

To jumpstart a lesson, follow these steps.

1 Restore the default program preferences as explained in the "Restoring default program preferences" section in this Getting Started.

2 Ensure that the Lessons folder is on your hard drive by referring to the earlier section "Accessing the Classroom in a Book lesson files."

3 Open Adobe Muse CC.

● **Note:** When you open a jumpstart lesson file, if you see a dialog box indicating missing, modified, or upsampled files, click OK.

4 Choose File > Open Site. Navigate to the Lessons folder on your hard drive and then to the specific lesson folder you are starting from. For instance, if you are jumpstarting Lesson 7, navigate to the Lesson07 folder in the Lessons folder and open the file named L7_start.muse. All of the jumpstart lesson files include "_start.muse" in their names.

These simple steps will need to be repeated for each lesson you want to jumpstart. However, if you choose the jumpstart method once, you do not have to continue using it for all subsequent lessons. For example, if you want to jumpstart Lesson 6, you can simply continue on to Lesson 7, and so on.

Additional resources

Adobe Muse CC Classroom in a Book is not meant to replace documentation that comes with the program or to be a comprehensive reference for every feature. Only the commands and options used in the lessons are explained in this book. For comprehensive information about program features and tutorials refer to these resources:

Adobe Muse CC Help and Support: You can search and browse Muse Help and Support content from Adobe at helpx.adobe.com/muse.html.

Adobe Forums: forums.adobe.com lets you tap into peer-to-peer discussions, questions, and answers on Adobe products.

Adobe Creative Cloud Learn: helpx.adobe.com/creative-cloud/tutorials-explore. html provides inspiration, key techniques, cross-product workflows, and updates on new features.

Adobe TV: tv.adobe.com is an online video resource for Adobe products, providing expert instruction and inspiration, including a How To channel to get you started with your product.

Resources for educators: www.adobe.com/education and edex.adobe.com offer a treasure trove of information for instructors who teach classes on Adobe software. Find solutions for education at all levels, including free curricula that use an integrated approach to teaching Adobe software and can be used to prepare for the Adobe Certified Associate exams.

Adobe Muse CC product home page: www.adobe.com/products/muse.html

Adobe Authorized Training Centers

Adobe Authorized Training Centers (AATCs) offer instructor-led courses and training on Adobe products. A directory of AATCs is available at training.adobe.com/training/partner-finder.html.

1 AN INTRODUCTION TO ADOBE MUSE

Lesson overview

In this lesson, you'll familiarize yourself with the Adobe Muse program interface as well as:

- Understand what Adobe Muse is
- Understand responsive web design
- Understand and navigate the different modes
- Work in Plan mode
- Work in Design mode
- Work with the Muse workspace
- Zoom and pan
- Preview a site

 This lesson takes approximately 30 minutes to complete. Before beginning, make sure to download the project files for this lesson by logging in or setting up an account at peachpit.com. Enter the book's ISBN (9780134547275) or go directly to the book's product page to register. Once on the book's page, click the Register Your Product link. The book will show up in your list of registered products along with a link to the book's bonus content. Click the link to access the lesson files for the book. Store the files on your computer in a convenient location, as described in the "Getting Started" section of this book. Your Account page is also where you'll find any updates to the chapters or to the lesson files.

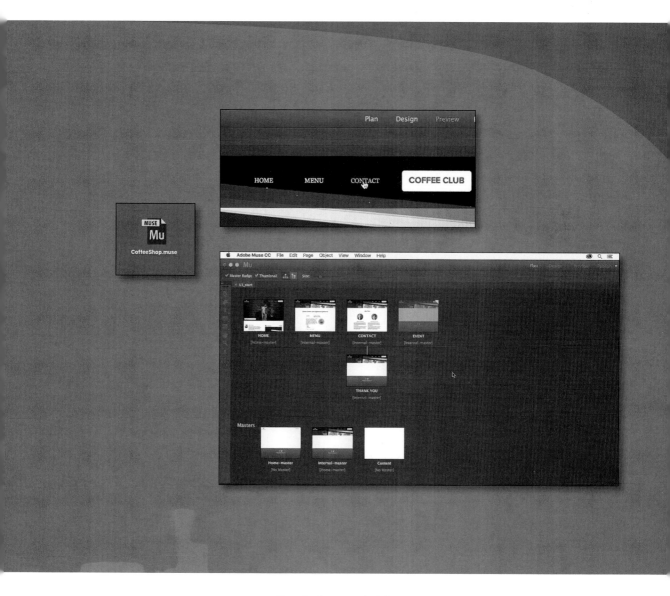

To make the most of Adobe Muse, you need to know
how to navigate the workspace. The workspace
consists of the Menu bar, Toolbar, Control panel,
Document window, default panels, and modes.

Introducing Adobe Muse

Adobe Muse CC is a perfect tool for designers who are looking to create websites of their own design that work and look great on any device. Using Adobe Muse, you can design and publish responsive HTML5 websites without writing code!

Over the course of this book, you'll walk through the process of creating a responsive website using Adobe Muse. Before you jump into building a website, however, you'll first explore the final site in your browser.

Tip: You can open the final site in Muse by choosing File > Open Site. Navigate to the Lessons folder, and open the CoffeeShop_final.muse file. You may see a warning for missing fonts or missing/modified images. You can dismiss these dialog boxes.

1   Open a browser on your desktop or device and type **http://musecoffeeshop.businesscatalyst.com/** to open the site you'll build.

    Explore the site by clicking links, scrolling through the pages, and more.

2   Close the browser and return to Adobe Muse.

    The site you just viewed was created in Adobe Muse and is a *responsive* website design, optimized for the best viewing experience on a wide range of device sizes.

Responsive Web Design in Muse

These days when you're hired to design a website, it goes without saying that the site design will need to be optimized for various screen (device) sizes.

Designing a website using responsive web design (RWD) means the layout changes based on the size, orientation, and even capabilities of the device you're using to view the site. Responsive web design takes the same content, like text, images, and video, and using web technologies such as CSS, HTML, and JavaScript, alters that layout so it works on any screen size. It allows you to provide an optimal viewing and interaction experience—easy reading and navigation with a minimum of resizing, panning, and scrolling—for your site across a wide range of devices.

In Adobe Muse, you can easily create a design that works across a range of device sizes *without* having to touch code. Here's an example of the responsive website you will create, as viewed on multiple device sizes.

In Lesson 6, you'll explore the responsive web design features in Muse and also learn about other methods for creating your site design.

An example Muse web workflow

Before you get started with your site in Muse, it's a good idea to understand a typical Muse workflow. In a web design workflow, you use Adobe Muse CC as a web page layout tool and a combination of Adobe Photoshop CC, Adobe Illustrator CC, and others for creating graphics. As with most creative programs, the Muse workflow is flexible and easily adapts to your work style.

Here's a typical Muse workflow from concept to published website:

1 Create a site concept.

At the outset of the creation process, you should gather information from those involved (like the client) including discussing the purpose of the site.

2 Create a Muse site file.

After creating a concept for your site, your first step within Muse is to create a new site file (File > New Site).

3 Plan your site (add and organize pages).

When you open your site file in Muse, you enter Plan mode, where you create a site map. Your *site map* shows the number of pages in your site, how the pages will be ordered, and how they connect to each other in the site navigation.

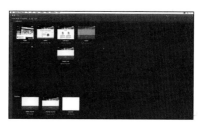

4 Wireframe your concept (*optional*).

With the site map created, some people choose to start by wireframing their web page layouts. A *wireframe* is a visual site outline. It shows the basic site structure, hierarchy of content, as well as the positioning of such basic elements as the header, footer, sidebar, navigation, and others—without specific formatting like fonts, colors, and styles. The benefit of starting with a wireframe is that it gives everyone involved (including the client) a simple way to envision the site layout and decide where content should be placed.

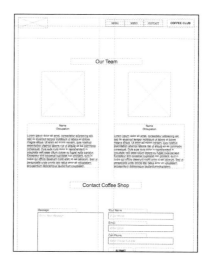

Note: The workflow steps are only a general guide and most likely won't be the same for every website you create. Your process may differ, depending on your needs.

Tip: For suggestions on the type of questions to ask clients in the initial stages of the website creation process, check out the PDF file named Client_questions.pdf in the Lessons > Lesson01 folder.

5 Design your pages.

After you plan your site, set up a site map, and, ideally also wireframe your pages, you can approach the page design in Muse. You can design directly in Muse, placing images in the following formats: .jpg, .gif, .png, .svg, .ai, or .psd, or start your design in Photoshop or Illustrator (or other); save the images in an acceptable format (.jpg, .gif, .png, .svg, .ai, or .psd); and then assemble the pieces in Muse.

If you're working with a responsive web design (called a "fluid width" layout in Muse), you will also check to ensure that your page designs work across a range of screen sizes.

6 Preview and test your pages.

As you design and add content to your pages, you can use Preview mode in Muse (and your default browser) to see how your site will look to visitors.

7 Publish your site.

The last step in the process is publishing your site. When your site is ready, you can share it with the world by hosting it using Adobe hosting, uploading the site content from within Muse to a host of your choice, or exporting your site as HTML and hosting it with a different hosting provider of your choice.

Web design vs. print design

If you're familiar with print design, you'll discover quickly in Muse that web design relies on many familiar print design concepts when it comes to text, graphics, color, and more. Soon thereafter, you'll also realize that web design offers its own set of challenges and design parameters that aren't as familiar, especially when it comes to responsive web design.

For instance, when you define colors in print, you typically choose from CMYK (Cyan, Magenta, Yellow, Black) or Pantone (spot) colors. When designing for the web, in Muse, you define colors using the colors RGB (Red, Green, Blue).

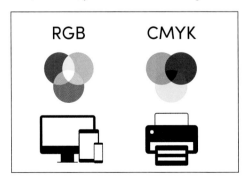

Touring the workspace

In the rest of this lesson, you'll learn the fundamentals of the Muse workspace by touring key features and becoming familiar with some commonly used tools.

The Muse workspace includes toolbars and panels that let you view, create, and edit Muse documents. You can also display multiple documents in a single window with tabs for each document. If you are familiar with the workspace in other Adobe applications, like InDesign or Illustrator, you may recognize a lot of commonality with Muse once you start designing your pages.

Understanding modes

When working on your site in Muse, there are three main modes you will be working in: Plan, Design, and Preview. When you select a mode, Muse displays it in the Application window. Each of these modes represents a stage in the website creation process, as explained in the previous section "An example Muse web workflow." As you design a website, you will most likely be switching back and forth between these modes. Next, you'll open an existing site and briefly explore the different modes.

Note: If you have not already downloaded the project files for this lesson to your computer from your Account page, make sure to do so now. See "Getting Started" at the beginning of the book.

Plan mode

The first mode you'll explore is called Plan mode because Plan mode is showing by default when a site is open in Muse.

1 Choose File > Open Site, and open the L1_start.muse file in the Lesson01 folder, which is located in the Lessons folder on your hard drive.

   The site you just opened is *similar* to the site you will create throughout the lessons in this book. In the upper-right corner of the Muse Application window, notice the links for the three main modes: Plan, Design, and Preview. You can tell you're in Plan mode because the word "Plan" is highlighted.

Note: You'll also explore Plan mode and its options further in Lesson 2, "Creating Your Site," when you create your own site file.

Note: You may see a warning for missing fonts or missing/ modified images. For now, you can dismiss these dialog boxes.

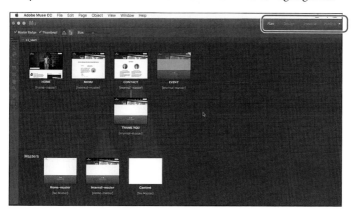

Plan mode is divided into two main sections: the site map area and the master page area (labeled "Masters"). The site map area contains thumbnail images of the current layout's pages organized into a hierarchy that shows how those pages connect to each other. Below each page thumbnail are the page name and, in brackets, the name of the master page associated with that page. The masters section, below the site map area, contains the default master page that every Muse site starts with. A master page can contain design elements that are shared across multiple pages of a site, like a header, footer, or Menu widget, and allows you to maintain consistency across the pages in your website.

You'll learn more about master pages in Lesson 3, "Working with Master Pages."

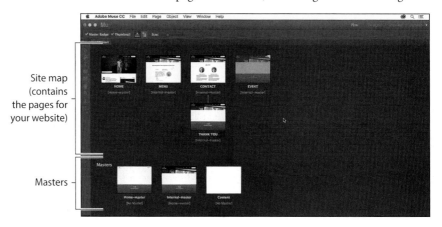

Design mode

▶ **Tip:** You can also enter Design mode by double-clicking a page thumbnail in Plan mode, by choosing View > Design Mode, or by pressing Command+I (Ctrl+I).

Design mode (also called Design view) is where you design the layout for each page of your site by adding text, images, slideshows, links, and much more.

1 In Plan mode, click the Design mode link in the upper-right corner of the Application window.

When you click the Design mode link, the first page of the website opens and appears in a separate tab at the top left of the Document window. In this case, the tab for the page shows HOME, which is the name of the page. The site also shows as a tab and is named L1_start, in this case.

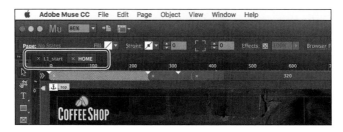

Notice that many more options, tools, and panels now appear as well. In Design mode, you'll see the Toolbar on the left (which is now active), Control panel on top, and panel groups that are docked on the right side of the Application window, similar to other Adobe applications, like InDesign CC. All of these features and more make up the Muse workspace. As with other Adobe applications, you can customize the workspace in Muse. You'll do that shortly. First, take a moment to familiarize yourself with the names of these workspace components in Design mode.

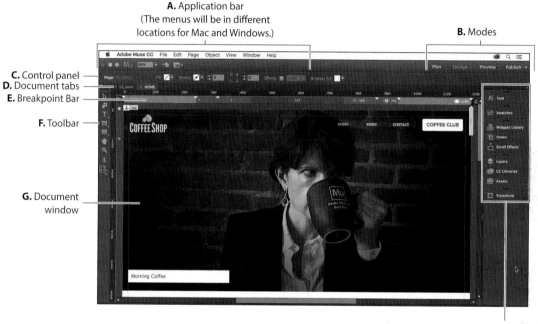

A. Application bar
(The menus will be in different locations for Mac and Windows.)

B. Modes

C. Control panel
D. Document tabs
E. Breakpoint Bar

F. Toolbar

G. Document window

H. Docked panels

A The **Application bar** across the top contains the mode switcher, menus, and other application controls.

B The **Modes** allow you to switch between different workspace layouts (modes) when working with Adobe Muse.

C The **Control panel** displays options for the currently selected object.

D **Document tabs:** Document windows can be tabbed and, multiple windows can be tiled for easy access.

E The **Breakpoint bar** displays all breakpoints for the current page and master page applied to that page.

F The **Toolbar** contains a series of tools such as shape tools and selection tools.

G The **Document window** displays the file you are working on.

H **Docked panels** are panels on the right side of the workspace, by default, that help you monitor and modify your work.

The Toolbar

Note: The Text tool has hidden tools, which are indicated by a little triangle off the lower-right corner of a tool icon. If you position the pointer over the Text tool, for instance, click and hold down, the available tools will appear in a submenu.

In Plan and Design modes, the Toolbar (Window > Toolbar) is docked on the left side of the application window and contains a series of tools. If you're familiar with other Adobe applications, like InDesign CC, you'll see some familiar tools. As you work through the lessons, you'll learn more about the functions of each tool.

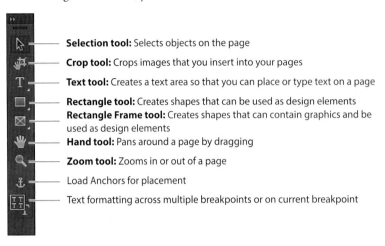

Selection tool: Selects objects on the page

Crop tool: Crops images that you insert into your pages

Text tool: Creates a text area so that you can place or type text on a page

Rectangle tool: Creates shapes that can be used as design elements
Rectangle Frame tool: Creates shapes that can contain graphics and be used as design elements
Hand tool: Pans around a page by dragging

Zoom tool: Zooms in or out of a page

Load Anchors for placement

Text formatting across multiple breakpoints or on current breakpoint

As in other Adobe applications, you can select a tool from the Toolbar by clicking it or pressing a keyboard shortcut. Let's do that now.

1   Hover over the Zoom tool (🔍) in the Toolbar. Notice that Muse displays the tool name and keyboard shortcut (Z, for the Zoom tool). Every tool in the Toolbar has a keyboard shortcut associated with it. Click to select the Zoom tool.

2   Press the V key to select the Selection tool (▶).

▶ **Tip:** The keyboard shortcuts in Muse, like those in InDesign CC and Photoshop CC, are spring-loaded tool shortcuts. This means that you can hold down a tool's shortcut key to switch to that tool temporarily. When you are finished using the tool, simply release the shortcut key to return to the previously selected tool. Spring-loaded tool shortcuts help you work faster, saving you time that adds up over the life of a project.

The Control panel

The Control panel offers quick access to options and commands related to the current page item or objects you select. By default, Muse displays the Control panel horizontally across the top of the Document window. You can open and close it by choosing Window > Control, if necessary. In the Window menu, a check mark to the left of the word Control indicates that the Control panel is open in the workspace.

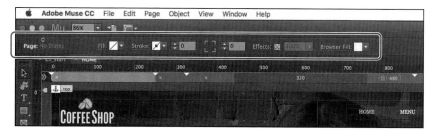

> **Tip:** You can drag the Control panel from the left end out into the workspace to make it a free-floating panel. To dock it again, drag it from the left end to just below the green Muse icon (the Mu) (or menu on Windows) towards the upper-left corner of the Application window.

Options displayed in the Control panel vary depending on the type of object you select. As you progress through each lesson, you'll also notice that most of the options displayed in the Control panel are also found within other panels in Muse.

When you first open a page, and nothing is selected, you see the word Page on the left end of the Control panel. This is called the *Selection Indicator* (see "Page" in the previous figure). When you select content on the page, the currently selected object is named here. For example, "Page" indicates that the options currently displayed in the Control panel will affect the large, white page box in the Document window (you'll learn more about the page area in a later lesson).

1   Choose View > Fit Page In Window so you can see the whole page.

2   With the Selection tool ( ) still selected, position the pointer over the "Coffee Shop News" text. You should see a tooltip with the words "Text Frame" appear next to the pointer, indicating that if you click, you'll select a text frame. Click to select the text frame.

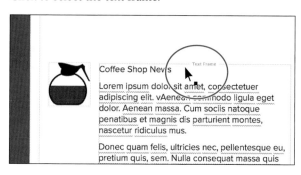

On the left end of the Control panel, you should now see the words "Text Frame" to indicate that you selected a text frame on the page. Notice also that the options in the Control panel have changed. Any changes you make in the Control panel will affect the selected object.

▶ **Tip:** You can get more information about each option in the Control panel by hovering over an icon or option label with the pointer to view its tooltip.

3 Choose Edit > Deselect All to deselect the text frame.

Throughout the lessons in this book, you'll be using the Control panel to format content on your pages and learn more about those options.

The Application Frame (Mac OS)

On Mac OS, Muse has an Application frame that is shown by default. The Application frame groups all of the workspace elements into a single, integrated window that lets you treat the application as a single unit. When the Application frame is turned on, you can move or resize the Application frame or any of its elements, and all of the elements within it respond to each other so that none overlap. If you work with two or more applications, you can position each application side by side on the screen or on multiple monitors.

If you are using a Mac and prefer a more free-form user interface, you can hide the Application frame. Choose Window > Application Frame to toggle the visibility of the Application frame.

The Breakpoint bar

Breakpoints in a responsive web design are how you define where design elements will change at different browser widths. Over the range of browser widths, from desktop down to mobile, whenever a design "fix" or change is needed, you set a breakpoint and make a design change. For instance, in a desktop browser, you may want three columns of text, but for the design to work on tablet, you might only need two columns. Breakpoints allow you to visualize your design in different browser widths, and test how the objects in a page respond to the change in browser widths.

The default purple bar that runs along the top edge of the page area is the Breakpoint bar. It displays all the breakpoints for the current page. In Lesson 6, "Responsive Web Design," you will learn everything you need to know to work effectively with the Breakpoint bar.

In the upper-right corner of the page area, you will see the scrubber (see the following figure). You drag the scrubber to view your page design at different page widths (screen sizes).

Breakpoint bar

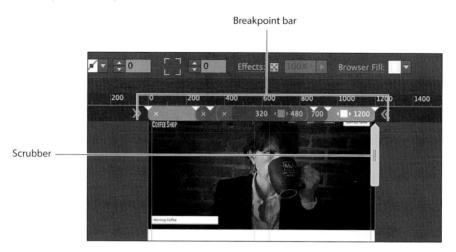

Scrubber

1 Drag the scrubber to the left to see the whole page area become narrower.

When designing a page or master page in responsive web design, you want to make sure the design "works" on different size browsers and devices, so you resize the page with the scrubber to preview the page at different browser widths, and see where it needs fixing. In other words, if two images were next to each other when the page was previewed at 1200 pixels, but they overlap at a smaller screen size, you would want to fix the overlap at the size that the content overlapped.

Note: If the page does not return to a width of 1200 pixels, you can also click on the "1200" in the Breakpoint bar to do so.

2   To reset the page to the original width of 1200 pixels, position the pointer in the page area. When the pointer changes to this ( ) and a tooltip shows "Click to jump to breakpoint," click.

When you click, the page width is reset to the original maximum width specified (1200 pixels), which happens to be the next, biggest breakpoint set. Muse won't let you edit your design content unless the page is the same width as an existing breakpoint. In Lesson 6, you'll learn much more about the different ways to change the width of the page to test your design.

Working with panels

Panels, which are listed in the Window menu, give you quick access to many tools and features that make modifying content easier. By default, some panels are docked and appear on the right side of the workspace.

Muse, like other Adobe applications, lets you manage your panels to make more important panels easier to access. Next, you'll experiment with hiding, closing, and opening panels.

1   Choose Window > Reset Panels to reset the panels to their default locations.

2   Click the Layers panel icon or label in the docked panels on the right side of the workspace to expand the panel, or choose Window > Layers. Notice that the Layers panel appears with other panels in a panel group.

3 Click the Assets panel tab in the Layers panel group to view the Assets panel.

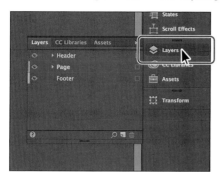 

The Assets panel is in the same panel group as the Layers panel.

4 Now click the Swatches panel icon or label. The Swatches panel appears by itself, and the panel group that contained the Assets panel is now hidden.

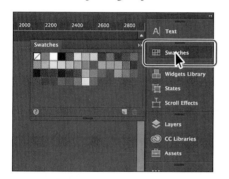

▶ **Tip:** To find a hidden panel, you can choose the panel name from the Window menu. A check mark to the left of the panel name indicates that the panel is showing in the workspace. If you choose a panel name that is already selected in the Window menu, the panel and its group are hidden.

5 Click and drag the gripper bar at the bottom of the Swatches panel down to resize the panel. Some, but not all of the panels can be resized in this way to reveal more panel content.

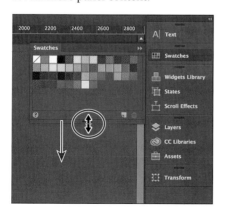 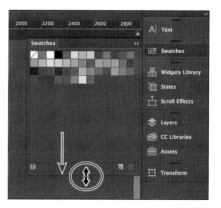

6 Click the Swatches panel icon (or panel tab) to collapse the panel group.

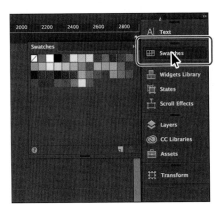 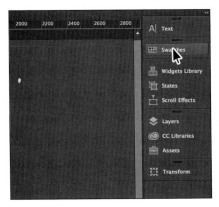

Working with the panel dock

On the right side of the workspace, the panels are in a dock, by default. A dock is a collection of panels or panel groups displayed together vertically. To show and arrange panels the way you like, you can dock and undock panels by moving them into and out of a dock, which is what you'll do next.

▶ **Tip:** You can also double-click the dark gray bar above the dock to collapse and expand the panels within.

1 Click the small double arrow at the top of the dock to expand the panels.

You can expand the panels using this method to show more than one panel group at a time.

 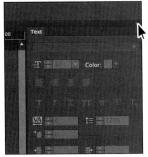

2 Click the double arrow again to collapse the panels.

3 To increase the width of all the panels in the dock, drag the left edge of the docked panels to the left. To decrease the width, click and drag the left edge of the docked panels to the right until the text for each panel name disappears.

4 Choose Window > Reset Panels to reset the workspace.

5 Click the small double arrow at the top of the dock to expand the panels so you can see the contents of the panels.

6 Click the Text panel tab to make sure it's selected. Double-click the panel tab to minimize the panel. Click the Text panel tab again to maximize the panel. This can be done to a panel that is docked or free-floating in the workspace (not docked).

▶ **Tip:** Press Tab to hide all panels. Press Tab again to show them all again. You can hide or show all panels except for the Toolbar and Control panel by pressing Shift+Tab to hide or Shift+Tab to show.

Editing panel groups

Panel groups can be docked, undocked, and arranged when either collapsed or expanded. Next, you'll resize and reorganize panel groups, which can make it easier to see more important panels.

1 Drag the Swatches panel by its tab away from the dock to make it a free-floating panel.

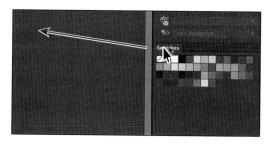 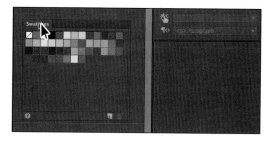

Tip: To close a free-floating panel, you can right-click a panel tab or title bar (above the tab) and choose Close. You can also right-click the panel tab of a docked panel and choose Close.

Notice that the Swatches panel has an X in the upper-left corner (Mac OS) or in the upper-right corner (Windows) for closing the panel, as well as a double arrow in the upper-right corner (Mac OS and Windows) for collapsing and expanding the panel. You can also move panels from one panel group to another. By doing so, you can create custom panel groups that contain the panels you use most often.

2 Drag the Swatches panel by the panel tab, the panel title bar above the tab, or the area behind the panel tab onto the Text panel tab in the dock. Release the mouse button when you see a blue line around the Text panel group to add the Swatches panel to the group.

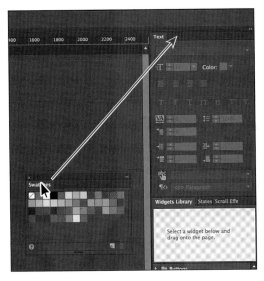
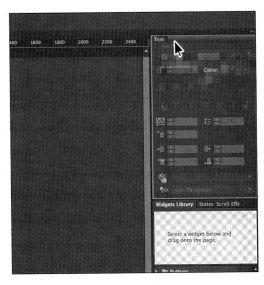

Note: You'll find that some panels have a fixed height, no matter how much you drag.

Note: This step shows how resizing a panel in the dock can affect other panels.

3 Click the Widgets Library panel tab to show the panel (if necessary), and position the pointer over the bottom of the Swatches panel. When the pointer changes to a double arrow, drag up to resize the group.

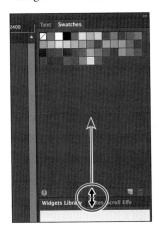

4 With the Swatches panel showing, drag from the darker gray area to the right of the Swatches tab to the left, away from the dock. This allows you to remove an entire group from the panel dock.

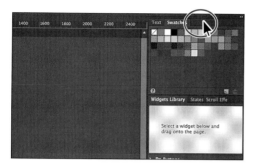 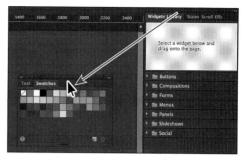

5 Drag the Swatches panel group from the same dark gray area or the panel title bar, back above the Widgets Library panel group. When a single blue line appears, release the mouse button to create a new group in the dock.

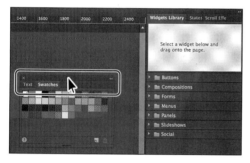 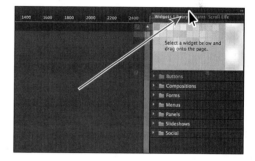

Next, you'll drag a panel from one group to another in the docked panels.

6 Click the States panel tab to show the panel. Drag the States panel tab up so that the pointer is over the *tabs* in the Swatches panel group. A blue border appears around the panel group. Release the mouse button.

Dragging panels into other groups allows you to create new panel groups to suit your work style.

Zooming and panning

When you're working on pages in a site, you'll often need to change the magnification level and navigate between pages. In the upper-left corner of the Muse Application window, the Zoom Level menu displays the magnification level, which can range from 5% to 4000%. Using any of the viewing tools and commands affects only the display of the page, not the actual size of the page and contents.

Using the view commands

1 Choose Window > Reset Panels to reset the panels to their default locations.

2 Choose View > Fit Page In Window to display the entire page within the Document window, if necessary.

Tip: You can zoom in using the keyboard shortcut Command+= (Ctrl+=). You can zoom out using the keyboard shortcut Command+– (Ctrl+–).

3 Choose View > Zoom In to enlarge the display of the page.

4 Choose View > Zoom Out to reduce the view of the page.

Note: The figures were taken in Mac OS. On Windows, the Zoom Level menu is to the right of the menus.

5 Choose 200% from the Zoom Level menu.

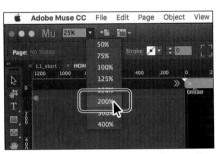

Each time you use the Zoom In or Zoom Out commands, the view of the page is resized to the closest preset zoom level. A list of those preset zoom levels is found in the Zoom Level menu in the upper-left corner of the Muse Application window.

6 Select the 200% value in the Zoom Level field and type **20**. Press Return (Enter).

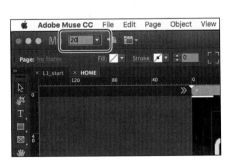

You can type values in the Zoom Level menu that range from 5% to 4000%. You don't need to type the % symbol.

Tip: You can also use the keyboard shortcuts Command+0 (Ctrl+0) to fit the page in the Document window.

7 Choose View > Fit Page In Window to display the entire page within the Document window.

Tip: You can also use the keyboard shortcuts Command+1 (Ctrl+1) to view the page at actual size (100%).

The View menu contains quick ways of fitting a page to your screen or viewing the page at actual size.

8 Choose View > Actual Size to display the page at actual size.

The page displays at 100%, which is the most accurate reflection of what your site will look like to visitors. The actual size of your page determines how much of it you can see onscreen at 100%.

9 Double-click the Hand tool (🖐) in the Toolbar to fit the page in the window.

This is the same thing as choosing View > Fit Page In Window.

Using the Zoom tool

In addition to the View menu options, you can use the Zoom tool to magnify and reduce the view level of your pages. The Zoom tool allows you to zoom into and out of specific areas of your pages.

1 Select the Zoom tool (🔍) in the Toolbar, and move the pointer into the Document window. Notice that a plus (+) sign appears at the center of the Zoom tool pointer.

2 Position the Zoom tool over some text on the page and click once.

The artwork displays at a higher magnification.

3 Click two more times, slowly, on the coffee pot icon to the left of the text you just clicked on, to increase the view again.

Notice that the specific area you clicked is magnified. You can reduce the view of the page in a similar manner.

4 With the Zoom tool still selected, position the pointer over the center of the page and hold down the Option (Alt) key. A minus (–) sign appears at the center of the Zoom tool pointer (🔍). Click a few times to zoom out.

5 Choose View > Fit Page In Window.

For a more controlled zoom, you can drag a marquee around a specific area of your artwork. This magnifies only the selected area. You'll try that next.

6 With the Zoom tool still selected, drag a marquee around the coffee pot icon to the left of the text. When you see the aqua box, called a *marquee*, around the area you are dragging, release the mouse button. The area with the marquee surrounding it is now enlarged to fit the Document window.

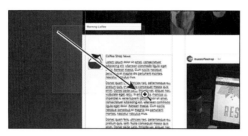

7 Choose View > Fit Page In Window.

The Zoom tool is used frequently during the editing process to enlarge and reduce the view of the page. For this reason, Muse allows you to select it using the keyboard without first deselecting any other tool you may be using.

8 Choose View > Actual Size to zoom in to the page.

Panning around in your page

In Muse, like other Adobe applications, you can use the Hand tool to pan to different areas of a page. Using the Hand tool allows you to push the page around much like you would a piece of paper on your desk.

1 Select the Hand tool (🖐) in the Toolbar.

2 Click and drag up or down in the Document window. As you drag, the page moves with the hand. Notice that at some point you cannot drag any further.

● **Note:** The spacebar shortcut for the Hand tool does not work when the Text tool is active and your cursor is in text. To access the Hand tool while the Text tool is selected, press Option (Alt).

3 Click any other tool except the Text tool (🅣) in the Toolbar and move the pointer into the Document window.

4 Hold down the spacebar to select the Hand tool temporarily, and then drag the mouse to bring the page back into the center of your view. Release the spacebar.

As with the Zoom tool (🔍), you can select the Hand tool with a keyboard shortcut without first deselecting the active tool.

Preview mode

As you create your designs in Muse, you can use Preview mode to see what your page will look like in a browser (without guides and visual indicators), test your links, view video and widget content, and more. As you'll learn in later lessons, you can also preview a page or your entire site in the default browser installed on your computer.

⬤ **Note:** With alternate layouts, which you'll learn a bit more about in Lesson 6, you can preview the page in different screen sizes and toggle between orientations. Preview mode does not emulate actual device behaviors for the Phone or Tablet alternate layouts. It gives you a sense of what the page content will look like in a specific device screen size and orientation. It is recommended to test directly on devices, if possible.

Next you'll preview a few pages in Preview mode.

1   With the HOME page showing in Design mode, click the Preview link in the upper-right corner of the Application window.

⬤ **Note:** You may see a warning dialog box. If that is the case, click OK.

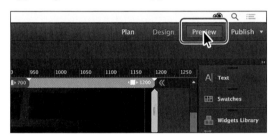

Any animations, links, slideshows, videos, and other web media are fully active in Preview mode. Also notice that Preview has a document tab at the top of the Document window (next to the HOME tab). You can leave Preview open, like you would a page, and simply refresh the preview area by clicking the Refresh button above the Document window. One thing to note, you cannot make edits to your pages while previewing them. You must return to Design mode to continue editing.

▶ **Tip:** You can also preview a page by pressing Command+P (Ctrl+P).

⬤ **Note:** When Design mode is active, clicking the Preview link in the upper-right corner of the Application window previews the active page in the Document window. If you do not have a page open, Muse previews the first page of the site.

2   Click the Contact link in the navigation at the top of the page to display the Contact page. Preview lets you test links between pages and navigate the site as you would in a browser.

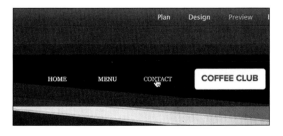

3 Press Command+I (Ctrl+I) to return to Design mode.

No matter which page is showing in Preview mode, when you return to Design mode, the same pages and site files that were open remain open.

4 Choose File > Close Site to close the L1_start.muse site file and any open pages associated with that site, without saving.

Why you preview websites

Unlike the print world, where you output to a single printing device, on the web there are many different browsers and multiple versions of each browser—not to mention different platforms, like Windows, Mac OS, Android, iOS, and tons of devices. Typically, when you're building websites, you should test your websites in as many of these environments as possible.

You can preview your site in Muse by clicking the Preview link in the upper-right corner of the Application window. Preview uses the browser technology from your operating system (the version of Safari or Internet Explorer [IE] you have installed) as a rendering engine.

The code that Muse generates is automatically cross-browser compatible, which lets you focus on your design and use Preview as a way to test your links and other content by browsing through it the way site visitors would.

As of the writing of this book, the Adobe Muse team currently tests and optimizes output for the following browsers:

- Firefox 11 for Mac OS and Windows
- Internet Explorer 8 and later for Windows
- Apple Safari 5 for Mac OS
- Chrome for Mac OS and Windows

Review questions

1 What is responsive web design?

2 What is "wireframing?"

3 Name the modes and briefly describe each.

4 Describe two ways to change a document view.

5 Briefly describe the benefits of working in Preview mode.

Review answers

1 Responsive web design (RWD) is designing a site so that the layout changes based on the size, orientation, and even capabilities of the device you're using to view the site. It takes the same content, like text, images, and video, and using web technologies like CSS, HTML, and JavaScript, alters that layout so as to provide an optimal viewing and interaction experience for your site across a wide range of devices.

2 A wireframe is a visual site outline. It shows the basic site structure, hierarchy of content, as well as the positioning of such basic elements as the header, footer, sidebar, navigation, and others—without specific formatting like fonts, colors, and styles. The benefit of wireframing is that it gives everyone involved (including the client) a simple way to envision the site layout and decide where content should be placed.

3 The three modes in Muse are Plan, Design, and Preview. Plan mode is used to edit your site map by adding and organizing pages, working with master pages, and creating alternate layouts; Design mode is used to edit your pages; and Preview mode is used to test your site.

4 You can choose commands from the View menu to zoom in or out of a document, or fit it to your Document window; you can also use the Zoom tool in the Toolbar, and click or drag over a document to enlarge or reduce the view. In addition, you can use keyboard shortcuts to magnify or reduce the display of artwork. You can also use the Zoom Level menu to change the magnification of the page within the Document window.

5 Preview mode enables you to see what your page will look like in a browser (without guides), test your links, view video and widget content, view pages optimized for phone and/or tablet (alternate layout pages) at a specific device size and orientation, and more.

2 CREATING YOUR SITE

Lesson overview

In this lesson, you'll take the first steps in creating your website and learn how to:

- Create a new site
- Edit site properties
- Work in Plan mode
- Add, edit, and organize pages
- Set page specific properties
- Add metadata

This lesson takes approximately 30 minutes to complete. To download the project files for this lesson, log in or set up an account at peachpit.com. Enter the book's ISBN (9780134547275) or go directly to the book's product page to register. Once on the book's page, click the Register Your Product link. The book will show up in your list of registered products along with a link to the book's bonus content. Click the link to access the lesson files for the book. Store the files on your computer in a convenient location, as described in the "Getting Started" section of this book. Your Account page is also where you'll find any updates to the chapters or to the lesson files.

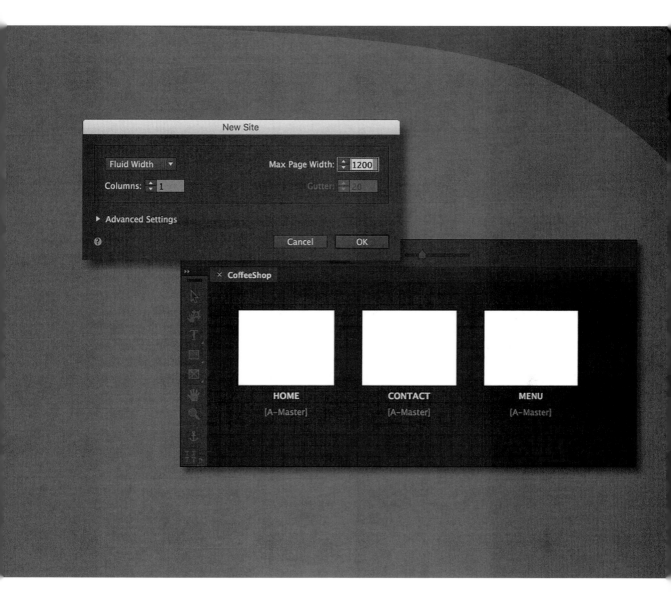

After creating your site file in Adobe Muse, you'll take advantage of Plan mode to quickly and visually add, delete, and organize pages in your site. You'll also add information about your pages, which is called *metadata*, for search engines to index and rank your site in search results.

Creating a new site

● **Note:** If you have not already downloaded the project files for this lesson to your computer from your Account page, make sure to do so now. See "Getting Started" at the beginning of the book.

In this lesson, you'll learn the fundamentals of creating an Adobe Muse site, adding and organizing pages in Plan mode, and adding metadata to your pages.

When you begin to work in Muse, you first create a site file with the extension .muse. That site file contains all of the pages, master pages, colors, styles, and more that you'll use in your website. Muse provides an environment where you can easily plan, design, and organize all of your web documents.

You need to create a Muse site before you can begin creating pages that belong to that site, and that's what you'll do first.

▶ **Tip:** With no sites open, you could also click the New button in the Start screen to create a new site.

1 Launch Muse. Choose File > New Site.

   The New Site dialog box appears. Here you'll choose an initial layout and set default page dimensions, margins, columns, and other attributes that become the default properties for the pages of your initial layout.

2 In the New Site dialog box, set the following options:

   • **Fluid Width** (the default setting)

      Fluid Width is chosen when you want the layout to resize with the browser window (this is responsive web design). The *Fixed Width* option, on the other hand, allows for static layouts that *do not* resize with the browser window. In the New Site dialog box, you choose one or the other. Later, you'll learn about mixing these layouts.

   • Max Page Width: **1200** (px)

      With a fluid width layout, you can limit how wide the page can get. None of the page content will be wider than the Max Page Width value you set, unless you set it to do so. When the page is viewed in a browser window that is wider than 1200 pixels, in this case, the page area remains 1200 pixels wide and simply centers in the browser window.

   • Columns: **1** (the default setting)

   • Gutter: **20** (the default setting)

● **Note:** The Gutter option is dimmed because there is only one column. The Gutter is the space between columns.

3 Click the arrow to the left of the Advanced Settings option to reveal more options. These options are not something you need to set right away to get started. You'll explore them next.

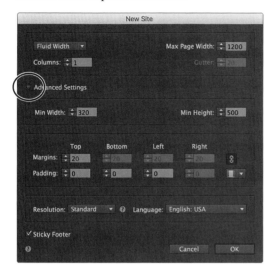

4 Click OK.

Muse opens the new site you created in Plan mode with a single page to start with.

5 Choose File > Save Site As. In the Save Adobe Muse File As dialog box, navigate to the Lessons folder. Type **CoffeeShop** in the Save As (File name) text field, and click Save. The site file is saved as CoffeeShop.muse in the root level of the Lessons folder.

Editing the site properties

When creating a site in Muse, you don't always get the site properties right the first time. You can easily edit the options you originally set for your site as well as edit the advanced settings at any point later on. That's what you'll do next.

1 With the CoffeeShop.muse site file still open, choose File > Site Properties. Click the Layout tab at the top of the dialog box, if it's not already selected.

The Site Properties dialog box displays the layout settings you specified when you first created the site as well as other optional properties, such as resolution and a Favicon Image option.

Tip: The Resolution setting in the Site Properties dialog box lets you use HiDPI (2x) images (some refer to them as "retina" images) in your site. Web designs you create in Adobe Muse can take full advantage of the display quality provided by high-resolution (HiDPI) screens, such as Apple Retina displays.

2 Change the Columns to **2**, in order to divide each page into 2 columns using guides that only show in Muse. Change the Gutter value to **80**.

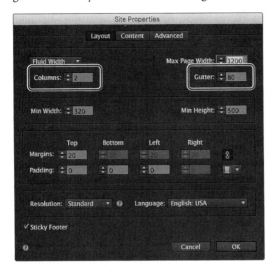

Tip: A favicon is a small image that displays to the left of your site's address in a browser's Address bar and other places.

3 Click the Content tab at the top of the Site Properties dialog box.

When you create text links to other pages, sites, and so on, Muse allows you to create hyperlink styles for the various states of those links that change the link appearance based on user interactivity. You can set and adjust the colors and other formatting options for those styles here, among a variety of other options. You'll create hyperlink styles in Lesson 8, "Adding Links, Buttons, and Graphic Styles."

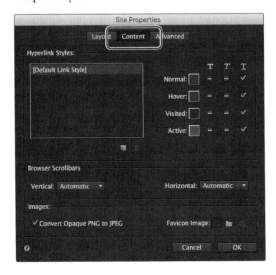

4 Click OK to close the Site Properties dialog box.

Editing the site map in Plan mode

Make sure Plan mode is selected in the upper-right corner of the Application window so you can see the site map. When you create a new site, by default, Muse creates one blank page called "Home" and one blank master page called "A-Master." These pages are the starting point for your site map and website.

In Muse, the site map in Plan mode shows the number of pages in your site, how the pages will be ordered, and how they connect to each other in the site navigation. After you add pages to your site map, you'll be able to see the relationship between pages at the top of the site map (called *parent* pages), and the pages beneath them called *child* pages. *Sibling* pages appear on the same level in the site plan. Below is an example of a site map in Muse with pages:

● **Note:** You won't see these pages in your site map. This is only for illustrative purposes.

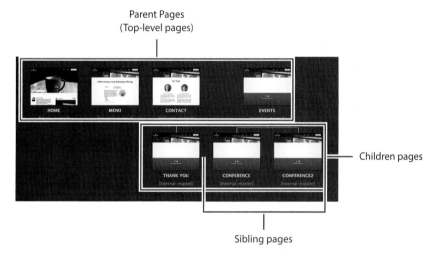

Parent Pages
(Top-level pages)

Children pages

Sibling pages

Adding, deleting, and arranging pages in your site

The site you create may contain a number of pages like the home page, a contact page, and more. In this section, you'll learn how to add as well as delete pages in your site. By adding pages to your site, you will be editing the site map. Keep in mind that you can edit your site map at any time in the process if your needs change, but a well-structured site map guides your process and also helps to determine site navigation.

An example site map in Plan mode

The menu that Muse populates based on a site map

Adding top-level pages

Let's start by adding some pages to your site. The pages you add will be in the main navigation for the site. First, you'll change the name of the Home page.

1 Position the cursor over the Home page name (*below* the thumbnail) in the site map area and double-click. Change the name to **HOME** and press Enter or Return to accept it.

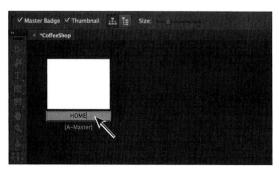

You might be asking why you just changed the name from "Home" to "HOME." When you add a navigation menu in Lesson 3, you'll see that Muse uses the names of the pages found in the site map as the names of the links in the menu. If the names are upper-case in the site map, they'll be upper-case in the menu.

▶ **Tip:** You can also choose Page > Add New Top Level Page to add a new page to the top level of the site map, or right-click a page thumbnail in the site map and choose New Sibling Page in the context menu that appears.

2 Position the pointer over the HOME page thumbnail and click the plus sign (+) to the right of the page thumbnail to add a new page to the right of the HOME page.

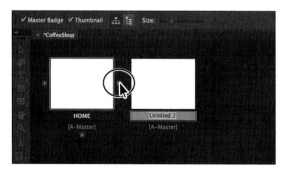

Clicking the plus sign (+) to the right or left of a page thumbnail adds a sibling page (a page on the same level). Clicking the plus sign (+) beneath the page thumbnail adds a child page (a page beneath, on the second level). After inserting a page, you can immediately change the name of the page.

3 Select the text "Untitled 2" beneath the new thumbnail, if necessary. Type **CONTACT**.

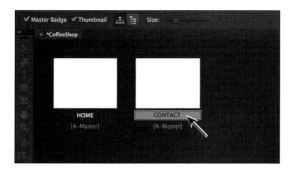

Note: If you cannot select the text "Untitled 2" beneath the page thumbnail, double-click the text to select it. You can also right-click the page thumbnail and choose Rename Page to edit the text.

When the site is published, by default Muse uses the name that appears beneath each page thumbnail in the site map as the page's title at the top of the browser window. Later, if you choose to add a navigation menu to your pages, Muse creates a navigation menu based on the top-level pages in the site map. You'll learn more about Menu widgets in Lesson 3.

4   Choose File > Preview Page In Browser to open the home page in the default browser installed on your machine.

Notice that Muse uses the page thumbnail name, "HOME," as the title of the page at the top of the browser window. You'll learn how to specify more descriptive titles for pages in "Adding page metadata" later in this lesson.

5   Close the browser and return to Muse.

6   Position the cursor over the CONTACT thumbnail, and then click the plus sign (+) to the right. Change the name of the new page to **MENU**.

You should now have a total of three pages: HOME, CONTACT, and MENU. These pages are considered parent pages, and are siblings of each other.

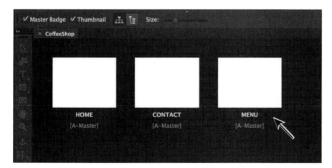

7   Choose File > Save Site.

Adding child pages

Like I said at the beginning of this section, child pages are typically lower-level pages that can be accessible on a web page via a menu that appears when you hover the pointer over the top-level navigation. You can add child pages to help further organize the pages in your site.

Once published, this site will contain a simple contact form. After users fill out the form, they will be taken to a "thank you" page that will be a child page of the contact page. You'll create the thank you page next.

Note: Over the course of the book you don't put anything on the THANK YOU page. After you learn about adding content to pages, you might want to add some text thanking users for filling out the form, some social media contact information, links to other relevant content, and more.

Tip: You can also choose View > Zoom In or View > Zoom Out in Plan mode to change the size of the thumbnails.

1 In the upper-left corner of the Application window, drag the Size slider to the right to make the page thumbnails larger. If the thumbnails no longer fit in the site plan area, horizontal and/or vertical scroll bars will appear.

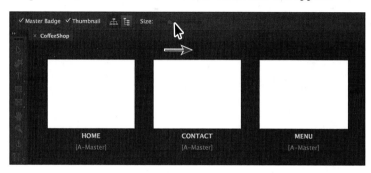

Tip: In Plan mode, you can collapse and expand child pages by clicking below the parent page on the expand/collapse icon (⌃) that appears. This allows you to hide pages temporarily, simplifying the Plan mode and reducing the amount of scrolling required.

2 Hover the pointer over the CONTACT page thumbnail, and click the plus sign (+) that appears *beneath* it.

3 Select the default name of the new child page, and type **THANK YOU**.

Notice that a line now connects the CONTACT (parent) and THANK YOU (child) pages, indicating their relationship.

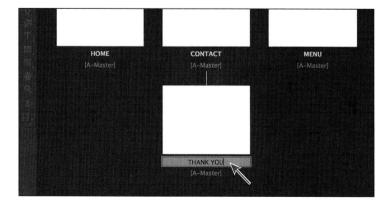

4 Hover the pointer over the THANK YOU page thumbnail, and then click the plus sign (+) to the right to add a new sibling page to the right.

Notice that the two new pages are now sibling pages of each other and are also child pages of the parent page CONTACT.

▶ **Tip:** Another way to add a child page is to right-click a page thumbnail and choose New Child Page. This command adds a new child page beneath the active page thumbnail.

5 Drag the Size slider in the upper-left corner of the Application window to the left until all the page thumbnails are visible in the site map area, if necessary.

6 Position the pointer over the new page thumbnail (mine is called "Untitled 5"). Click the Delete button (x) that appears off the upper-right corner of the thumbnail to remove the page from the site map.

▶ **Tip:** Another way to delete a page is to right-click a page thumbnail and choose Delete Page. You can also choose Edit > Undo Delete Page if you want the page back.

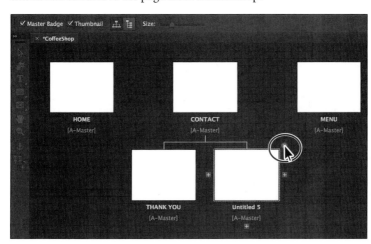

Know that you don't have to finalize the site map before you begin adding content to existing pages. You can always add, delete, and rearrange pages at a later time.

● **Note:** If you were to delete a parent page, such as CONTACT, Muse does not delete the children of that page; instead, it promotes them to the level of the deleted parent page.

7 Choose File > Save Site. Saving your work often is a good habit to get into no matter what program your working in.

Arranging pages in the site map

You can organize your site however you feel will benefit the end user most. Suppose you are building a site for your portfolio. The parent pages could include the Home page, Contact page, Projects page, and so on. The child pages for the Projects parent page could consist of different types of projects, like web and print. It always helps to explore the web and notice how other sites are organized.

With pages in your site map, you can rearrange them, when necessary, to create a more organized site map. This structure can help you immensely when you add a Menu into your pages, as you'll see in Lesson 3.

1   If necessary, drag the Size slider to the left until all the page thumbnails are visible in the site map area.

⬤ **Note:** Relocating a parent page moves all of its child pages at the same time.

2   Click and drag the MENU page thumbnail to the left of the CONTACT page. When you see an orange drop zone to the left of the CONTACT page, release the mouse button. The CONTACT page thumbnail and its THANK YOU child page now reside to the right of the MENU page thumbnail in the site map.

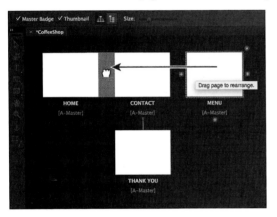 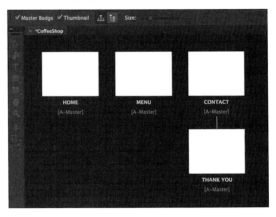

▶ **Tip:** You can always choose Edit > Undo Rearrange Page to return the page thumbnail to where it was.

▶ **Tip:** You can press and hold the Option (Alt) key as you drag a page thumbnail to duplicate a page.

As you drag pages in the site map, pay attention to the colored drop zones that appear around other page thumbnails. The orange drop zone indicates where the page will be in the site map when you release the mouse button. For instance, if you drag a page thumbnail beneath another thumbnail and the orange drop zone appears, the page you are dragging will become a child of the page that shows the drop zone.

3   Click the Vertical Site Map Display button (🗎) above the site map, to the left of the Size slider.

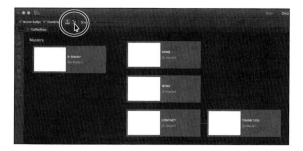

In Muse, you can choose to view the site map and master pages in a horizontal (default) or vertical layout. Sites with more pages and complex hierarchies may find it easier to navigate pages with a vertical site map showing.

4 Click the Horizontal Site Map Display button (⊞) above the site map, to the left of the Size slider to return the Plan mode layout to the default horizontal layout.

5 Choose File > Save Site.

Setting page properties

When you create your site and edit the *site* properties, you set default properties for all pages in your site (including the master page). In addition to editing properties for the entire site, you can also edit properties for a master page or on a page-by-page basis. In this exercise, you'll edit the page properties for a single page in your site map. The MENU page will have more than two columns of text, and it's the only page that needs this number of columns. You'll edit the page properties in order to have guides in place to help align the MENU page content into columns.

● **Note:** You'll learn what master pages are and how to work with them in Lesson 3, "Working with Master Pages."

1 In Plan mode, hover the pointer over the MENU page thumbnail, right-click and choose Page Properties.

▶ **Tip:** If a page is open in Design mode, you can also choose Page > Page Properties to set properties for that page.

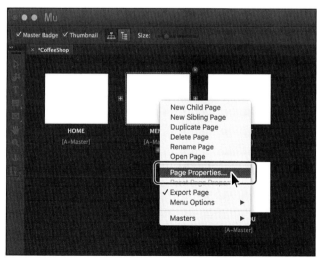

In the Page Properties For MENU dialog box, you'll see familiar options, like Min Height and Columns. Any changes you make in this dialog box will only affect the MENU page and will override the default site properties set when you first created the site or edited by choosing File > Site Properties.

2 In the Page Properties For MENU dialog box, make sure the Layout tab is selected at the top of the dialog box. Change the Columns to **4**, and the Gutter to **40**. Leave the dialog box open and continue to the next section.

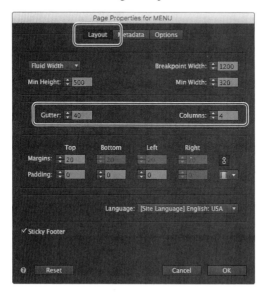

Adding page metadata

In addition to setting page properties in the Page Properties dialog box, you can also add metadata to each of your pages. *Metadata* is a great way for you to provide search engines, such as Google and Bing, with information about your site.

Adding metadata is also a first step on the long road of *search engine optimization (SEO)*, the process of trying to improve the visibility of a website in search engines in unpaid search results. The goal is to have search engines rank your site higher than other sites, meaning that search engines perceive your site as more relevant to the search terms someone enters and place it higher in their returned lists of results. Metadata can also make site content more accessible to visitors using screen readers and other assistive devices to search the web.

In Muse, you can add three types of metadata to describe the page content to a search engine:

- The **title** appears at the top of the browser window when you preview a page or visit it on the web and can appear in the search results for search engines. For instance, when you visit Adobe.com, you can see the title of the page at the top of the browser window. The title is also generally shown as the title in search results (at least for Google).

  You'll learn about setting the title in the next section.

- The **description** briefly describes the page content or provides information about a blog post, such as author and date or byline information. In some cases, search engines may show a portion of this description in their results. If you search for "Adobe" on Google.com, for instance, in the search results you would see the site title and a description below that. Some search engines also display the description metadata that you add to each page.

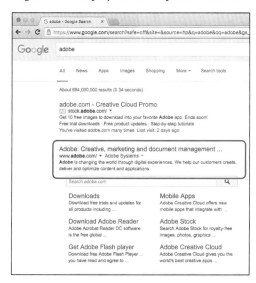

- **Keywords** are words and phrases that relate directly to the content on your site and that someone is likely to type in when searching for your business or website in a search engine. These days, search engines like Google don't take keywords into account in web search ranking.

Adding metadata to your pages doesn't guarantee that your site will be ranked higher than others by a search engine, but using a relevant title and description in your pages typically doesn't hurt and is considered the best practice. In addition, search engines may display some of this metadata information to users in their search results, which might draw in extra visitors. Let's add some metadata now.

1 Click the Metadata tab at the top of the Page Properties For MENU dialog box to view the metadata options.

2 In the Description field, type **Hillsborough North Carolina coffee house featuring fair trade locally roasted coffees, with an organic menu of pastries, great tasting sandwiches and salads**.

The description doesn't have to be a sentence. As a matter of fact, it can be a good place to include general information about the page. If it's a product page, for instance, you could include prices in the description.

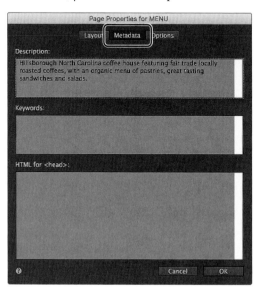

We will leave the keywords blank for this project. If you would like to add them for your site, be sure to prioritize the list of keywords, from most to least important, and to separate each keyword or key phrase with a comma. Choose keywords that are relevant to the specific page you're working on, and use them sparingly. Also, definitely avoid keyword "stuffing," which is loading a web page with keywords or numbers in an attempt to manipulate a site's ranking in search engine results.

Skip over the HTML for <head> field. It is used to add code to a section of the HTML page that is generated when you preview, publish, or export a site. Leave the Page Properties For MENU dialog box open and continue to the next section.

Writing meaningful descriptions

Because meta descriptions aren't displayed in the pages visitors see, you might be tempted to let this content slide. Resist that urge. High-quality descriptions are more likely to be displayed in Google search results; therefore, taking the time to write meaningful descriptions can go a long way toward improving the quality and quantity of your search traffic. A description can be as long as you'd like, but most sites keep it within 160 characters to avoid being cut off in search engine results.

To make your descriptions more effective, remember to:

- Write a unique, specific description for each page of your site.
- Include facts about the content on the page that are not represented in its title.
- Make the descriptions easy to read.
- Make sure your descriptions are unique and represent the content on the page.

Setting page options

The Options section in the Page Properties dialog box allows you to adjust the title for a page, edit the HTML page name, and more. You'll do that next.

1 Click the Options tab at the top of the Page Properties For MENU dialog box to view the other options.

As you can see in the Options section, the Page Name is the name you originally gave the page in Plan mode. You can change the name here, but remember that Muse displays this name in the navigation menu you'll add later. By default, Muse uses a page's name as its title. As you'll see in this exercise, you can use the Page Properties dialog box to change the title to be more descriptive. Your title provides visitors and search engines with useful information about your site. The title appears at the top of the browser window when you preview a page or visit it on the web. It can also appear in the search engine results.

2 In the Page Title field, deselect the option Same As Page Name. Change the Page Title to: **The Coffee Shop | Menu**.

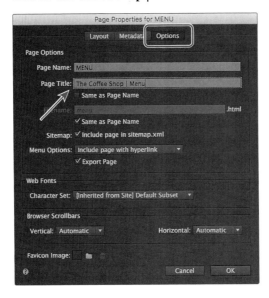

By default, Muse sets the Page Title field to be the same as the Page Name field. Deselecting Same As Page Name enables you to enter a unique, more descriptive title in the Page Title field. Make sure your page title effectively communicates the topic of the page's content. Ideally, you should add a unique page title to each of your pages. By specifying a relevant title and adding the text "| Menu" to the end, you give the search engine information about the page and orient visitors to the current page.

Below the Page Title field is the Filename field. The name of the HTML file that Muse generates when you publish the site will be the same as the page name. For a page named "Team" in the site map, for example, Muse names the HTML file "team.html." The exception to this rule is the Home page. Conventionally, the first page of a website, which is usually the Home page, has the filename index.html. You cannot edit the filename for the Home page, so this option is dimmed. Editing the filename is necessary only under special circumstances. For example, you can edit filenames as requested by a web developer on your team.

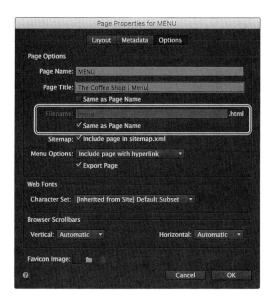

In Lesson 3, you'll explore the settings available in the Menu Options.

3 Click OK.

4 In Plan mode, position the pointer over the THANK YOU page thumbnail, right-click, and choose Page Properties.

5 Click the Options tab at the top of the Page Properties For THANK YOU dialog box. Deselect the option Include Page In Sitemap.xml. Click OK.

When you export your Muse site or upload your Muse site to a third-party host provider, Muse auto-generates an XML site map for your site (a file named sitemap.xml) that contains a list of all the site pages and assets. This file helps search engines index your site content more easily and can be useful for improving your site's search engine ranking.

By default, all pages in your site are included in the XML sitemap. You can exclude a page from the XML file (if you don't want search engines to find it) by deselecting the Include Page In Sitemap.xml option in the Page Properties dialog. For instance, the THANK YOU page does not need to be indexed since it only contains thank you information for users who have filled out a contact form.

6 Choose File > Save Site.

▶ **Tip:** After setting page properties, you might later realize that you don't want those properties (like metadata or columns) to be different from other pages in your site. You can always reset the page properties to the default site properties. While a page is open in Design mode, you can choose Page > Reset Page Properties or right-click in a blank area of the page or gray area outside of the page area and choose Reset Page Properties.

As you progress through the lessons, feel free to add unique titles, descriptions, and keywords to each page in the site. In the next lesson, you'll learn about working with master pages, which make it easier and faster to apply consistent content and formatting to multiple pages.

Review questions

1   When you create a new site in Muse, briefly describe the differences between "Fluid Width" and "Fixed Width" in the New Site dialog box.

2   Name the two main parts of Plan mode.

3   What is the purpose of the site map in Plan mode?

4   What is a top-level page?

5   What are the three types of metadata that you can add in the Page Properties dialog box?

Review answers

1   Fluid Width is chosen when you want the layout to resize with the browser window (responsive web design). The Fixed Width option allows for static layouts that do not resize with the browser window. In the New Site dialog box, you choose one or the other.

2   The two parts of Plan mode are the site map area (pages area) and the masters area.

3   Building a site map in Plan mode is a critical first step in the website creation process because it determines the number of pages in your site, how the pages are organized, and how they connect to each other in the site navigation dynamically generated in Menu widgets.

4   A top-level page appears in Plan mode in the top tier of the site map. Top-level pages are the main sections of the site and automatically appear in the menu items of Menu widgets (unless they are set to Manual).

5   Three types of metadata that Muse allows you to insert into your pages in the Page Properties dialog box (Page > Page Properties) are a description, keywords, and a page title. The page name and filename can also be used by search engines to help rank your page and are also considered metadata.

3 WORKING WITH MASTER PAGES

Lesson overview

In this lesson, you'll work with master pages and learn how to:

- Edit master page properties
- Edit master page guides
- Edit page fill and browser fill
- Add header and footer content
- Create and duplicate master pages
- Work with layers
- Add and edit a menu
- Edit the appearance of a submenu ▪◀
- Test your pages

This lesson takes approximately 60 minutes to complete. To download the project files for this lesson, log in or set up an account at peachpit.com. Enter the book's ISBN (9780134547275) or go directly to the book's product page to register. Once on the book's page, click the Register Your Product link. The book will show up in your list of registered products along with a link to the book's bonus content. Click the link to access the lesson files for the book. Store the files on your computer in a convenient location, as described in the "Getting Started" section of this book. Your Account page is also where you'll find any updates to the chapters or to the lesson files. If you are starting from scratch in this lesson, use the method described in the "Jumpstart" section in "Getting Started."

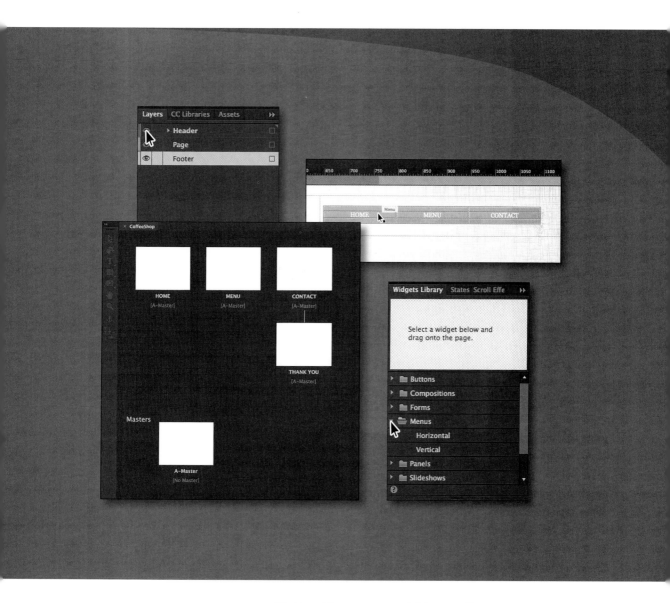

Working with master pages in Adobe Muse allows you to control the appearance of pages; set up consistent areas of your pages, such as headers and footers; and maintain design consistency across the pages in your website.

Working with master pages

● **Note:** If you have not already downloaded the project files for this lesson to your computer from your Account page, make sure to do so now. See "Getting Started" at the beginning of the book.

When you first create a site in Muse, the site has one page as well as a single master page. Master pages contain repeating design elements, like a logo and navigation, which are automatically applied to other pages, in the same place on the page. When you change a master page, all pages based on that master reflect those changes. Using a single master page or a few different master pages for different site sections makes it easier to create consistent pages and a cohesive site. Content on a master page is locked on the pages in the site and can only be selected within the master page itself, not in the website pages.

Below the site plan area in Plan mode, you can access the default master page that every Muse site is initially based on. That default master page is named "A-Master." Over the course of this lesson, you'll learn how to create, duplicate, delete, apply, and add content to master pages in your site.

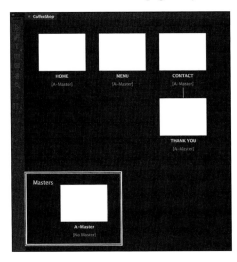

Editing master page properties

● **Note:** If you are starting from scratch using the Jumpstart method described in the "Jumpstart" section of "Getting Started," your workspace may look different from the figures you see in this lesson.

In the previous lesson, you set up the site file and edited the properties for the site and a few of the pages. Just as you can for a single page, you can also edit those same properties for a master page. The difference is that any page that has that master page applied will have the same properties as the master page by default. If you set page properties, they override shared master page properties *and* site properties. Master page properties ultimately override site properties.

Setting page properties on a master page can save time because it lets you set properties across multiple pages simultaneously instead of editing them page by page.

With your site still open in Plan mode, look at the page thumbnails in the site map. Below each thumbnail you see [A-Master], which indicates that the default master page, A-Master, is applied to that page.

1 With the CoffeeShop.muse site open, in Plan mode double-click the A-Master thumbnail in the masters area at the bottom of the Application window to open the A-Master page.

The A-Master page opens as a new tab in the Document window in Design mode. As you saw in the first lesson, with a page or master page open, the workspace shows many more features, including the Control panel, Toolbar, and panels.

2 Choose View > Fit Page In Window, and then choose View > Zoom Out.

3 Choose Page > Page Properties with the A-Master page open in Design mode.

4 In the Page Properties For A-Master dialog box, with the Layout tab selected, change the Min Height value to **800**. This makes each page with the A-Master page applied at least 800 pixels tall.

▶ **Tip:** To edit the page properties for the A-Master page, you could also stay in Plan mode, right-click the A-Master thumbnail, and choose Page Properties.

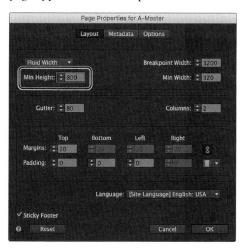

The Min Height set on the A-Master page overrides the Min Height set in the Site Properties. Another option worth pointing out is Sticky Footer. Selected by default, Sticky Footer forces the footer to "stick" to the bottom of the browser window, even if the browser window is taller than the minimum height of the page. This is useful when the site is viewed on a large display.

● **Note:** Clicking Reset in the Page Properties dialog box or choosing Page > Reset Page Properties will set the page properties to mirror the site properties and remove any page/browser fill changes you made.

5 Click the Metadata tab at the top of the Page Properties For A-Master dialog box.

The metadata options for the master page include an area for adding HTML content to the <head> section of the HTML file that is generated for each page based on the master page.

6 Change the Page Title Prefix to **Coffee Shop** – (with one space before and after the dash).

Each page with the A-Master page applied will now be affected. For instance, the HOME page will now have a title of "Coffee Shop – HOME."
"Coffee Shop - " is added to the beginning of each page title.

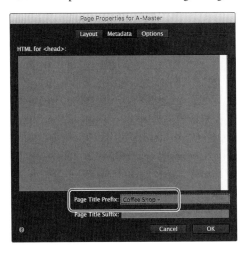

7 Click OK and leave the A-Master page open.

Editing the master page guides

Like other websites designed with HTML and CSS, individual pages in your Muse website may have varying heights based on the unique content on each page, but all can feature the same header and footer regions. These regions ensure that the header content, such as your logo, always remains in place at the top of the page and the footer content, such as social media content, always displays directly below the page content regardless of the height of a given page. By adjusting the page guides on a master page in Design mode, you can easily specify consistent header and footer areas across multiple pages.

Using the page guides on the master, you can also set the padding on the top and bottom of the page (the distance between the browser window edge and the page edge), and the minimum height of the page (called the Min Height). You already saw some of these settings when you edited the page properties. The master page guides simply give you a visual way to edit those same properties.

1 Choose View > Hide Breakpoints to temporarily hide the Breakpoint bar.

2 Choose View > Show Guides, if necessary.

If you see View > Hide Guides, then the guides are already showing, which is what you want. Here's a quick guide to page guides:

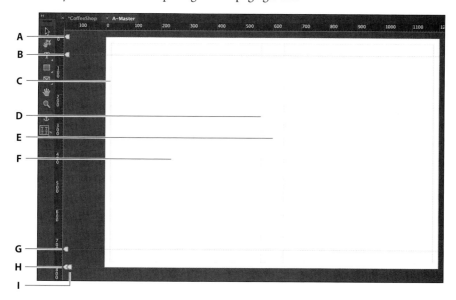

A Top of Page: Defines padding above the page and is the same as the Padding Top setting in the page or site properties.

B Header Guide: Defines the bottom of the header area. Items inserted on a master page above this guide appear at the top of the page.

C Margin guides: Defines an area of the page that can be used to keep content like text away from the edge of the browser window so it's more readable.

D Column guides: Divides the page area into columns of content.

E Gutter: Specifies the distance between columns.

F Page area: Indicates where you can add the unique content for each page.

G Footer Guide: Defines the top of the footer area. Items below the footer guide always appear at the bottom of the page. Elements associated with the footer stay at the bottom of the page below the Footer guide regardless of content height (by default), and elements placed in the footer on a master page are locked (cannot be selected or edited) on the pages of the site.

H Bottom of Page: Defines the minimum page height. This is the same as the Min Height setting in the page or site properties. You set the minimum height in an earlier step when you edited the master page properties. This guide is a visual way to edit that value.

I Bottom of Browser: Defines padding below the page and is the same as the Padding Bottom setting in the page or site properties.

3   Choose View > Fit Page In Window.

4   With A-Master page open in Design mode, off the left side of the page, click and drag the blue Header guide handle down until the Y: value shows 100 in the measurement label, and then release the mouse button.

The Y: value, in this case, indicates how far from the top edge of the page area the Header guide is located. Setting it to 100 makes the header area 100 pixels tall.

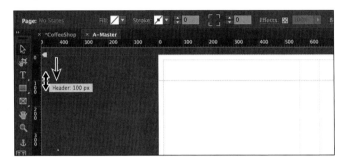

5   Click and drag the Footer guide up until the measurement label reads approximately 600 px.

6   Choose View > Show Breakpoints to see the Breakpoint bar again.

7   Choose File > Save Site.

With the key areas of the master page mapped out, next you'll start adding content to it.

Editing the appearance of the browser and page fills

When you design for the web, you must consider not only the page design and content, but also the area behind and around the page area, called the *browser fill* in Muse. By default, Muse uses fluid width layouts. When viewed in a desktop browser, if a visitor makes the browser window wider than the Max Page Width we set, the page will not be wider than the Max Page Width and will stay in the center of the browser window. There will be a gap on either side of the page horizontally. You can specify something to fill that space, such as a background color and/or an image, other than the default solid white color for the browser fill.

1   With the A-Master page open, choose View > Fit Page In Window, if necessary.

2   Choose View > Zoom Out.

3   Drag the scrubber (off the upper-right corner of the page) to the left, just a bit.

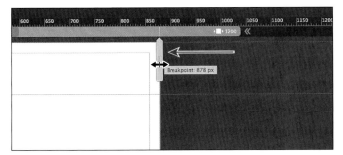

Notice how the page gets narrower. The scrubber lets you simulate browser width. In this case that means a narrower browser.

4   Drag the scrubber to the right, just beyond the 1200 you see in the purple Breakpoint bar above the scrubber.

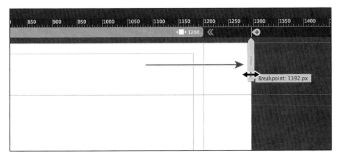

Notice how, when you pass the maximum page width set (1200 pixels), the page area no longer resizes, but you still see white on either side of the page area now. This is the browser fill. The browser fill can contain a single color, gradient, an image, or a combination of those, which appear behind (and in this case) on the sides of the page area's content. The dark gray zone outside of the white area is beyond the edge of the browser and cannot be edited.

Note: For now, don't worry about why you are clicking in the page area. In Lesson 6, you will explore responsive web design and understand why this is important.

5 Click in the white page area when the pointer looks like this ✎ and "Click to jump to breakpoint" appears in a tooltip next to the pointer.

The page width is reset to the Max Page Width setting of 1200 pixels so you can continue working. If you skip this step, you won't be able to make edits going forward.

Setting the browser fill appearance

Note: You'll learn more about creating and saving colors in Lesson 7, "Shapes, Color, and Effects."

In the Control panel, notice the word Page on the left end of the panel. This is called the *Selection Indicator*. As you learned in Lesson 1, the Selection Indicator indicates that the page is selected and that *most* of the formatting options you change in the Control panel will affect the appearance of the page area. The Browser Fill menu allows you to add a color and/or image to the background of the browser window, which resides behind the page area. Next, you'll change the browser fill.

1 Click the Browser Fill link in the Control panel to see the fill options for the browser.

Here you can change the color of the browser fill or add a gradient, as well as add or adjust a background image.

2 Select the Gradient Fill Type to see a gradient appear in the browser fill.

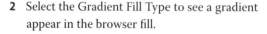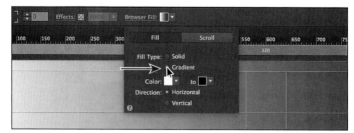

A gradient in Muse can consist of two colors with varying levels of opacity and can either be in a horizontal or vertical orientation. If you apply a gradient to the browser fill, notice that several other options disappear.

3 Select Solid for the Fill Type. Click the Add Image link to the right of the Image option. Navigate to the Lessons > images folder, select the image titled page_bg.jpg. Click Open.

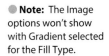 **Note:** The Image options won't show with Gradient selected for the Fill Type.

This step inserts a *subtle* image into the background of the browser window, which appears behind the content of the page. You'll typically create the background image in a separate application, such as Adobe Photoshop or Adobe Illustrator, and place it in an accepted web format (.jpg, .gif, .png, .psd, .ai, or .svg). You'll learn more about image types in Lesson 5, "Working with Graphics."

4 Choose Scale To Fill from the Fitting menu, if necessary, and select the bottom, center point of the Position reference point indicator (⊞).

Tip: You have several fitting options in the Fitting menu. I encourage you to explore them all!

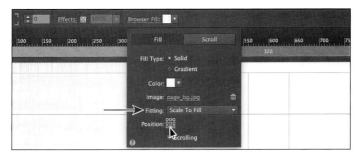

Tip: For some tips on working with background images on your pages, see the PDF named "Background_tips.pdf" in the Lessons > Lesson03 folder.

Muse now inserts the image once in the browser background. The image will also always be at the bottom of the browser window and fill the browser window, without distorting the image.

5 In the Browser Fill menu, deselect the Scrolling option. Press the Esc key to hide the menu.

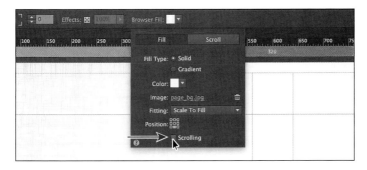

With Scrolling deselected, the background image stays in place if the user scrolls the page content using the scroll bars in the browser. The page content scrolls on top of the fixed background image. If you'd rather have the image scroll with the page, leave Scrolling selected.

6   Choose View > Preview Mode to preview the background image in the page.

7   Click the Design mode link in the upper-right corner of the Application window, to return to the A-Master page in Design mode.

Editing the page appearance

Next, you'll edit the appearance of the page area. Like the browser fill, you can assign a background color and image to the page area along with other options to match your design. In addition, you can adjust the opacity of the page area to allow the browser fill to be visible behind it. By default, the page area has no fill or stroke (border). You'll edit the page area to get an idea of what is possible, and then you'll remove it.

1   With "Page" showing in the Selection Indicator on the left end of the Control panel, click the Fill link in the Control panel to show the Fill menu.

▶ **Tip:** You can also apply a gradient fill to the page area instead of a solid color in the Fill menu. The Fill menu also includes an option for a background image for the page area. The options are similar to the options for the browser fill, and the image will appear in the page area on top of the page fill color.

2   In the Fill menu, click the Color option and then click a color swatch (one of the small color squares) to apply a fill to the page. You could also change the RGB color values to create a color you want.

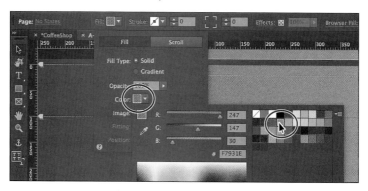

3   Click the arrow to the right of the Opacity value (100%) in the Fill menu and drag the slider to the left until 30 appears in the field. (You can also simply enter the value.) This makes the page area transparent.

4 In the Document window, drag the scrubber to the right, past 1200 in the Breakpoint bar, to see the browser fill behind and around the page area.

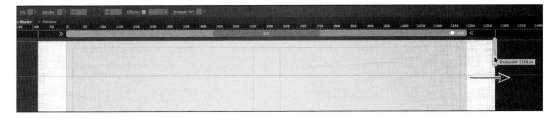

5 Click in the page area to preview the page width at 1200 pixels again. That way you can make edits to the design again.

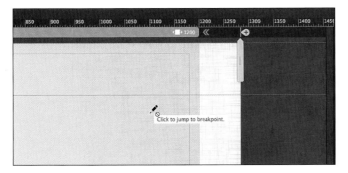

6 Click the Fill link in the Control panel to show the Fill menu. Click the Color option and select the None (⬜) color swatch to remove the page color.

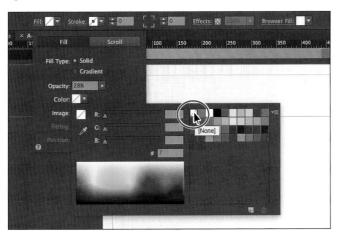

● **Note:** You may be asking whether or not it's necessary to set the Opacity back to 0 (zero). As far as the code that is generated, it is not. But, it wouldn't hurt.

7 Choose File > Save Site.

Now that the appearance of the page area and browser fill is set, you can start to add content like a logo to the master page.

Adding content to the master page

Next, you'll add some design content to the master page. In most cases, you'll add header content, like a logo and nav bar (menu), and footer content, like social media icons and more, to the master page because those elements should appear on every page. As was mentioned earlier, you don't have to add content to the master, but when you need consistent content across pages, it's a real time saver.

Adding a logo to the header

The header of most websites contains a variety of content: a logo, a menu bar (also called a navigation or nav bar), possibly social media links, and more. For learning purposes, we'll add a logo to the header. You'll learn all about web graphics and working with them in your site in Lesson 5, "Working with Graphics."

1 With A-Master still open in Design mode, choose View > Fit Page In Window, and then, if necessary, scroll up to see the header area above the Header guide.

● **Note:** SVG (Scalable Vector Graphics) is a *relatively* new format used in web design for vector web graphics.

2 Choose File > Place. Navigate to the Lessons > images folder. Select the image named logo.svg, and click Open.

Like Adobe InDesign, placing an image shows this cursor (⌐) with a preview of the graphic in Muse. With this cursor, you can click to place an image on the page at 100% its original size or click and drag to size the image as you place it.

3 Position the cursor in the page area and click to place the image on the page.

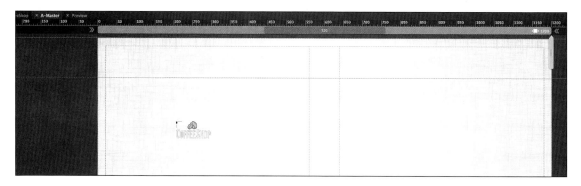

When you place images, Muse, like InDesign, creates a link to the original image. It also creates an image frame and places the image within it. You can use the frame to crop the image, and you can move the image within the frame. You'll learn more about working with images in Lesson 5.

4 Select the Selection tool (▶) in the Toolbar and drag the image from its center to above the Header guide. Drag it so the left edge of the logo snaps to the margin guide and the top snaps to the top margin guide. See the following figure for placement help.

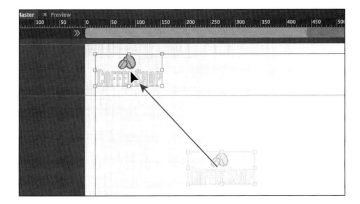

5 Click the Plan link in the upper-right corner of the Application window to show Plan mode again.

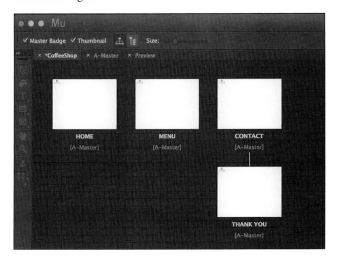

It may be a little difficult to see, since the logo is so small and the background image is subtle, but notice that each page thumbnail now shows the background image and logo you added to the A-Master page. You could change the size of the thumbnails by dragging the Size slider to make them larger.

6 Double-click the HOME page thumbnail to open that page in Design mode.

If you try clicking the logo in the header, you won't be able to. You can't select or edit master content on your pages, as in InDesign.

7 Choose File > Close Page and return to Plan mode, if it's not already showing.

● **Note:** You can choose View > Plan Mode or click the Plan link in the upper-right corner of the Application window to return to Plan mode.

Creating a new master page

Although a consistent, cohesive site design can be important, that doesn't mean every page has to look exactly alike. Sometimes a group of pages within a site need its own identity. For example, you may want to design the home page or individual product pages with a slightly different look and feel from the rest of the pages. Muse lets you create multiple master pages for this exact reason. You can either create a new, blank master page based on the site properties or even duplicate an existing master page and make changes to it.

Next, you'll create a new, blank master page that you may use later, but first you'll change the name of the existing A-Master.

● **Note:** Why put the word "master" in the master page name? When pages are open in Design mode, the page names appear in tabs at the top of the Document window. Having "master" in the name makes it easier to differentiate, but you can name the pages however you like.

1   In Plan mode, double-click the A-Master page name *beneath* the master thumbnail and change the name to **Home-master**. Press Return (Enter).

Notice that the text in brackets beneath each page thumbnail, called the *master badge*, changed from "A-Master" to "Home-master." Changing the name of master pages can be really useful. For instance, naming them can help you keep track of what they are used for. We named the master page "Home-master" because it will be the master for only the home page.

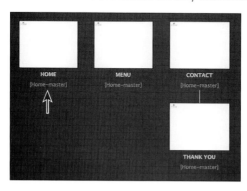

2   Choose Page > Add New Master Page.

Muse creates a new, blank master page in the Masters area with the same properties (width, column, and so on) as found in the site properties (File > Site Properties). It also gives it a generic name like "A-Master," which you can easily change.

3 Name the new master page **Internal-master** by double-clicking the name beneath the page thumbnail, if necessary, or right-clicking the page thumbnail and choosing Rename Page.

Tip: You can reorder the master pages by dragging the master page thumbnails right or left. This has no effect on the site; it can just be easier to either group similar master pages or put the most often used master pages together.

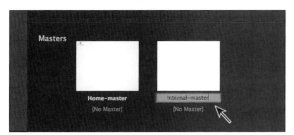

This blank master page could be something you use to create a different master page design for all pages except the home page, for instance.

Tip: You can also duplicate masters so you have the same content to start on a new master page. To do so, Right-click (Ctrl-click) a master page thumbnail and choose Duplicate Page to create a duplicate of that master.

4 Double-click the Internal-master thumbnail to open the page in Design mode.

5 With the Rulers showing (View > Show Rulers, if necessary), click and drag from the top horizontal ruler down into the page area. When you see a value of 230 px in the gray measurement label, release the mouse button to create a horizontal guide to use later.

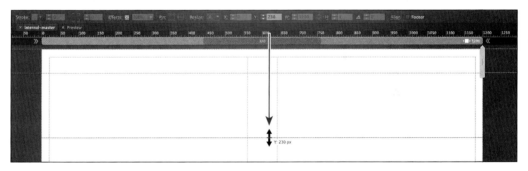

Tip: You can toggle the visibility of guides by choosing View > Hide Guides or View > Show Guides. You can also lock guides so you don't accidentally select them by choosing View > Lock Guides.

6 Choose File > Save Site.

7 Choose View > Plan Mode to return to Plan mode.

Applying master pages

When you create a new master page, either a blank master or by duplicating an existing master page, that new master page isn't applied to any of the pages in your site map. You can apply master pages to any number of pages, and even have a unique master page for each page. In the case of the CoffeeShop site, you will apply the Internal-master page to every page *except* for the HOME page.

1 With Plan mode showing, drag the Size slider in the Control panel above the site map, making sure that the page thumbnails still all fit in the sitemap area.

2 Drag the Internal-master page thumbnail onto the MENU page in the site map. When the MENU page thumbnail shows a highlight, release the mouse button.

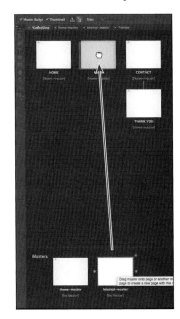

Note: When you apply a different master page to a page in the site map, the previous master page content is removed from the page and replaced entirely by the new master page content.

Notice that the text in brackets beneath the MENU page thumbnail changed from "Home-master" to "Internal-master," indicating that the Internal-master page is now applied to the MENU page and the design content from the Internal-master is now on that page. Right now, the MENU page thumbnail will be blank since the Internal-master page currently has no design content.

3 Right-click the CONTACT page and choose Masters > Internal-master to apply the Internal-master page to the CONTACT page.

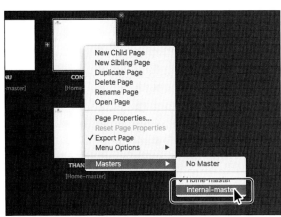

4 Repeat the previous step for the THANK YOU page.

5 In the Control panel, deselect Master Badge.

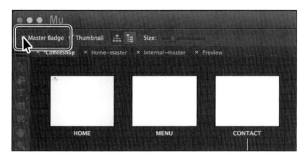

Notice that the master page names associated with the pages no longer appear beneath the page thumbnails. Sometimes, perhaps when you're discussing the site map with a client or colleague, you want to look at the site map and just see the page thumbnails. Muse lets you show and hide the master badge for all pages.

6 Select Master Badge to show them again.

7 In the Control panel deselect Thumbnail, and you'll see that the thumbnails turn into simple gray boxes.

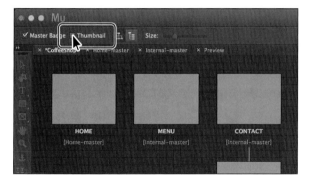

At times, you may also want to focus on the site map structure and not be distracted by a preview of the page in each thumbnail.

8 Select the Thumbnail option again to see the thumbnail previews once again.

9 Choose File > Save Site.

Basing one master on another

In Adobe Muse, you can apply one master page to another master page. That way, shared elements can be displayed in multiple master pages. For instance, in our example, on the Home-master page there is a logo that needs to be on every page in the site. We can apply Home-master to the Internal-master page and all elements from the Home-master page will appear on the Internal-master page, plus you can add unique elements to the Internal-master page.

1 Right-click (Ctrl-click) the Internal-master thumbnail and choose Masters > Home-master.

You should see the content from the Home-master page appear in the Internal-master thumbnail as well as all of the thumbnails for the pages based on the Internal-master page.

2 Double-click the Internal-master page thumbnail to open it in Design mode.

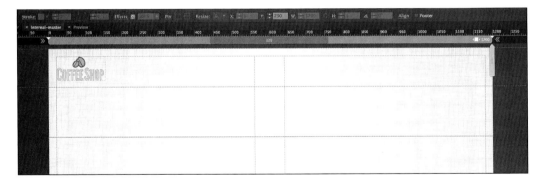

The content from the Home-master page is locked and cannot be selected on the Internal-master page. In order to edit the logo, for instance, you would need to open the Home-master page and make the change there. The logo on the Internal-master page would update as well. This can be a great time saver for master content that needs to appear on every page. You only have to edit each element once, and all instances of it are updated on the site automatically.

3 Choose File > Close Page to return to Plan mode.

Using layers

Now that you have some properties set for your master page, and a little design content in the form of a logo, you'll explore layers. As you add content to your site in Adobe Muse, each new object is stacked on top of the previous object in what is referred to as a *stacking order*. The first object you create on the page is on the bottom of that stack.

● **Note:** In Lesson 7, "Shapes, Color, and Effects," you'll learn more about stacking order and how to arrange content.

To organize your page elements and make your site designs easier to edit later, you can use layers in Muse. Think of layers as transparent sheets of paper stacked on top of each other, with each one containing different content. If you are familiar with layers in other programs like Adobe InDesign or Adobe Illustrator, you'll be able to jump right into working with layers in Muse. Each new Muse site starts with one default layer called *Layer 1*, which all content is placed on. The layers in the Layers panel are shared across all pages (including masters) and alternate layouts (which we haven't discussed).

● **Note:** If you decide to use layers in your Muse site, be sure to actually use them! I can't tell you how many times I've decided to use layers in my site, and then forgotten to ensure that the content for the header, for instance, is on the header layer. You'll see what is meant by this as you go through the lessons.

Creating layers

You don't *have* to work with layers, but they can make your life easier in the future when you're making edits or attempting to arrange your content's stacking order. Next, you'll begin setting up layers to more easily organize your page content. This includes creating as many layers as necessary and naming them to keep track of the content on each layer.

1   In Plan mode, double-click the Home-master page thumbnail to open it.

2   Choose Window > Layers to show the Layers panel on the right side of the workspace.

3   Double-click the "Layer 1" name in the Layers panel and change the name to **Page** in the Layer Options dialog box. This layer contains the master page content. Leave the other options at their default settings and click OK.

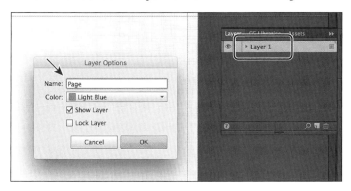

4 Click the New Layer button () at the bottom of the Layers panel to add a new layer named "Layer 2" above the existing layer. We'll discuss the importance of layer ordering shortly.

Every new layer that you create, by default, will have no content on it. Also, objects on master pages appear at the bottom of each layer. Master elements can appear in front of document page objects if the master elements are placed on a higher layer, but by default they are located on the bottom of the stacking order.

▶ **Tip:** To delete a layer, you can select it in the Layers panel and either click the Delete Selected Layer button (🗑), drag the layer(s) to the Delete Selected Layer button, or right-click the layer and choose Delete Layer. Deleting a layer will delete all content on the layer.

5 In the Layers panel, double-click the name "Layer 2" (your layer name may be different) to open the Layer Options dialog box. Change the following options in the dialog box:

• Name: **Header**

• Color: **Red** (the default setting)

• Show Layer: **Selected** (the default setting)

• Lock Layer: **Deselected** (the default setting)

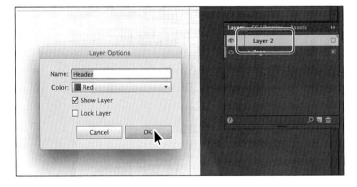

▶ **Tip:** You can also press Option (Alt) and click the New Layer button to create a new layer, and then open the Layer Options dialog box in one step. You can also right-click a layer name and choose Layer Options.

Notice the options in the Layer Options dialog box. You can assign a color to each layer. When content is selected on the pages, the color of the bounding box will match the color of the layer it's on. You can also lock a layer and hide a layer, but that can also be done directly within the Layers panel.

6 Click OK.

7 Click the New Layer button () at the bottom of the Layers panel to add another new layer named "Layer 3" above the existing layer.

8 In the Layers panel, double-click the name "Layer 3" (your layer name may be different) to open the Layer Options dialog box. Change the name to **Footer** and click OK.

There should now be three layers in the Layers panel: Footer, Header, and Page. Layers you create are shared across all pages, so later, if you need to edit or add a layer, you can open any page or master page to do so.

9 Choose File > Save Site.

Organizing layers and content

With a few layers created, you can begin to organize them to meet your needs. For instance, you could make it so that a logo in the header of a page is "stuck" to the top of the browser window. This is called "pinning" content. It will always be visible, even if the user scrolls down on the page. That means that the header content would need to always be *on top* of the page content for this site. To do that, you would change the ordering of the layers in the Layers panel. In this site, you'll make it so that the layer order follows the top to bottom ordering of page content: header, page, footer.

1 In the Layers panel, drag the Footer layer beneath the Page layer. When a line appears beneath the Page layer, release the mouse button.

▶ **Tip:** A fast way to locate content in the Layers panel is to select the content on the page, and then click the Locate Object button (▣) at the bottom of the Layers panel.

2 With the Selection tool (▶) selected, click the logo in the header to select it, if necessary.

With the logo selected, notice the blue box around it. Look in the Layers panel and you'll see the Page layer has a blue color bar to the far left of the layer name. This color helps to identify objects on that layer. Also notice the little blue square to the far right of the Page layer name. With the logo selected, the square with a color fill indicates which layer contains the logo (in this case).

3 Click the disclosure triangle (the little arrow) to the left of the Page layer name in the Layers panel to show the contents of that layer. The Layers panel reveals the image currently on the page (the logo).

Similar to layers in InDesign and Illustrator, Muse shows each object in your design in the Layers panel. Each layer that has content on it has a disclosure triangle to the left of the layer name. When collapsed, you can click the disclosure triangle to expand the contents of the layer and see the list of objects and their stacking order on that layer for the active page. Groups, widgets, and certain widget parts also have disclosure triangles that you can click to expand the set and display their contained objects. You can reorder these objects, lock and unlock them, and add or remove them from groups.

4 Click the disclosure triangle to the left of the Page layer name to hide the layer content.

The logo is a part of the header content which means it should be on the layer named Header to keep things organized, but it's now on the Page layer. The logo needs to be moved to the Header layer.

● **Note:** With the logo now on the Header layer, the logo bounding box will now be red to match the layer color.

5 With the logo still selected on the page, drag the small blue square to the right of the Page layer name *straight up* to the empty square on the Header layer. When the square on the Header layer shows a highlight, release the mouse button to move the logo to the Header layer.

6 Click the eye icon to the left of the Header layer name in the Layers panel to hide the logo temporarily.

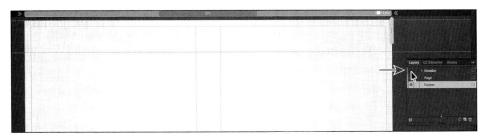

As you work in Muse, it can be helpful to hide entire layers or selected content on layers to focus on or more easily select the design content at hand.

7 In the Layers panel, click the now blank area where the eye icon was to show the Header layer content again.

Leave the Home-master page open so you can add a navigation menu to it in the next section. As you progress through this and later lessons, you'll continue to work with layers and discover other useful layer features.

Adding a navigation menu

When designing for the web, site navigation plays a key role in your design process, and the prime navigation system of any website is its menu bar. To help you create a menu, Muse offers Menu widgets. Although you can create a series of links to connect the pages manually, Menu widgets are a fast and flexible way to add navigation. Like other widgets, you simply drag a Menu widget onto your page. From there, you can customize it with your own content and formatting.

Note: You'll learn more about working with widgets in Lesson 9, "Working with Widgets."

Inserting a Menu widget

With the Home-master page still open, next you'll add a navigation menu to it. Since the Internal-master page is based on the Home-master page, the menu will also appear on the Internal-master.

1 Scroll up in the page, if necessary, to see all of the header content on the Home-master page.

2 Open the Layers panel by choosing Window > Layers, if necessary. Select the Header layer in the Layers panel, if it's not already selected.

3 Open the Widgets Library panel by choosing Window > Widgets Library. Click the folder icon or arrow to the left of the Menus category to reveal the Menu widgets.

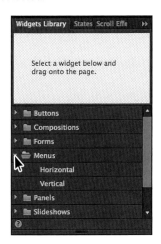

   Muse offers two types of Menu widgets: Horizontal and Vertical. Depending on your design and where the menu will be positioned on the page, you'll choose one or the other. You can always change your mind later and switch between the two if necessary.

4 Drag the Horizontal Menu widget into the right side of the header area. See the figure for general placement. You'll reposition the menu later.

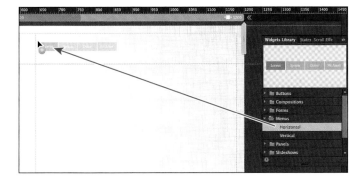

With the Menu widget on the page, notice that Muse automatically filled in the names of your pages in the menu, following the same order as the page thumbnails in Plan mode. Muse creates menu items with links to all of the *top-level* pages in your site map. Any child pages (the THANK YOU page, in your site) will not be shown by default. Be careful and accurate when naming those thumbnails; any errors in the site map names will appear in your menu!

5 Choose File > Save Site.

Excluding pages from the menu

Every time you create a new top-level page in Plan mode, Muse automatically adds it to the menu. Sometimes, however, you may want to test a page before making it accessible to visitors or hide a seasonally specific page during the offseason, for instance. In Plan mode you can specify pages to exclude from the navigation to ensure these pages are not listed as menu items in the Menu widget.

Next, you'll add a new page to the site map that you'll use for an event in the future.

1 Choose View > Plan Mode to return to Plan mode.

With the menu now on the Home-master page, it appears on every page in the site because Home-master is applied to the Internal-master page. Internal-master is applied to all of the interior pages of the site.

2 Hover over the CONTACT page thumbnail, and click the plus icon (+) to the right of the thumbnail to add another page.

3 Name the page **EVENT**.

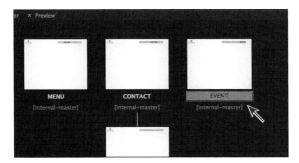

This page will contain information about an event happening in the future. You won't be adding any content to this page.

4 Click the Home-master page tab above the site plan area to show the master page in the Document window. Notice that the new page, EVENT, was automatically added to the right end of the menu.

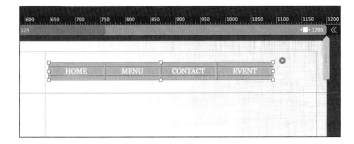

In the menu, each button with a page label and link is called a *menu item*. Muse automatically creates links to those pages so you won't have to do so later. This new page is being set up ahead of time for an event that hasn't happened yet, so it doesn't yet need to appear in the Menu widget.

5 Choose View > Plan Mode.

6 Right-click the EVENT page thumbnail and choose Menu Options > Exclude Page From Menus so that the page no longer appears in the menu.

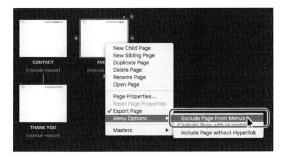

By default, any new pages are added to the menu, but by choosing Exclude Page From Menus for the EVENT page, only that single page is excluded from the menu.

7 Click the Home-master page tab to return to the page to see that the EVENT page no longer shows in the menu.

8 Choose Edit > Deselect All.

9 Choose File > Save Site.

▶ **Tip:** When you're creating a menu that has submenu content, like a "products" section of your menu, you may not want visitors to click the parent page (products). You may prefer that visitors click only the children pages in the submenu. In Plan mode, right-click a page thumbnail, like the products page thumbnail, and choose Menu Options > Include Page Without Hyperlink so that the page still appears in the menu but no longer links anywhere.

Editing the Menu widget options

With the number, naming, and order of pages set, you can now define how the menu behaves. Just remember, anything you've done up to this point can be changed later, if necessary.

1   With the Selection tool (►) selected, click to select the Menu widget on the page. Click the blue arrow button off the right end of the menu to reveal the Options menu, and set the following options:

    •   Menu Type: **All Pages**

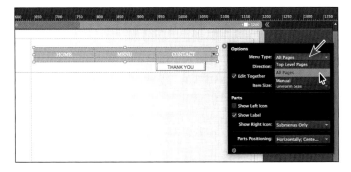

Notice that by choosing All Pages, the child pages from the site map appear in the menu as a submenu (the THANK YOU page in your site).

    •   Change Menu Type back to **Top Level Pages** to see only the parent pages again.
    •   Direction: **Horizontal** (the default setting)
    •   Edit Together: **Selected** (the default setting)
    •   Item Size: **Uniform Size** (Each menu item will be the same width. This will be important in a later lesson when you test the responsive web design.)
    •   Show Left Icon: **Deselected** (the default setting)
    •   Show Label: **Selected** (the default setting)
    •   Show Right Icon: **Off**
    •   Parts Positioning: **Horizontally; Center-Aligned** (the default setting)

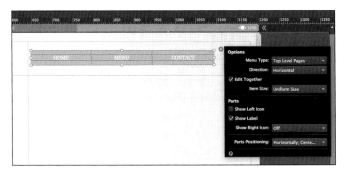

Formatting the Menu text

When you insert a Menu widget into your pages, the default font of the menu text is a serif font like Georgia. In Lesson 4, "Adding and Styling Text," you'll learn all about text and formatting. For now, you'll simply change basic formatting.

1   In Design mode, click away from the Menu widget to deselect it. Position the pointer over the menu and when the word "Menu" appears in a tooltip next to the pointer, click to select the menu (see the first part of the following figure). Position the pointer over the HOME text in the menu bar. When "Menu Item" appears in a tooltip next to the pointer, click to select the menu item.

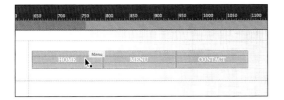 

The words "Menu Item" appear in the Selection Indicator on the left end of the Control panel when the menu item is selected. If you were to click once more on the HOME text, you would select the Label. You can change the text formatting when selecting the menu item or the label.

2   Choose Window > Text to open the Text panel on the right side of the workspace. Click the Font menu in the Text panel, and choose Lucida Sans from the Standard Fonts (with fallbacks) category.

▶ **Tip:** You can edit the text formatting, such as font family, size, and more, without ever selecting the text in the menu. By selecting the entire Menu widget, any changes you make to text formatting will affect all of the text in the Menu widget.

All of the menu items update to use the same font. This occurs because Edit Together is enabled in the Options menu.

3   In the Text panel, change the Size to **14** by clicking the arrow to the left of the size field or by typing the value directly into the field.

4 Click the Color option in the Text panel, and change the color to white by clicking the white color swatch, if necessary.

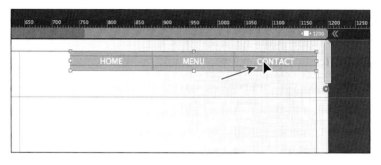

5 Click the Text panel tab to collapse the panel.

6 With the menu item still selected, press Esc to select the entire menu.

You can also click away from the menu with the Selection tool and click the menu to select it again.

▶ **Tip:** If you need to nudge the menu, press an arrow key on your keyboard. Or press Shift while pressing an arrow key to make it move ten pixels at a time.

7 Drag the menu to the right. When it snaps to the top and right edge of the rightmost column and Smart Guides appear, release the mouse button. See the following figure for placement help.

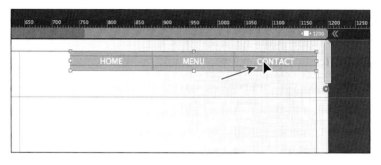

8 Click the Preview link in the upper-right corner of the Application window and position the pointer over an item in the menu. Notice that the background color changes to a darker gray.

When interacting with the menu, the appearance changes that you see are called the menu *states*. Editing the appearance of these states is an important part of designing your menu and is the task you'll perform after you edit the menu appearance a bit more.

9 Click the Design mode link in the upper-right corner of the Application window to return to the Home-master page.

Editing the appearance of the Menu widget and items

You can change the look of your menu by changing appearance settings. When an entire Menu widget is selected, you can change its dimensions, appearance, and location. With the sub-elements of a widget selected, you can format the contents (such as insert other objects, like images, text, and rectangles) as well as update each element's appearance and dimensions within the confines of the widget. First, you'll edit the size and appearance of the entire widget.

1 Choose View > Smart Guides to temporarily turn them off.

Smart Guides are turned on by default, and they are temporary snap-to guides that appear when you create or manipulate objects in Muse. They help you align, edit, and transform objects relative to other objects, margins, the page, and more. If you don't want content to snap, you can temporarily turn them off.

2 With the entire menu still selected and the Selection tool (⬏) selected, drag the left, middle point of the menu to the right until the measurement label shows a width of approximately 300 px. You want to leave a little space on the left and right of the text to account for font size differences in browsers.

▶ **Tip:** You can change the width or height of the menu by dragging a bounding point or change the values in the Width and Height fields in the Control panel or in the Transform panel (Window > Transform).

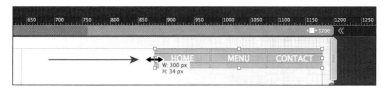

3 Choose View > Smart Guides to turn them back on.

Aside from changing the width and height of the menu, you can also change the background of the menu by applying a fill (color, gradient, or image). The fill appears behind the menu items. By default, the menu has no stroke and no fill.

4 With the menu still selected, click the word HOME to select the individual menu item.

The words "Menu Item" will appear in the Selection Indicator on the left end of the Control panel. Now that the general menu appearance is finished, you can edit the appearance of each of the menu items as well.

5 Click the Fill color in the Control panel and select the None swatch (▨) in the list of swatches to remove the fill color. Leave the HOME menu item selected.

▶ **Tip:** To make each of the menu item containers look different, deselect Edit Together in the Menu Widget options. Then select each menu item within the Menu widget, adding different fills, strokes, background images, rounded corners, and more.

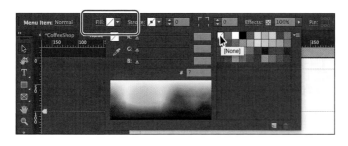

In addition to changing the fills, you can also apply strokes, including gradients, solid colors, and background images, in each of the menu items. You can also apply effects like drop shadows or rounded corners to the menu items. You'll learn about effects and rounded corners in Lesson 7. Right now, the menu items might be hard to see. You'll change that shortly.

Editing the menu item states

As discussed earlier, a state is the appearance of content (in this case, a menu item) on a web page based on user interaction. For example, if a visitor puts the pointer over an item in the menu, a menu item's background color might change from one color to another. You can edit the various states of Menu widget items by selecting the correct menu part and using the States panel, which is what you'll do next.

▶ **Tip:** To view the States panel, you can also click the Normal link on the left end of the Control panel where you see "Menu Item: Normal."

1 Open the States panel by choosing Window > States.

With the HOME menu item still selected in the menu, in the States panel, you'll see that each menu item has four states.

2 Click the Rollover state, and Muse shows what the Rollover state looks like on the page in the menu.

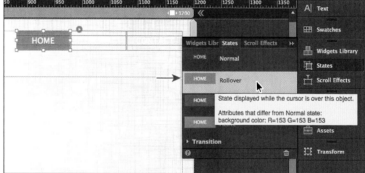

▶ **Tip:** In Lesson 8, you'll learn how to save formatting as a graphic style that you can apply throughout your document, making changes like these even easier.

Once you select a state in the States panel or States menu, you can then edit the appearance of the state using any number of appearance options, such as text properties, fill, stroke, and more.

● **Note:** Clicking the Reset To Default button (the trash can icon in the lower-right corner) in the States menu or the States panel with either the Rollover state or Active state selected will make the selected state look like the Normal state. With the Mouse Down state selected, clicking the Reset To Default button will make it look like the Rollover state.

3 With the Rollover state selected in the States panel, click the Reset To Default button (🗑) at the bottom of the States panel.

This makes the attributes the same as the Normal state for every menu item.

4 In the Text panel (Window > Text), click the Text Color and change the RGB color values to R=**200**, G=**200**, B=**200** (a light gray).

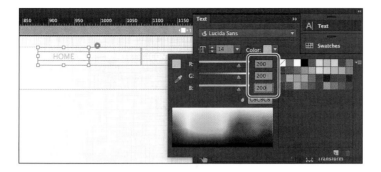

Next, you'll change the Mouse Down state. In this case we want the Mouse Down state to have the same appearance as the Rollover state.

5   Select the Mouse Down state in the States panel. Click the Reset To Default button (🗑) at the bottom of the States panel. This makes the attributes of the Mouse Down state the same as the Rollover state for every menu item.

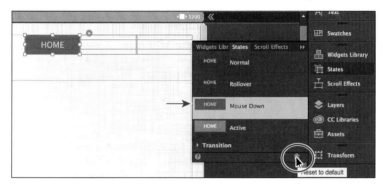

6   Select the Active state in the States panel that is still showing.

The Active state indicates the appearance of the menu item of the page currently showing in the browser window (it's a link in the menu).

7   Click the Reset To Default button (🗑) at the bottom of the States panel. This makes the attributes of the Active state the same as the Normal state for every menu item.

8   In the Text panel, change the RGB color values to R=**200**, G=**200**, B=**200** (a light gray).

9   Choose Edit > Deselect All.

Editing the appearance of a submenu ▇◀

To learn how to edit the appearance of a submenu, check out the video titled "Editing the Appearance of a Submenu" that is a part of the Web Edition. For more information, see the "Web Edition" section of Getting Started at the beginning of the book.

▶ **Tip:** When you first applied the light gray color to the rollover state, you could have saved the color as a swatch to save time and ensure consistency.

Testing your pages

During the course of the exercises, you've previewed the file by selecting Preview mode. This allows you to test links, hide all hidden items, and navigate the site like visitors will. Although Preview mode is very useful, it does not show a few elements in the site, such as the page title and favicon.

To give you the full user experience, Muse lets you test a page or your entire site in a browser outside of the program. That's what you'll do next.

1 Choose File > Save Site.

2 Choose File > Preview Site In Browser.

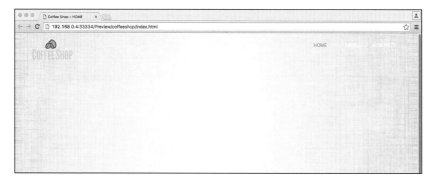

Preview Site In Browser allows you to navigate between pages for an overview of the site. Choosing File > Preview *Page* In Browser, the other alternative, allows you to see only the current page in the Document window or the first page of the site if there are no open pages. When previewing a single page, links to other pages in the site will not work because you are only previewing the appearance of that single page.

3 Close the browser window, and return to Muse.

4 Close all open pages (including Preview), and make sure that Plan mode is displayed for the next lesson.

   To close Preview, you can either click the X on the Preview tab or click the Preview tab and choose File > Close Preview.

You have now laid the groundwork for a fully responsive site! In the next few lessons, you'll add text and graphics to your site. Then, in Lesson 6, with some content on your pages, you'll explore what makes a site responsive and the tools necessary to make it happen.

Review questions

1 What are the benefits of using master pages?

2 What purpose do the Header and Footer page guides serve on the master pages?

3 Describe how layers can be useful in your Muse site.

4 Where on a page does a background image in the browser fill appear?

5 Name the two ways that you can apply master pages to pages in Plan mode.

Review answers

1 Master pages can be used to more efficiently update a site, because common site elements are easy to locate and only need to be updated once. You can use one default master page throughout your website, or you can create multiple master pages and apply them individually to other pages or master pages.

2 The Header and Footer page guides define the areas where the header and footer content appear on the page. They also determine how large either of those areas is. Content that is placed on a master page and appears above the Header guide or below the Footer guide is locked on each page (cannot be selected or edited unless you're editing on the master page that contains that content).

3 Layers allow you to organize content and make your projects easier to update. You can create and edit specific areas or kinds of content on the page without affecting other areas or accidentally changing other content. You can also place content that rarely updates in one layer while keeping content that you'll update frequently on a different layer of the same page. Using layers also allows you to set the stacking order to arrange elements to display above or behind each other.

4 When you set a background image as the fill content using the Browser Fill menu in the Control panel, the image appears in the background of the browser window, behind the page area.

5 You can apply master pages to pages in your site by dragging a master page thumbnail in Plan mode onto a page thumbnail in the site plan area. You can also apply a master page to a page in the site map by right-clicking a page thumbnail in the site plan area and choosing Masters > [*name of the master to apply*].

4 ADDING AND STYLING TEXT

Lesson overview

In this lesson, you'll add text to your pages and learn how to:

- Type and place text
- Change text attributes
- Work with fonts
- Create and edit lists
- Create and edit paragraph styles
- Create and edit character styles
- Create and edit list styles
- Work with the Spell Checker

 This lesson takes approximately 60 minutes to complete. To download the project files for this lesson, log in or set up an account at peachpit.com. Enter the book's ISBN (9780134547275) or go directly to the book's product page to register. Once on the book's page, click the Register Your Product link. The book will show up in your list of registered products along with a link to the book's bonus content. Click the link to access the lesson files for the book. Store the files on your computer in a convenient location, as described in the "Getting Started" section of this book. Your Account page is also where you'll find any updates to the chapters or to the lesson files. If you are starting from scratch in this lesson, use the method described in the "Jumpstart" section in "Getting Started."

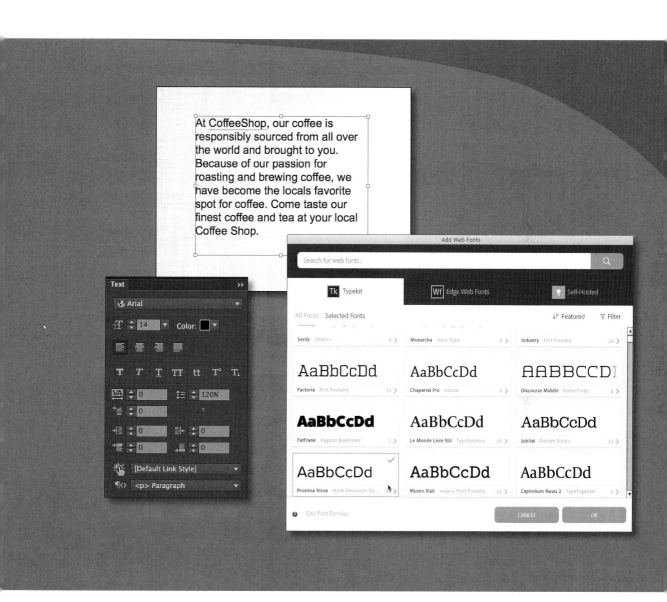

Adobe Muse provides numerous tools for
creating, editing, and formatting text, whether
it's created within the program or imported from
another program.

Adding text

Note: If you are starting from scratch using the Jumpstart method described in the "Jumpstart" section of "Getting Started," your workspace may look different from the figures you see in this lesson.

With your master pages and pages created, you'll now turn your attention to adding some text to your pages. Muse offers several ways to add text to your web pages. From typing text directly on your page to placing or pasting text from other applications, adding text to your design is simple.

As in InDesign, text that you insert into your pages in Muse is contained within a text frame (see the following figure). You can resize, reposition, rotate, and transform those text frames and their content (which can include text, images, and rectangle shapes) almost any way you like.

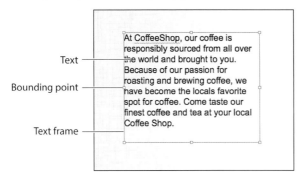

Text —
Bounding point —
Text frame —

At CoffeeShop, our coffee is responsibly sourced from all over the world and brought to you. Because of our passion for roasting and brewing coffee, we have become the locals favorite spot for coffee. Come taste our finest coffee and tea at your local Coffee Shop.

In this first section, you'll insert text in various ways, and then format that text.

Note: If you have not already downloaded the project files for this lesson to your computer from your Account page, make sure to do so now. See "Getting Started" at the beginning of the book.

Typing text

The first method you'll use to insert text into your pages is to create a text frame and type heading text into it.

1 With the CoffeeShop.muse site still open, in Plan mode double-click the MENU page thumbnail to open it in Design mode.

For the next section, the rulers along the top and left side of the Document window need to be showing.

2 Choose View > Show Rulers, if necessary.

3 Choose Window > Reset Panels.

4 Select the Text tool (**T**) in the Toolbar. Position the pointer near the center of the page, click and drag down and to the right, and then release the mouse button. A blinking cursor will appear within the text frame.

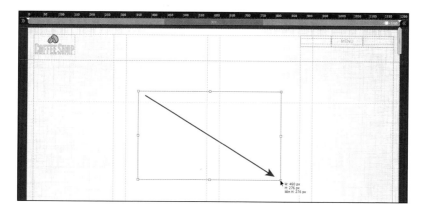

Notice that as you create the text frame it snaps to guides and red lines, and other visual aids display, depending on where you drag the frame and what its edges touch. The snapping feature and visual aids are part of Smart Guides and are turned on by default.

About Smart Guides

Smart Guides are temporary snap-to guides and visual aids that appear when you place, create, add, or manipulate objects. They help you align, edit, and transform objects relative to other objects, page guides, or both by snap-aligning and displaying gap measurements to help you consistently space your objects.

Smart Guides are turned on by default, but you can easily turn them off. With a page open in Design mode, choose View > Smart Guides. However, be aware that when you turn off Smart Guides, you also turn off the snapping feature and visual aids.

5   Type **Coffee Company Food Offerings** in the text frame.

6   Click and drag from the horizontal ruler above the page, down into the page until you see roughly 320 px in the measurement label. This created a horizontal guide to align content to.

The 320 px value is the pixel distance from the top edge of the page.

7   Select the Selection tool (⬆) in the Toolbar. Click and drag the text frame from the center until its top edge snaps to the guide *you just made,* and the left edge snaps to the left edge of the first column guide. You can tell when the top and left edges of the frame are snapped to the guides when red lines appear. See the following figure for placement help.

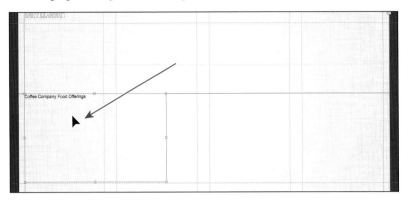

8   With the Selection tool, double-click within the text frame to select the Text tool (**T**) in the Toolbar and enable text editing.

● **Note:** You may want to zoom in to see the text more clearly.

9   Insert the cursor before the word "Offerings," and type **& Beverage** and then a spacebar space.

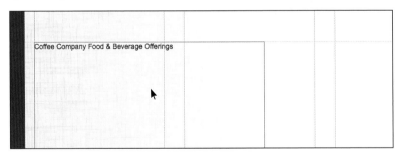

▶ **Tip:** With the Text tool selected and the cursor in text, you can press the Esc key to switch to the Selection tool and select the text frame.

10 Select the Selection tool and drag the bottom-middle point of the text frame up a little to make the text frame shorter.

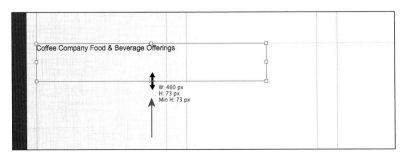

Placing text

In Muse, you can also place text (File > Place) from a file created in another application, provided that file was saved as a .txt file. Because .txt files typically don't contain formatting, Muse applies default formatting to the text when you place the file.

1　Choose File > Place. Navigate to the Lessons > Text folder. Select the file named Menu.txt (or Menu), and click Open.

Note: Currently you cannot place (File > Place) text into an existing text frame in Muse.

　The cursor you see indicates that you can either click to create a text frame that the text is placed into or you can click and drag to draw a frame with the proportions that you want.

2　Position the pointer below the heading you just created and click. A text frame is created and the text is placed within.

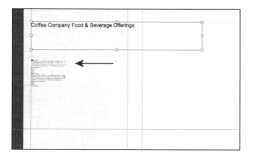 

3　With the Selection tool (⬉) selected, drag the right, middle bounding point of the text frame to the right to snap to the right edge of the second column. See the following figure for sizing help.

Note: In Muse, Dynamic Spelling (Edit > Spelling > Dynamic Spelling) is turned on by default. That means any words not found in the Muse dictionary are underlined in red. In the figures going forward, the word "CoffeeShop" has a red underline. If your looks different, that's okay.

　Later, after you format the text, you will copy this text frame to create another column of text.

4　Choose Edit > Deselect All and then choose File > Save Site.

Now that you have text on the page, you'll make sure that it is on the correct layer, and then begin to format it using the text formatting options available in Muse.

Move content between layers

When you create layers, it's important to continue working with them. Otherwise, everything you create will wind up on the last selected layer and do you no good. Next, you'll ensure that the text content you just created is on the correct layer.

Tip: You can also Shift-click between the frames to select them both. This method may be preferable if there is a lot of content on the page.

1   With the Selection tool (▶) selected, drag across the two text frames you created to select them both.

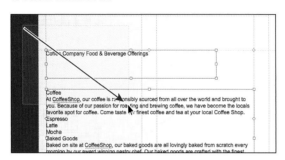

Notice the red edges of the selected bounding boxes. In the Layers panel (Window > Layers) you'll see a small red square to the right of the Header layer name. This square is another way to see which layer the selected content is on and also a way to select that content on the page from within the Layers panel.

Tip: You can also click the empty box to the far right of a layer name in the Layers panel to select all of the content on that layer.

Tip: To move content between layers, you can also select content on the page. In the Layers panel, drag the little red box on the Header layer straight down to the hollow box on the Page layer. When the hollow box highlights, release the mouse button.

2   Choose Object > Move To Layer > Page.

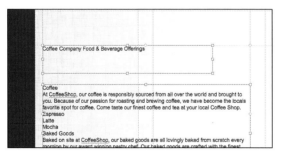

Note: Currently, you cannot select content on the Header layer because the content on the Header layer is on a master page. It cannot be selected unless the master page is showing in Design mode.

You just moved the text from the Header layer to the Page layer. You can also right click selected content and choose Move To Layer > Page (in this case). Notice that the colored edges of the selected text frames on the page changed from red to blue. You can use the color of a layer you set in the Layer Options dialog box to determine which layer selected content is on, which also may make it easier to see the bounding boxes for transforming artwork.

3   Choose Edit > Deselect All.

4   Choose File > Save Site.

Formatting text

In this section, you'll work with a wide range of text formatting options available to you in Muse, from changing font size to adjusting paragraph spacing. You can find these formatting options in the Control panel (Window > Control) and Text panel (Window > Text).

The Text panel contains more formatting options than the Control panel, but the Control panel can be more convenient because it's always showing (by default).

*   Open the Text panel by choosing Window > Text, and take a look at some of the formatting features available. With either a text frame selected, or text selected within a frame, the options in the Text panel become available.

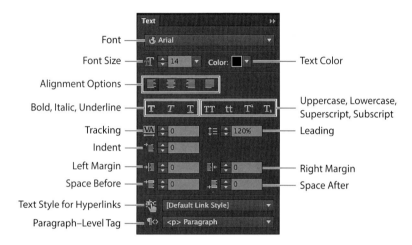

Note: Some of the features will be dimmed in the panel you see unless a text frame or text is selected.

▶ **Tip:** To learn more about the Paragraph-Level Tag menu, see the Paragraph_tags.pdf file in the Lessons > Lesson04 folder.

The first formatting you'll change is font size. Muse uses Arial as the default font and 14 pixels as the default font size, whether you type or place your text onto your pages.

Adjusting font size

In print work, most of us use the unit *points* to set the size of text. In Muse, the font size unit used is *pixel* to correspond with web standards.

▶ **Tip:** Clicking text twice with the Text tool selects a word, clicking three times selects the paragraph, and clicking four times selects all of the text within a frame.

1 Select the Text tool (**T**) in the Toolbar, and insert the cursor in the text frame that begins with the text "Coffee… At CoffeeShop, our coffee is…"

2 Choose Edit > Select All.

3 Choose 18 from the Font Size menu in the Control panel. The text frame may expand to fit the resized text.

▶ **Tip:** You can dynamically change the font size of selected text using keyboard shortcuts. To increase the font size in increments of two pixels, press Command+Shift+> (Ctrl+Shift+>). To reduce the font size, press Command+Shift+< (Ctrl+Shift+<).

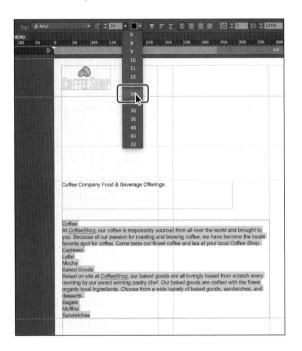

▶ **Tip:** If you have a text frame to which you want to apply all the same text formatting, you can select the text frame with the Selection tool rather than using the Text tool to select the text and edit the formatting.

4 With the Text tool still selected, position the cursor over the "Coffee Company Food & Beverage Offerings" text. Click three times to select the text.

▶ **Tip:** To change the font size by one-pixel increments, you can also click the arrows to the left of the Font Size field in the Control panel or Text panel.

5 In the Font Size menu in the Control panel, select 14 and type **28**. Press Return (Enter) to accept the change.

If the text is wrapping in the text frame, you can select the Selection tool and drag the right, middle point to the right until all of the text fits on one line. Know that you will fix that in a later lesson if you decide not to do it now.

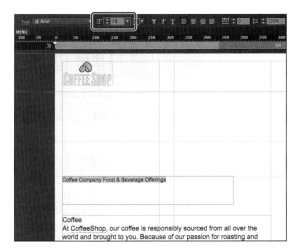

Note: The figure shows the text just *before* pressing Enter or Return.

6 Select the Selection tool (▶) in the Toolbar and click the larger text frame. Drag the bottom, middle bounding point up until a dotted line appears. You won't have to drag far.

 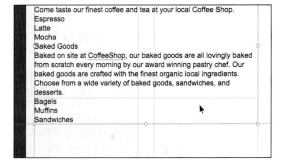

The dotted line across the text frame near the bottom indicates a minimum height for the text frame. When you drag the frame shorter than the text and the dotted line appears, Muse inserts a style property called *min-height* in the code. This tells the browser that the frame must be at least that tall and can expand in height if the content dictates it.

7 Drag the same bottom, middle bounding point down until the dotted line disappears.

8 Choose File > Save Site.

Selecting a font

For years, web designers and developers had to rely strictly on "web safe" fonts, or fonts that came installed on Mac OS and Windows machines. We used web safe fonts in our designs because a font we used on a web page needed to be installed on the machine of the visitor viewing your website for it to work. These days you can use a variety of methods, like hosted fonts, for getting the font you want in your page designs.

Using a hosted font in your design will cause the web fonts needed to download to the users machine and display the content as text in the chosen font. This has lots of advantages, one being the large variety of fonts we can now use in our designs. In this section, you'll change the font that is applied to the text by default. Adobe Muse offers three categories of fonts that you can use:

- **Standard fonts (with fallbacks):** Most systems or devices have these fonts installed, which increases the likelihood of them displaying correctly on your visitors' devices. These are also referred to as "web safe" fonts.

- **System fonts:** These fonts are those located on your machine. If you apply one of these to text on your pages, Muse converts that text to an image when your site is previewed, published, or exported.

- **Web fonts:** These are fonts hosted by a company such as Adobe Typekit, Edge Web Fonts, or Self-Hosted fonts. When a hosted font is viewed, your site visitor's browser downloads the font from that company's server, so the font appears on your web page regardless of whether that site visitor owns the specific font. Using Muse, you get access to a wide variety of fonts hosted by Adobe Typekit.

Applying a standard font

The first category of font you'll use is a standard font that you'll apply to the placed text on the MENU page.

1 Double-click the placed text frame, that contains the text, "Coffee... At CoffeeShop, our coffee is..." to switch to the Text tool (**T**).

2 Insert the cursor in the text, if it isn't in the text already, and choose Edit > Select All.

3 Click the Font menu in the Control panel.

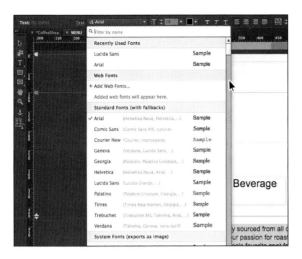

In the Font menu that appears, you'll see a sectioned list with each of the three font categories available: Web Fonts, Standard Fonts (with fallbacks), and System Fonts (exports as image). Web fonts and system fonts are grouped by font family. Individual weights and styles (e.g., Bold, Italic, Bold Italic, etc.) of multiface font families appear in submenus. At the top of the menu is a filter by name field that you can use to search for fonts by entering a font name or partial font name, as well as a recently used fonts list.

4   In the menu, click the Standard Fonts (with fallbacks) category shortcut to scroll to those fonts. Position the pointer over the Lucida Sans font in the list that appears.

Note: You can filter the font list by font family (e.g., Myriad Pro), weight or style (e.g., Bold Italic), a combination of these (e.g., Myriad Pro Bold Italic), or use partial names in any order (e.g., It Bold Myr Pro).

▶ **Tip:** You can configure the number of recently used fonts to display, and you can clear the list by choosing Adobe Muse CC > Preferences (Edit > Preferences) and clicking Clear Recent Fonts.

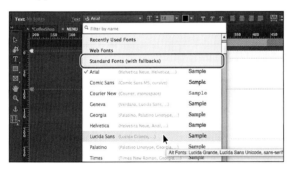

A yellow tooltip appears. In the tooltip, you'll see the words "Alt Fonts..." and a list of fonts. Keep in mind that selecting a web safe (standard) font doesn't guarantee it will work, because visitors need to have the font (Lucida Sans in this example) on their devices. The alt (alternate) fonts are second, third, and subsequent choices the browser will use if Lucida Sans isn't available. You cannot change alt fonts in Muse. Just know that Muse selects alternate (fallback) fonts that are similar to your first choice font.

5   Click the Lucida Sans font to apply it to the text.

System fonts

System fonts refer to fonts that you have installed on your computer (and are not considered Standard fonts). Applying a system font converts the text into an image when the site is previewed, published, or exported. As you are designing pages, the system font text remains editable.

One downside of applying a system font is that text is converted into an image on the live site, which can take longer to load than text content. Also, because the text is now an image, search engines can't read it.

You can tell that a system font is applied to text in Muse when a small "T" with an image icon appears in the lower-right corner of any text frame. That icon indicates that the text will become an image when you preview, publish, or export the site.

Adding Typekit web fonts

The next type of font you'll apply to text is a web font (also called a hosted font). You'll need an Internet connection to choose a web font the first time. Choosing a web font in Muse will download a local version of the font so that you can preview it in Muse when you're working on your site. The code for your page will contain a link to the Typekit servers that allows site visitors to view the font in the browser, but you don't need to worry about that. Even if you decide to export the site content and host the site elsewhere, you can still use the web fonts that you apply to your design content within Muse.

● **Note:** The font list you see under the Web Fonts category may not be the same as in the figure and that's okay.

1   With the Text tool (**T**) selected, select the "Coffee Company Food & Beverage Offerings" heading text. Click the Font menu in the Control panel. In the Font menu click the Web Fonts category to see the options. Click the +Add Web Fonts option that appears to open the Add Web Fonts dialog box.

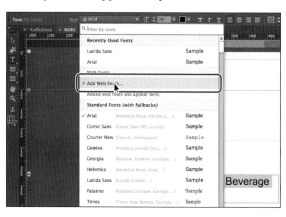

2   Click the Get Started button in the Add Web Fonts dialog box to begin selecting Typekit web fonts.

3   In the Add Web Fonts dialog box, type **Estilo** in the Search For Web Fonts field at the top of the dialog box. You'll see that on each of the tabs (Typekit, Edge Web Fonts, and Self-Hosted) below the field, a number appears next to the name on the tab. The Typekit tab will show (3) most likely (circled in the following figure). This indicates that 3 Estilo fonts were found on Typekit.

4   With the Typekit tab selected, click to select the Estilo Pro font in the list and a blue check mark appears next to the font name indicating that it will download and appear in your web fonts list when you're finished.

● **Note:** Because the Typekit library is constantly being updated, it may have changed since I wrote this lesson; the fonts I ask you to choose may not be available. Feel free to choose other fonts if you like. Just know that you'll need to substitute your font when you see any references to the selected fonts later in the lessons.

● **Note:** If you click the bottom part of a font in the list (where the font name is), you will get a preview of all of the font styles in the font. If that happens, you can click Select and then click All Fonts to return to the list.

5   Clear the word Estilo from the search field by clicking the X on the right end of the search field.

6 Click the Filter button. Click the Sans Serif button in the Classification options.

Filtering allows you to see only specific font types, such as serif or sans serif. To stop filtering, you can click the filter button again and deselect the filter option.

▶ **Tip:** If you are having a difficult time finding the same fonts I chose, you can click the Featured button and sort by name or search for the names in the Search For Web Fonts field at the top of the dialog box.

7 Click the Acumin Pro font, and then any other font you want, to select them both. I selected Proxima Nova. You may want to scroll in the list of fonts. Both fonts will show a blue check mark. Click OK.

8 When the Web Fonts Notification dialog box appears, click OK.

The Web Fonts Notification dialog box indicates that the fonts you've chosen have been downloaded and added to the Font menu. The fonts will appear in the Font menu no matter what site file is open, allowing you to apply them to any site.

Managing Typekit web fonts

While designing your site, you may want to add more Typekit fonts, or even remove a few from the font list in Muse. Next, you'll learn how to add and remove a Typekit font from the list.

1 Choose File > Add/Remove Web Fonts.

This is just another way to access the Add Web Fonts dialog box. I will sometimes use this menu command when I work on a Muse site so I can load Typekit fonts I know I need even before I begin designing.

2 Click the Get Started button in the Add Web Fonts dialog box.

3 Click Selected Fonts in the dialog box (circled in the following figure).

This shows a list of all of the web fonts that you've downloaded.

4 Making sure Acumin Pro and Estilo Pro are still selected, click the Proxima Nova font (or the extra font you chose) to deselect it and remove that font family from the Web Fonts menu. Click OK.

5 Click OK in the Web Fonts Notification dialog box that indicates that the font family was removed.

Note: For each font you choose, the entire font family is downloaded. This means that if there are any font styles, such as bold or black, those font styles are downloaded as well.

Note: The figure shows just before clicking the Proxima Nova font. Once you click, the font is longer in the listing.

Note: Any font styles in a family, like Bold, that are applied to text when you remove them in the Add Web Fonts dialog box will remain in the Web Fonts section of the Font list. Also, if you remove fonts that are used in a site file that is not currently open, when you open that site after removing the font, it will be downloaded again automatically.

6 With the header text still selected, click the Font menu in the Control panel, and then click the Estilo Pro > Medium font, or a font you selected. You may need to scroll in the list to see the fonts.

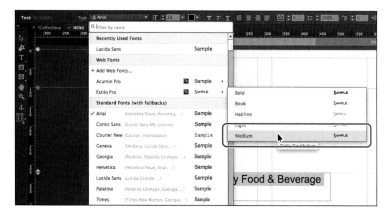

Self-Hosted web fonts

The Self-Hosted Web Fonts feature, accessible in the Add Web Fonts dialog box (File > Add/Remove Web Fonts), allows you to access and use web fonts you may have purchased from third-party providers.

In order to use your own self-hosted web fonts, Adobe Muse requires you to obtain the web font in the following formats (to properly render across all browsers):

- Web Open Font Format (.woff)
- Embedded OpenType (.eot)
- Scalable Vector Graphics (.svg)

When you publish a site, the associated font files are published to the selected host server along with all other site content. Hosting and rendering web fonts real time, is called self-hosting. Fonts obtained in this manner are called Self-Hosted Web Fonts.

Changing other text formatting

With the main generic formatting complete, you can begin to fine-tune some of the text to better suit your design. As mentioned earlier, you can change the formatting options in either the Text panel or the Control panel, depending on what tool or content is selected in Muse and the resolution of your screen. For this part of the lesson, you'll use the Text panel.

1 Open the Text panel by choosing Window > Text or clicking the word Text in the docked panels on the right side of the workspace, if necessary.

I dragged the Text panel from the dock closer to the text to make it easier to see the panel relative to the text.

2 Click in the first paragraph of the text that begins with "At CoffeeShop, our coffee is…" to insert the cursor. Click three times to select that paragraph only.

In the Text panel, notice that the Leading value (⊟) is 120%. That means that the distance between the lines of text is 120% of the font size of the text.

3 Change the Leading value to **140%** in the Text panel.

▶ **Tip:** Pressing the Shift key and clicking an arrow to change the Leading value you will change the value by 10% every time you click, not 1%.

You don't have to type the percent sign (%) because Muse will assume that the unit is percent. You can also enter a value for the leading with px (for pixel), like **32px**, instead of a percent, and Muse will keep it as a pixel value in the code that is generated.

4 With the Text tool (**T**) selected, insert the cursor into the text, "Coffee Company Food & Beverage Offerings." In the Text panel, click the Align Center button (▤) to align the text to the center of the text frame.

Muse offers four alignment options: Align Left, Align Center, Align Right, and Align Justify. The Align Justify option justifies the entire paragraph (makes it look like a block of text) except for the last line of text in that paragraph. Next, you'll adjust the spacing between the letters in the heading.

5 Select the Selection tool (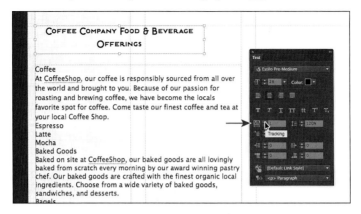) in the Toolbar and ensure that the text frame that contains the "Coffee Company Food & Beverage Offerings" text is still selected. In the Text panel, change the Tracking option (☒) to **1**.

In Muse, *tracking* is the distance between characters (not just letters). When you select the entire text frame, Muse changes the spacing between all characters in the text frame. If you come from the print world, tracking in Muse is the web equivalent of tracking and kerning. Muse tracking uses pixel values rather than the typical print unit of points. On the web, we typically use tracking for text like headlines, not entire stretches of body copy. Just keep in mind that every small kerning adjustment adds code to the HTML pages that Muse creates for you when you preview, publish, or export as HTML, which can ultimately increase download times for your pages.

6 With the Selection tool selected, drag the text frame that contains the text, "Coffee Company Food & Beverage Offerings" into the horizontal center of the page. Make sure the top edge is still aligned with the guide you created previously. When a vertical smart guide appears in the center of the page between the columns, you'll know it's centered horizontally.

● **Note:** The pixel values you see off the left and right edges of the text frame may be different and that's okay.

7 Choose File > Save Site.

There are lots of other text formatting options in the Text panel and Control panel to explore, like Left and Right Indents, Space Before and Space After, and more. Feel free to try them out!

Changing the color and case of text

The last bit of text formatting you'll learn about is changing text color and changing text case from lowercase to uppercase and vice versa.

1   Select the Text tool (**T**) and select the first word "Coffee" in the text frame below the heading you just centered.

2   Click the Color option in the Text panel (or Control panel) and change the RGB values to R=**117**, G=**76**, B=**0** to change the color of the text.

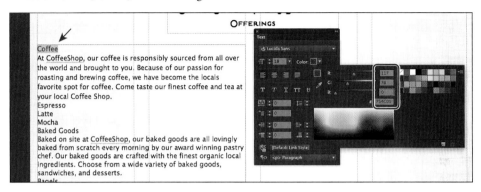

Note: You'll learn more about creating and editing colors in Lesson 7, "Shapes, Color, and Effects."

3   With the "Coffee" text still selected, choose Edit > Change Case > UPPERCASE to capitalize the selected text from "Coffee" to "COFFEE."

▶ **Tip:** You could also right-click on the text and choose Change Case > UPPERCASE or click the Uppercase button (TT) in the Text panel.

4   Choose File > Save Site.

Now that you've explored basic text formatting options in Muse, you'll learn how to add bulleted and numbered lists to your page designs.

Creating a list

In Adobe Muse you can easily create both bulleted and numbered lists from your text. In this section, you'll explore working with bulleted lists.

1   With the Text tool (**T**) selected, drag to select the three lines of text, Espresso... Latte... and Mocha.

2 Click the Bullets button (🔳) in the Control panel to apply a bullet list to the selected text.

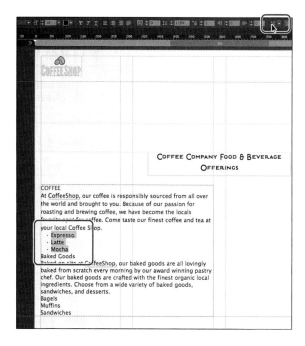

3 Choose Window > Bullets to open the Bullets panel and change the following options:

- Click the arrow to the right of the Bullets button (circled in the following figure). This is where you can select another available bullet. In this case, leave it at the default bullet character.

- Color: 50% Grey swatch

- Indent For Right Edge of Bullets (➡●): **20**

In the Bullets panel, you can apply a list and edit bullet properties like size and color, as well as placement.

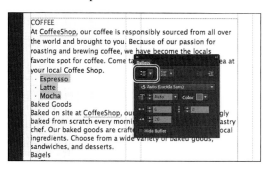

4 Choose Edit > Deselect All.

Creating Type Styles

Using styles in Muse, you can quickly apply consistent formatting to text and make global changes across multiple pages in your site. After you create a style, you can update all of the text throughout your site that uses that particular style simply by editing the saved style. Styles you create on one page are available on every other page in a site. This is very similar to how styles in InDesign and Illustrator work. When you publish your site, Muse converts your styles to CSS (Cascading Style Sheets) rules.

Muse supports three types of text styles:

- **Paragraph** styles retain text and paragraph attributes; apply them to an entire paragraph.

- **Character** styles retain text attributes only; apply them to selected text, such as a single character or word.

- **Bullet** styles retain formatting from lists using the Bullet Styles panel.

Note: As a best practice, apply text formatting using paragraph styles and character styles; doing so requires less effort in Muse and also makes a site that has the potential to download faster on the web. Also, text styles are shared between layouts and can be very useful when you're editing layouts.

Creating and applying paragraph styles

The first type of text style you'll learn about is paragraph styles. Paragraph styles save formatting from an entire paragraph and encompass all of the formatting options found in the Text panel, including font size, alignments, indents, and more.

Next, you'll create a paragraph style to save the formatting for heading text and another style for the main body text so that you can apply that formatting elsewhere easily. Remember, after you create a style, it appears in the Paragraph Styles panel, no matter which page of the site is open.

1 Choose Window > Reset Panels.

2 Choose Window > Paragraph Styles to open the Paragraph Styles panel.

Take a minute to become familiar with the options in the Paragraph Styles panel. As you progress through this exercise, you'll learn about each of these options.

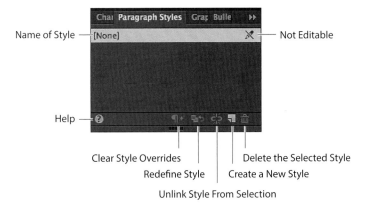

Name of Style — [None]
Not Editable
Help
Clear Style Overrides
Redefine Style
Unlink Style From Selection
Delete the Selected Style
Create a New Style

3 With the Text tool (**T**) selected, click three times in the first paragraph that begins with "At CoffeeShop, our coffee is…" to select it.

4 Click the Create A New Style button (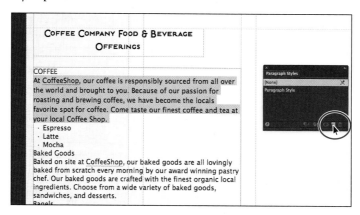) at the bottom of the Paragraph Styles panel.

Muse saves the formatting from the selected text as a paragraph style and adds it to the Paragraph Styles panel. By default, Muse names the new style "Paragraph Style," but you can, and should, rename it to make sense to you.

⬤ **Note:** You do not have to select an entire paragraph to create a paragraph style. You can simply insert the cursor in the text, and then click the Create A New Style button.

5 In the Paragraph Styles panel, double-click the style named "Paragraph Style" to open the Paragraph Style Options dialog box.

⬤ **Note:** The order of text attributes in the Style Setting field may be different than what you see in the figure, and that's OK.

6 Change the Style Name to **Body**.

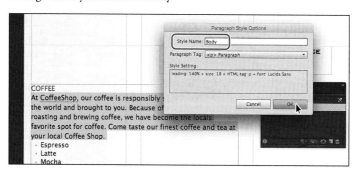

In the Paragraph Style Options dialog box, notice that the formatting options that were saved from the paragraph text appear. Also, you'll see the Paragraph Tag menu. To learn more about the Paragraph Tag menu, see the Paragraph_tags.pdf file in the Lessons > Lesson04 folder.

7 Click OK.

When you create a new style from selected text, Muse does not automatically apply the style to that text; edits to the style don't automatically affect the paragraph on which you originally based the style. To apply the new style to its paragraph of origin, you must apply the style after you make it. Double-clicking to name the style does that for you, and also lets you assign a more meaningful name to the style.

You can always tell which style is applied to text by selecting that text or inserting the cursor in it and looking in the Paragraph Styles panel where the applied style's name will be highlighted.

8 Position the cursor over the Body style in the list.

A yellow tooltip appears, listing the style settings, which can help you to differentiate between styles with similar names.

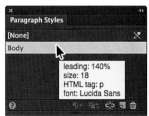

● **Note:** The order of your settings in the tooltip may be different, and that's OK.

9 With the Text tool selected, select the header text "COFFEE." Repeat steps 4 to 7, creating a new paragraph style named **Heading**. Make sure that in the Paragraph Style Options dialog box you choose <h1> Headline from the Paragraph Tag menu.

Choosing <h1> Headline from the Paragraph Tag menu means that in the HTML code that Muse generates, the HTML tag for the text with the Heading style applied will be an <h1> tag (called a heading 1). That can be very useful for search engine optimization because an <h1> tag carries more importance than a <p> (paragraph) tag, which is set by default. Setting a paragraph tag can also make it easier for screen readers and other assistive devices to navigate the content. You are not required to choose <h1> Headline to make your site work.

Note: If the resolution of your screen allows it, you may also see the Paragraph Style menu in the Control panel. This is another way to apply paragraph styles to your text.

Tip: You can remove formatting from text by applying the [None] paragraph style to it.

10 Insert the cursor into the paragraph that begins "Baked on site at CoffeeShop, our baked goods are…" In the Paragraph Styles panel, click the Body style to apply it to the text.

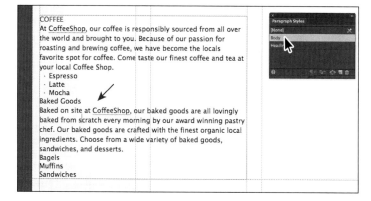

You can either insert the cursor in text or select the entire paragraph (or more) to apply paragraph styles.

11 Insert the cursor into the paragraph that contains the "Baked Goods" text. In the Paragraph Styles panel, click the Heading style to apply it to the text.

Notice that the "Baked Goods" text is *not* uppercase like the "COFFEE" heading text. The method you used to change the case of the COFFEE headline (Edit > Change Case > UPPERCASE) cannot be saved in a paragraph style. Next, you will edit the Heading style to fix this.

Editing paragraph styles

After you create a paragraph style and begin working in your pages, you may change your mind later on and want to change the settings in the style. In Muse, when you change style settings, every paragraph that has that paragraph style applied will update. In Muse, in order to change a paragraph style you need to redefine the style. To *redefine* a style, you edit the formatting for text that has the paragraph style applied. Then you redefine the style based on the changes. This makes the paragraph style match the new settings, and all other paragraphs with that style applied automatically update to match.

1 With the Text tool (**T**), select the heading text "Baked Goods." In the Control panel, change the Font to Estilo Pro Book and the Font Size to **22**.

2 In the Text panel (Window > Text), click the Uppercase button (TT) to capitalize all of the letters, and change the Space After to **10**. Using this method of capitalizing can be saved in a paragraph style.

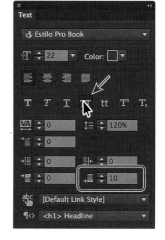

Look in the Paragraph Styles panel. You can tell that the style named Heading is applied because it is highlighted. You'll also now see a plus (+) to the right of the name. The plus indicates local formatting on the selected text. *Local formatting* means that there is formatting on the selected text that is different from the paragraph style applied to it.

3 Position the pointer over Heading + in the Paragraph Styles panel. A yellow tooltip appears displaying the style settings, a dashed line (-----), and then size: 22, space after: 10, case: uppercase, font: Estilo Pro Book. Settings listed below the dashed line indicate formatting on the selected text that is not a part of the applied paragraph style. Yours may be in a different order and that's okay.

▶ **Tip:** To remove the extra formatting (clear the overrides) on selected text, you can right-click the style name in the Paragraph Styles panel and choose Clear Overrides or click the Clear Style Overrides button ( ) at the bottom of the Paragraph Styles panel.

Note: The figure shows the text after clicking the Redefine Selected Style button.

4   Click the Redefine Selected Style button () at the bottom of the Paragraph Styles panel.

Tip: To redefine a style, instead of clicking the Redefine Selected Style button, you can right-click the style name and choose Redefine Style.

Notice that the plus is gone from the right of the Heading style name. Also, the "COFFEE" heading has updated to reflect the new formatting since that text also has the Heading style applied.

5   With the Text tool, select the entire first paragraph that starts with the text "At CoffeeShop, our coffee is…" In the Text panel, change the following:

- Font: **Acumin Pro Light** (or another font you want)

- Font Size: **16**

- Space After: **12**

Tip: For any value in a field that you want to change, you can select the value in the field (like the 140% in the Leading field) and press the up or down arrow to change the value. You can also press and hold the Shift key while pressing the up or down arrows to change the value in larger increments. Additionally, while a field is selected, you can press the up or down arrow keys on your keyboard, or Shift-click the up and down arrow keys to increase/decrease the value by 10.

6   Click the Redefine Selected Style button (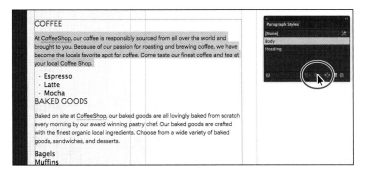) at the bottom of the Paragraph Styles panel to update the Body style.

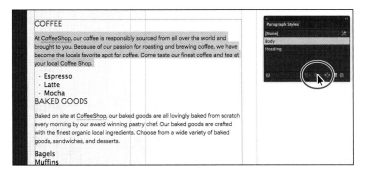

7   Choose File > Save Site and leave the first paragraph selected for the next section.

Duplicating and deleting paragraph styles

In Muse, you may wind up creating multiple paragraph styles that are very similar to each other. For instance, you may want to create two versions of the Body style, maybe one for mobile and one for desktop design, with the only difference being the font size. In that case, instead of creating a whole new style you can duplicate an existing style and adjust the formatting.

1 In the Paragraph Styles panel, right-click the style named Body, and choose Duplicate Style to create an exact copy of the style. Not surprisingly, Muse names it "Body copy."

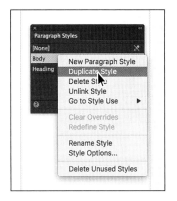

2 Right-click the new style (Body copy) and choose Rename Style. Change the name of the style to **Body 18**, and press Return (Enter).

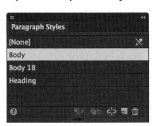

Renaming a style by right-clicking does not apply the new style to any selected text. To change the new Body 18 style, you'll redefine the style. First, you need to apply the style to text.

3 Click Body 18 in the Paragraph Styles panel to apply it to the selected paragraph. The paragraph will not change in appearance because the applied style (Body 18) is just a duplicate of the original Body style with the same attributes.

4 Change the Font Size in the Control panel to 18 by typing **18** and pressing Return (Enter).

5 Click the Redefine Selected Style button (![icon]) at the bottom of the Paragraph Styles panel to update the Body 18 style to match the selected text.

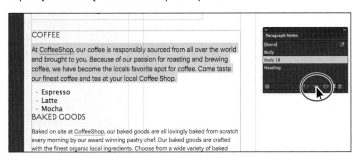

With both styles (Body and Body 18) applied to the text now, it's time to decide which to use for the body copy. In this case, you'll use the Body style instead of the Body 18 style. To do so, you can simply apply the Body style to the selected text and keep both styles, or you can delete one of the styles (if you no longer need it), and Muse allows you to choose a style to replace it with. You'll delete the style Body 18 to see how that works.

6   With the paragraph still selected, in the Paragraph Styles panel, the Body 18 style should be highlighted since it's applied to the selected paragraph. Click the Delete The Selected Style button (🗑) at the bottom of the panel (circled in the following figure).

> **Tip:** To delete a style, you can also right-click the style name and choose Delete Style.

> **Tip:** If you start to lose track of which of your styles are actually in use in your site, Muse offers a quick solution. Right-click a style name in the Paragraph Styles panel or the Character Styles panel, and choose Delete Unused Styles to delete all the styles that you are not using. Bear in mind that you'll need to clean out the Paragraph Styles and Character Styles panels separately.

7   In the dialog box that appears, choose Body and click Replace.

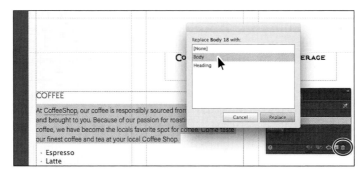

The Body 18 style is gone and the two paragraphs now have the Body style applied. Notice that the text now displays using the specified font size.

> **Tip:** You can also unlink a paragraph style by selecting text that has a paragraph style applied and then clicking the Unlink Style From Selection button (⛓) at the bottom of the Paragraph Styles panel. Unlinking a style from text can be helpful when you want to apply the styling to the text but later don't want the text to update if the style updates, for example.

8   Choose Edit > Deselect All.

9   Choose View > Hide Guides to temporarily hide the guides.

10 Choose View > Hide Frame Edges, to get a better sense of what the text looks like on the page.

11 Choose View > Show Guides and choose View > Show Frame Edges to show the guides and frame edges again.

Creating and applying a character style

Paragraph styles apply attributes to an entire paragraph, while character styles can include only the following formatting options: font, font size, color, styles (such as italic, bold, underline), and tracking. You access character styles from the Character Styles panel (Window > Character Styles) no matter what page in the site is open.

Next, you'll format the company name, "CoffeeShop," and apply that formatting throughout the page using a character style.

1   Click the Character Styles panel tab on the right side of the workspace (or choose Window > Character Styles). Once again, I pulled the panel out of the dock, closer to the text.

2   With the Text tool (**T**) selected, select the "CoffeeShop" text in the first paragraph.

3   Click the Font menu in the Control panel and choose the font Acumin Pro > Light Italic.

4   Click the Underline button (**T**) in the Control panel.

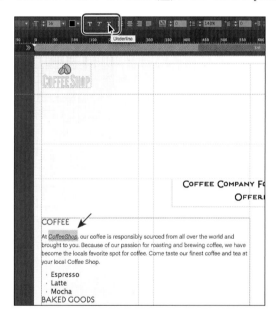

5   With the text "CoffeeShop" still selected, click the Create A New Style button (⊞) at the bottom of the Character Styles panel.

Position the pointer over the new style named "Character Style," and you'll see the saved formatting appear in a yellow tooltip, just like in a paragraph style.

6   Double-click the new style named Character Style. In the Character Style Options dialog box, change the Style Name to **company name** and click OK.

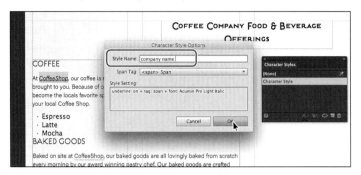

▶ **Tip:** You may also see the Character Style menu in the Control panel. This is another way to apply a character style.

As with a paragraph style, by double-clicking the name of the new character style right away, you also apply it to the selected text from which the style was made.

7   Select the text "CoffeeShop" in the paragraph after the "BAKED GOODS" heading.

8   Click the style named "company name" in the Character Styles panel to apply that formatting to the text. Leave the text selected.

Editing a character style

Editing a character style and the rest of the options in the Character Styles panel work identically to the Paragraph Styles panel. You need to redefine a character style to update the formatting, and change any text with the style applied.

1   With the "CoffeeShop" text still selected, remove the underline on the text by clicking the Underline button (🔲) in the Control panel.

2   Click the Redefine Selected Style button (🔲) at the bottom of the Character Styles panel.

Notice that the plus is gone from the right of the "company name" style name and that the other CoffeeShop text has updated to reflect the new formatting. Next, you'll make two columns from the text by copying the text frame to the next column.

3   Choose Window > Reset Panels if you dragged any panels away from the dock.

4   Select the Selection tool ( ). With the text frame still selected, press the Option (Alt) key and drag the frame to the right column. When the top of the frame copy is aligned with the top of the original, release the mouse button and then the key. Smart guides will help you to align the frames. See the following figure for placement help.

5   In the original text frame in the left column, select the Text tool (**T**) and select from the BAKED GOODS heading to the end of the text. Press Backspace or Delete to remove it.

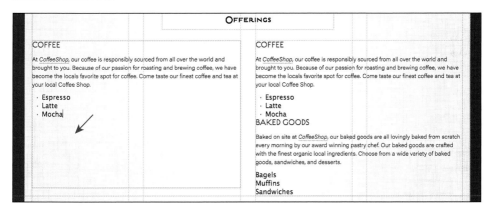

● **Note:** You most likely will see that the text frame does not shrink vertically when you delete the text. That's because earlier in the lesson you resized the text frame vertically. If you place text, without modifying the vertical height, then add or delete text from the frame, the text frame will grow and shrink depending on what you do with the text.

6 In the copied text frame in the right column, select all of the text above the BAKED GOODS heading. Press Backspace or Delete to remove it.

You may need to insert the cursor just before the "B" in BAKED GOODS and press Backspace or Delete a few times to remove any extra paragraph returns.

Currently in Muse, there is no way to thread or link text frames together.

7 Choose File > Save Site and leave the MENU page open.

Pasting text between Muse sites

When you copy and paste text from one site to another site, formatting is retained. Muse copies any necessary text styles into the second site. This can be a great way to quickly duplicate styles from one site to another.

When you copy and paste images between sites, the pasted images are linked to the same location as the original copied images. You'll learn more about linking in Lesson 8, "Adding Links, Buttons, and Graphic Styles."

If you paste text with a style that has the same name as a style in the page that you are pasting the text into, the existing style overrides the new style you are pasting. This is another reason why it is a best practice to rename styles with unique and descriptive names.

Working with bullet styles

In Muse, you can save bulleted or numbered list formatting as a bullet style using the Bullet Styles panel. This is useful for applying similar formatting to lists, and for updating list formatting later. One interesting thing to note about Muse bullet styles is that the style applies formatting to an entire list within a text frame. If you have a list with multiple levels, the formatting from each level is saved within the style. Text formatting such as font size, font family, color, etc. are not saved in a bullet style; only formatting associated with the list is saved. Next, you'll create a list style from the bullet list you created earlier so you can easily apply it to other text.

1 With the Text tool (**T**) selected, insert the cursor in the bullet list text in the left column.

2 Choose Window > Bullet Styles to open the Bullet Styles panel. In the Bullet Styles panel, click the Create A New Style button (⊡) at the bottom of the panel to create a list style from the text that the cursor is in.

3 Double-click the new "Bullet Style" style name in the Bullet Styles panel. Change the name to **Menu Items** and click OK.

Note: By double-clicking the style name, you apply the style to the entire list.

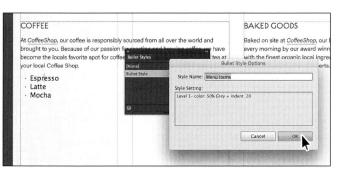

Notice that the Menu Items style in the Bullet Styles panel is applied to the text.

4 Select the "Bagels… Muffins… Sandwiches" text in the right column. Click the Bullets button (▦) in the Control panel to apply a bullet list to the text.

Note: In order to apply a list style to text, that text needs to already be a list.

5 In the Bullet Styles panel, click the Menu Items style name to apply the formatting to the selected text.

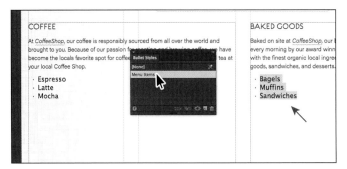

If you need to update a bullet list style, you can do so by redefining the style just like a character or paragraph style.

▶ **Tip:** To change the spacing between the bulleted list items, you can edit Space After formatting from within the Text panel.

6 Open the Paragraph Styles panel (Window > Paragraph Styles) and, with the bullet list text still selected, click the Body style to apply the formatting.

7 Select the Bullet list text "Espresso... Latte... Mocha..." in the left column and click the Body style in the Paragraph Styles panel to apply the formatting.

8 Choose Page > Page Properties. In the Page Properties For MENU dialog box, with the Layout tab selected, change the Min Height (minimum height of the page) to 1100. Click OK.

The page has space beneath the text now, and the page still has the ability to grow in height if you add more content to the page beneath the text.

9 Choose File > Save Site.

10 Choose File > Close Page to return to Plan mode.

Working with the Spell Checker ▰◀

To learn how to work with Spell Checker, check out the video titled "Working with the Spell Checker" that is a part of the Web Edition. For more information, see the "Web Edition" section of Getting Started at the beginning of the book.

Review questions

1 Name four ways that you can add text to your pages in Muse.

2 Explain the purpose of Smart Guides.

3 What are the three categories of fonts that you can use in Muse?

4 What is the difference between a character and a paragraph style?

5 What must be applied to text before you can apply a bullet style?

Review answers

1 In Muse, you can type text directly into your pages after creating a text frame using the Text tool; you can paste text from almost any other application (the formatting will be lost); you can choose File > Place to place a .txt file; or you can copy text from another Muse site and paste the text into the site, retaining the formatting (and styles) of the text content.

2 Smart Guides are temporary snap-to guides and visual aids that appear when you create or manipulate objects. They help you align, edit, and transform objects relative to other objects, page guides, or both by snap-aligning and sometimes displaying gap measurements that help to space multiple objects evenly.

3 The three categories of fonts that you can use in Muse are web fonts, standard fonts, and system fonts.

4 Paragraph styles apply attributes to an entire paragraph, but character styles can be applied to selected text only. Character styles can include only formatting options like the following: font, font size, color, styles (italic, bold, underline), and tracking.

5 In order to apply a bullet style to selected text, you first need to apply a bulleted or numbered list to that text.

5 WORKING WITH GRAPHICS

Lesson overview

In this lesson, you'll add personality to your pages by adding graphics. Specifically, you'll learn how to:

- Place different types of images
- Work with image frames
- Transform images
- Wrap text around an image
- Align, group, arrange, and lock content
- Fix missing and modified links
- Add alternative text and a tooltip to images

 This lesson takes approximately 60 minutes to complete. To download the project files for this lesson, log in or set up an account at peachpit.com. Enter the book's ISBN (9780134547275) or go directly to the book's product page to register. Once on the book's page, click the Register Your Product link. The book will show up in your list of registered products along with a link to the book's bonus content. Click the link to access the lesson files for the book. Store the files on your computer in a convenient location, as described in the "Getting Started" section of this book. Your Account page is also where you'll find any updates to the chapters or to the lesson files. If you are starting from scratch in this lesson, use the method described in the "Jumpstart" section in "Getting Started."

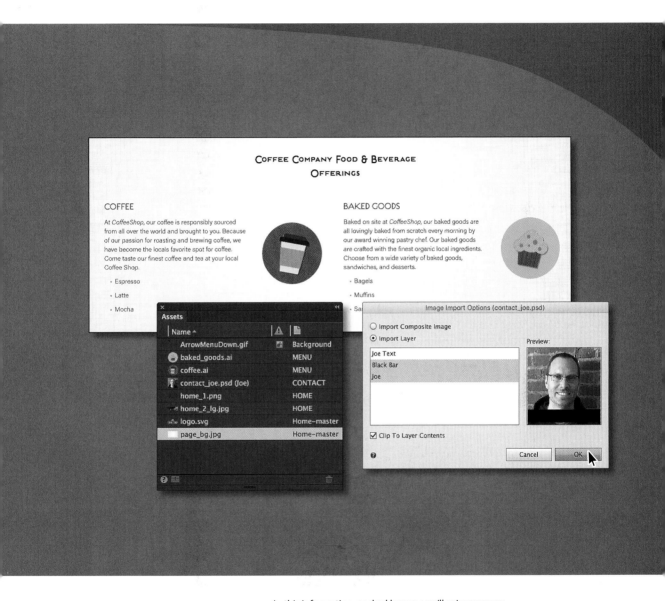

In this information-packed lesson, you'll spice up your website design and learn how to place images and easily move, scale, rotate, and more.

Web image basics

● **Note:** If you are starting from scratch using the Jumpstart method described in the "Jumpstart" section of "Getting Started," your workspace may look different from the figures you see in this lesson.

Whether you need to add interest to your pages to sell products, call attention to a promotion, or showcase your latest post, images can help. You simply need to choose the right image for the task. As you'll see, the key to the effective use of images is finding a balance of size and color to achieve the desired optimal quality.

Although you can save images in a multitude of file formats in programs like Adobe Illustrator or Adobe Photoshop, Muse allows you to place .gif, .jpg, .png, .svg, native Illustrator (.ai), and native Photoshop (.psd) files on your pages. Any Photoshop files (.psd) that you place are automatically converted to .gif, .jpg, or .png files once the site is published, exported, or even previewed. Illustrator files (.ai) you place are automatically converted to .svg files (with a .png fallback) when the site is published, exported, or even previewed.

These formats are optimized for use on the web and are compatible with most browsers. Each format, however, has different capabilities and strengths. To understand which is best for your site design, take a closer look at some important factors in the Web_images.pdf file in the Lessons > Lesson05 folder.

● **Note:** If you have not already downloaded the project files for this lesson to your computer from your Account page, make sure to do so now. See "Getting Started" at the beginning of the book.

Working with images

Muse offers several methods for getting images into your web design, including placing and pasting. *Placing* an image into your Muse site using the Place command (File > Place) creates a link to the image file, which means that if you later update the image file outside of Muse, the instances of that file will update in your Muse site. *Pasting* image content into your pages embeds that content into the site, meaning changes to the original image file will not update in Muse. To learn more about pasting content into Muse, see the sidebar, "Copy and paste image content into Muse" in this lesson.

Before you jump into placing images, it can be useful to gather your images into the same folder as your Muse site file to keep the files neat and organized. It's often helpful to create a dedicated subfolder named **images**. Copying all image files used for a site into a single images folder that exists in a folder with the .muse file can make it much easier to later collaborate with others on a site project. You can also place images (File > Place) from other locations as well.

As you'll see in later lessons, you can export or publish the site, and optimized images are gathered into a single folder, or, in the Assets panel, you can collect all original assets in a folder on your hard drive.

Placing an image

In Muse, a placed image is contained within a frame. In Muse, much like Adobe InDesign, you can draw a frame first, perhaps to use as a placeholder or for wireframing, and then place the image into that frame later. You can also place an image without creating a frame first and Muse will create a frame and place the image within.

In this first exercise, you'll use the Place command (File > Place) to insert an image on the home page, allowing Muse to create a frame and place the image within.

1   With the CoffeeShop.muse site still open, in Plan mode, double-click the HOME page thumbnail to open it in Design mode.

2   Choose View > Fit Page In Window.

3   Choose Window > Reset Panels.

4   In the Layers panel, select the Page layer so that the new images you place appear on that layer.

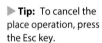

5   Choose File > Place. In the Import dialog box, navigate to the Lessons > images folder. Select the image named home_1.png, and click Open.

Tip: To cancel the place operation, press the Esc key.

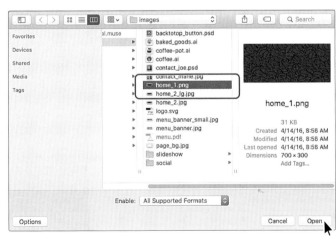

Move the pointer onto the page. You should now see the loaded graphics cursor with a handy thumbnail preview of the image that you are about to place. The upper-left corner of the image will align with the upper-left corner of the graphics cursor when you click on the page to place the image.

6 About halfway down the page, click and drag to place the image. When the measurement label next to the pointer shows a value of 50%, release the mouse button to place the image. Its vertical position doesn't matter right now.

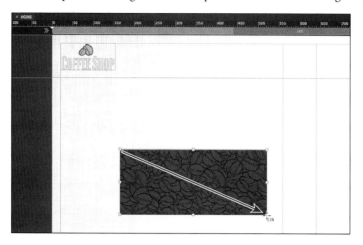

Notice that as you drag to place the image, you are sizing the image along with the frame.

7 Choose Edit > Undo Place to remove the image from the page and put it back in the graphics cursor for placement.

8 Position the pointer on the left side of the page, about half way down and click to place the image.

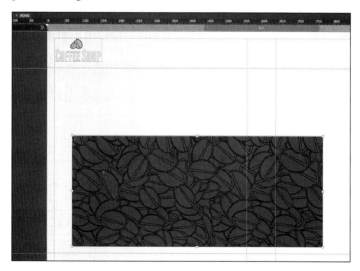

By simply clicking when placing, you create an image frame the same size as the image and place the image in the frame at 100% of its original size. Notice that the image is a bit wider than the column. That's okay, you'll adjust it later.

Note: In Muse, it's best to place images at 100% of their original size or smaller. When you enlarge an image, it can become jagged on the edges and blurry, depending on the original resolution of the image. As you'll see later in this lesson, Muse shows a warning in the Assets panel when a raster image is scaled larger than 100%.

About linked files

If you place a .gif, .jpg, .svg, .ai, .psd, or .png image, Muse links to the original image, wherever it lives. All linked files are optimized, if necessary, and gathered into a single folder when the site is published. Similar to working in an InDesign file, it's best practice to keep all site assets in a single project folder that also contains the Muse site file.

Once you place an image, an optimized version of the image is contained within the .muse site file. Unless you need to make changes to linked images, you can publish, preview, or export *without* the linked images.

Placing Adobe Illustrator (.ai) files

Adobe Muse allows you to place native Adobe Illustrator (.ai) files, as well as SVG (Scalable Vector Graphics) files into your Muse site. You can also copy content from Adobe Illustrator into a Muse web page. As was mentioned previously, Illustrator files (.ai) you place are automatically converted to .svg files (with a .png fallback) when the site is published, exported, or even previewed.

In this section, you'll place a few Illustrator (.ai) images. Before placing the images, you'll create several frames with the Rectangle Frame tool (⊠), and then place images into them. Using the Rectangle Frame tool or Ellipse Frame tool, you can create either rectangular or elliptical empty image frames on the page. These can be placeholder image frames that you can fill later by dragging or pasting graphics into them at any time when the content is ready.

> **Note:** By default, shapes created with the Rectangle Frame tool or Ellipse Frame tool have a Resize value of Responsive Width And Height by default. This will make more sense in Lesson 6.

1   Click the Plan mode link to access the page thumbnails. Double-click the MENU page thumbnail to open the page in Design mode.

2   Choose View > Fit Page In Window.

3   In the Layers panel (Window > Layers), make sure the Page layer is selected so that the new images you place appear on that layer. Click the Layers panel tab to hide it.

4   Select the Rectangle Frame tool (⊠) in the Toolbar. Pressing the Shift key, above the text on the page, click and drag a frame that has a width and height of approximately 150 pixels. Release the mouse button and then the key.

5 Select the Selection tool (↖). Pressing the Option (Alt) key, drag the frame to the right of the original to create a copy. Release the mouse button and then the key.

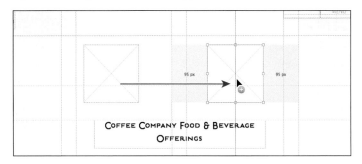

There are now two image frames on the page. This could be a way to save time and mock up a design before you have the images in hand. Once you have the images, you can insert one into each of the frames, which is what you'll do next.

6 Choose File > Place. In the Import dialog box, navigate to the Lessons > images folder. Select the image named baked_goods.ai. Command–click (Ctrl–click) the image named coffee.ai to select both images. Click Open.

With the loaded graphics cursor showing, you should see a number next to the right edge of the image thumbnail (2), indicating how many images are loaded in the graphics cursor.

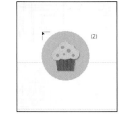

▶ **Tip:** If multiple images are showing in the loaded graphics cursor, pressing the Esc key will remove the selected image from the loaded graphics thumbnail.

7 Press the right or left arrow keys to cycle between the images, stopping when you see the thumbnail of the coffee cup image you are ready to place. Position the loaded graphics cursor over the frame on the left. A highlight will appear on the frame edge. Click to place the coffee image.

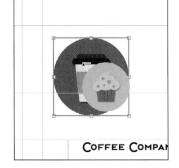

8 Position the loaded graphics cursor over the empty frame on the right. A highlight will appear on the frame edge. Click to place the muffin image. Later, you'll position these images, so leave them where they are for now.

9 Choose File > Save Site.

● **Note:** As of the writing of this book, you cannot click to place a layered PSD file into an empty image frame when you select Import Layer in the Image Import Options dialog box when placing the PSD. If you choose Import Composite Image in the Image Import Options dialog box when placing the PSD, then you can do it.

Placing SVG files

SVG is an image format we use on websites for vector graphics. It's great for logos, page elements, and much more, because it usually has small file sizes that compress well, you can scale it to almost any size without losing quality, they look great on retina displays, and more. Adobe Muse allows you to place SVG (Scalable Vector Graphics) files into your Muse site or copy content from Adobe Illustrator into a Muse web page (which is typically converted to SVG when the site is exported, published, or previewed).

Placing a Photoshop (.psd) file

Placing a Photoshop file (.psd) in Muse offers the same linking and updating benefits as placing a .jpg, .gif, .svg, .ai, or .png file, plus a few extras. If the Photoshop file has content in more than one layer, for example, and you place it in your site via File > Place, Muse lets you choose whether to place the composite image (all layers) or selected layers. This means that, for instance, you can create a complete page design in Photoshop with page-specific content on individual layers, and then place only the layer you need for each page. Alternatively, you could create multiple versions of a button or logo on separate layers, for instance, and place the version you like best.

When you publish, preview, or export the site, Muse converts the Photoshop content to a suitable format for the web but does not publish or export the original .psd file. Don't let your imagination run wild, though; for all other images that you place, you still need to consider file size, resolution, and color when creating Photoshop content. Next, you'll place a .psd file on a page.

1 Click the Plan mode link to access the page thumbnails. Double-click the CONTACT page thumbnail to open the page in Design mode.

2 Choose View > Fit Page In Window.

3 In the Layers panel (Window > Layers), make sure the Page layer is selected so that the new image you place appears on that layer. Click the Layers panel tab to hide it.

4 Choose File > Place. In the Import dialog box, navigate to the Lessons > images folder and then to the image named contact_joe.psd. Click Open.

The Image Import Options (contact_joe.psd) dialog box opens. This is where you go to place the composite image with all of the layers showing or only selected layers.

● **Note:** Choose carefully! If you later want to turn layers on or off in the .psd in Muse, you must place the file again or relink it (more on this later in this lesson).

5 Select Import Layer. Select the "Black Bar" layer, Command–click (Ctrl–click) the "Joe" layer to select both Photoshop layers. Select Clip To Layer Contents, and click OK.

Suppose you designed an entire web page in Photoshop, and you only want to place a logo from one of the layers in the .psd into Muse. The logo is only a small part of the larger design. Selecting Clip To Layer Contents crops the placed image to the size of the selected layer(s) content instead of making it the size of the entire design. The original .psd file remains unchanged.

6 Position the graphics cursor in the first column of guides (on the left), and click to place the image. With the image content selected on the page, look at the left end of the Control panel and you'll see the word Group.

If you choose to place the composite Photoshop file or select a single layer when placing, a single image is placed. If you choose more than one layer, as you did here, the layers are individual images that are grouped together by default and placed in the same relative position and stacking order as the original Photoshop file.

7 With the image selected, choose Object > Ungroup to ungroup the objects.

8 Click somewhere in a blank area of the page to deselect all content. Position the pointer over the images and a Hint label appears with the words "Image Frame," indicating that you'll select an image frame if you click. Click to select the black bar. In the Selection Indicator on the left end of the Control panel you should now see "Image Frame," indicating that it's a single image. Delete the image.

● **Note:** After placing an image, Muse switches to the Selection tool automatically, regardless of which tool was selected before.

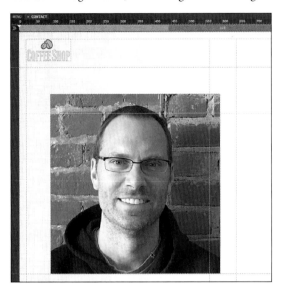

9 Choose File > Save Site and leave the CONTACT page open.

Copy and paste image content into Muse

If you want to copy and paste graphic content into a page in Muse from within the same site, from site to site, or from another program, consider these factors first:

- If you copy an image you placed on one page of your site and paste it to another page, the newly pasted image and the placed image will link to the original image file on your hard drive. Changes to the original source file will change the image copies on both pages.

- If you copy an image you placed on one site and paste it into another site, the placed image and pasted image will link to the original image file. Changes to the original source file will change the copies on both sites.

- If you copy and paste image content from Photoshop, Illustrator, Fireworks, or other programs, Muse flattens the image content, removing any transparency and layer information, and embeds the image in the site. The pasted image does not link to an image file outside of Muse and appears in the Assets panel as "Pasted Image" or "Pasted SVG."

Transforming images

Images in Muse, like text, live in rectangular frames that are referred to as *image frames*. The frame that contains an image can have a stroke, fill, or other formatting or transformations applied to it. As you've already witnessed, if you move the frame on the page, the image moves as well. You can resize the frame and image together or separately to create some interesting effects.

Getting images into your site design is only the first step. Unless you hit perfection on the first try, you may need to adjust the image's placement, size, rotation, or cropping. Using several tools and methods, you can transform the rectangular frame of the image, edit the image independently of the frame, or transform both the image frame and image together.

Scaling images using the Selection tool

You'll first focus on exploring image transformation using the Selection tool ($\blacktriangleright$), which offers many fast, powerful transformations. The first type of transformation you'll perform is to scale an image.

Tip: You can also begin typing the name of a page in the Go To Page dialog box to filter the names of pages.

1 Choose Page > Go To Page (Command+J [Ctrl+J]). Click the arrow to the right of the field and choose HOME. Click OK.

   The HOME page was already open as a tab at the top of the Document window. This menu command is just one way of many in Muse to navigate pages.

2 Choose View > Fit Page In Window, if necessary.

Note: You could choose Edit > Undo Resize Item to return this image to its previous size.

3 With the Selection tool ($\blacktriangleright$) selected, click to select the home_1.png image on the page, if necessary. Click and drag the bottom-right point on the image frame in toward the center of the image until the measurement label shows *approximately* 85%.

With the Selection tool selected, if you drag a point on a frame to resize it, you also resize the image. If you want to return the image to 100%, you can simply drag a corner of the image until 100% appears in the measurement label. No matter how many times you resize an image, you can always get it back to 100%. Later in the lesson, you'll explore the Assets panel, where you can tell if an image has been resized.

4 In the Control panel, click the Constrain Width And Height Proportionally button ( ) so that when you edit either the width or height, the other value will change as well. Change the Width value to **600**, if necessary.

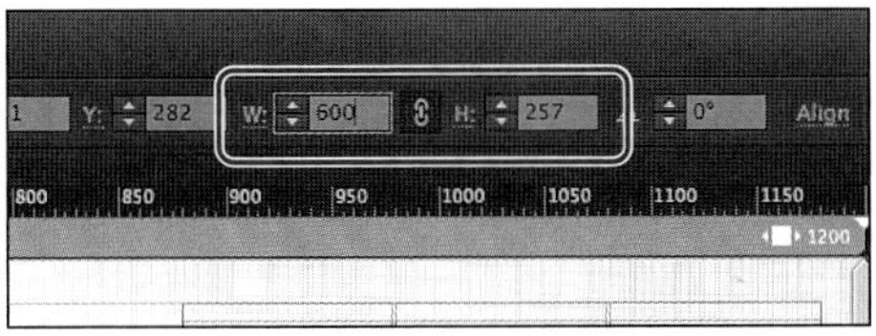

Changing the width of the image frame has the same effect as dragging to resize. The image within the frame is also scaled. If the Constrain Width And Height Proportionally option was *not* turned on, the image would be distorted in the frame if you changed the width or height of the frame.

Note: At smaller screen resolutions, you may not see the necessary options in the Control panel. If that is the case, you can either click the word "Transform," click the X or Y to reveal the Transform panel, or open the Transform panel by itself (Window > Transform).

5 Choose Page > Go To Page (Command+J [Ctrl+J]). Click the arrow to the right of the field and choose Home-master. Click OK.

6 Choose View > Fit Page In Window, if necessary.

7 With the Selection tool ( ) selected, click to select the logo in the upper-left corner. Click and drag the bottom-right point on the image frame in toward the center of the logo. When you see a width of approximately 115 pixels release the mouse button to resize the logo.

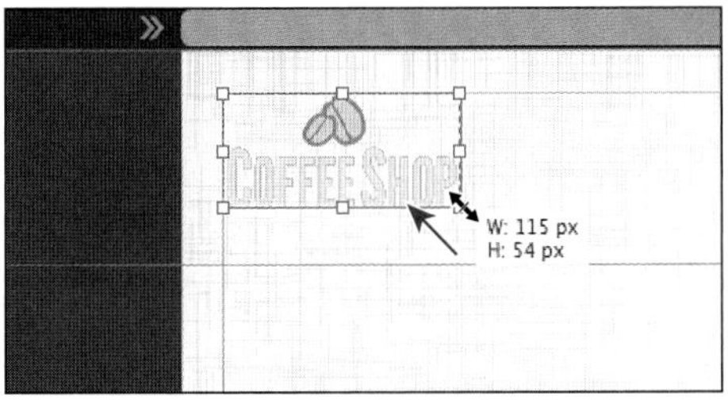

Did you notice that the measurement label only showed a width and height, *not* a percent (%) like you saw with the previous image? That's because the logo is SVG. SVG and placed .ai files are infinitely scalable and still retain their clarity, so you don't have to worry about scaling these types of files larger than 100%. The exception to that rule is if there is raster content in the .ai or SVG.

Note: When you open a site that contains at least one image that has been scaled larger than 100%, a warning dialog box appears.

8 Choose File > Close Page, and then choose File > Save Site.

Cropping an image using the Selection tool

There may be times when you'll want to crop out (hide) part of an image on your pages as well. You can crop using several methods. In this section, you'll crop using the Selection tool.

1 Click the HOME tab at the top of the Document window to show that page in Design mode.

Note: Cropping an image in Muse does not crop the original image file.

2 Click the image of the coffee beans on the page to select it, if necessary. With the Selection tool (▶) selected, press and hold the Command (Ctrl) key, and drag the bottom, middle bounding point of the frame up a bit to crop part of the image. Release the mouse button and then the key.

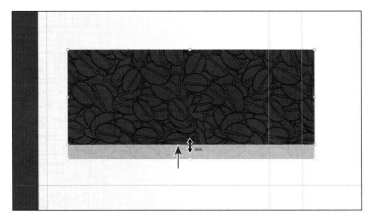

Rather than resizing the frame and image together, dragging while pressing Command (Ctrl) lets you resize the frame only. In this case, you are cropping a part of the image so that it no longer shows (but is still there). You could also make the frame larger than the image if you wanted a background color or background image applied to the image frame to create a border effect.

3 Double-click the image with the Selection tool (▶).

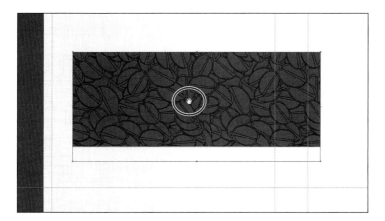

Notice that the once blue rectangle (because it's on the Page layer) with eight bounding points turns into another color rectangle (brown in this case) with smaller points. Also notice that the pointer has changed from a black arrow to a hand when the pointer is positioned over the image. The brown frame extends beyond the blue image frame and shows the size of the image within the frame. These indicators will help you resize the image within the frame and reposition it.

4 While pressing the Shift key, click and drag the image from the center straight up a little. Be careful not to drag too far, you want to make sure that the image is still filling the frame. Release the mouse button and then the Shift key.

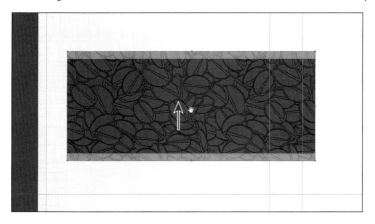

You're moving the image in the frame; not editing the frame. You'll see that the cropped (hidden) part of the image that is outside of the frame looks lighter or semitransparent as you drag the image. If you drag an image far enough in the frame, a fill color or background image you applied to the frame will show. The Shift key constrains the movement of the image inside the image frame to 90 degrees.

5 Position the pointer over the bottom-right corner point of the image (the brown frame) and the pointer changes to a double arrow. Drag away from the center of the image until the measurement label shows 90% to resize the image, not the frame.

Resizing an image this way automatically constrains the proportions of the image, preventing you from distorting it.

6 Press the Esc key to select the blue image frame, not the image.

You can see that the image is cropped within the frame and is now a little larger than it was. Don't worry that it's not in the center; you'll fix that soon.

Using the Fitting commands

Another way to resize an image is to use the Fitting commands built into Muse. These commands allow you to fill a frame with an image or fit the image to the frame while keeping the image in proportion.

1 With the image frame still selected on the HOME page, choose Object > Fitting > Fit Content Proportionally.

This command fits the entire image in the frame and centers it *without cropping it*. Notice the gaps on the right and left of the image frame. Because the frame doesn't have the same proportions as the image, Muse left a gap between the frame and image on two sides.

2 Choose Object > Fitting > Fill Frame Proportionally.

This command ensures that the image fills the frame and is centered with no gaps, but a portion of the image will be cropped if the proportions of the frame don't match the image proportions.

Note: Using a Fitting command will most likely make the image smaller or larger than 100%. Don't forget, making an image larger than 100% can reduce image quality. In Muse, when you look at an image on the page, you can't tell if it's larger than 100% of its original size. You can do that by selecting the image on the page and looking in the Assets panel, which you'll explore shortly.

Using the Crop tool

You can also crop or resize an image with the Crop tool. Found in the Toolbar, the Crop tool (🔨) enables you to move, resize, and crop an image and its frame together or separately, much like the Selection tool methods discussed previously.

1 Click the CONTACT page tab at the top of the Document window to show the page in Design mode.

2 Select the Crop tool (🔨) in the Toolbar. Drag across the contact_joe image to select it, if necessary. Position the pointer over the upper-right bounding point of the image frame. When the pointer changes to double arrows, press and hold Shift+Option (Shift+Alt), then drag the point toward the image center. When you crop a bit of the image, release the mouse button and then the keys.

Note: When resizing an image frame using the Crop tool, pressing the Shift key constrains the proportions and pressing the Option (Alt) key allows you to resize the image frame from the center.

The Crop tool allows you to resize the frame without resizing the image like the Selection tool, but unlike the Selection tool, you don't have to hold down a modifier key with the Crop tool (unless you want to constrain the proportions of the cropping or crop from the center, like you just did).

3 Position the pointer over the image. When the Content Grabber appears in the center of the image (the two concentric circles, as shown in the following figure), position the pointer over it. When the pointer changes to a hand (🖐), click and drag down to reveal a little more of the top of the image.

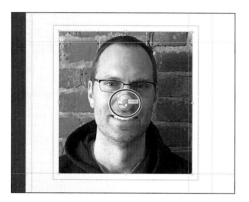 

▶ **Tip:** If you position the pointer over the image, away from the image center, the pointer changes from a crop icon (🔧) to an arrow (▶). This allows you to move the frame and the image together.

In this case, the Content Grabber allows you to temporarily select the image, not the image frame. The Smart Guides help to align the image as you drag it. By simply clicking and dragging the Content Grabber, you can move the image within the frame, but the frame is still selected.

4 Click the Content Grabber in the center of the image to select the image, not the frame.

You can tell that the image (not the frame) is selected when you see the rectangle (brown in this case) around the image again. With the image selected, you can drag the image and reposition it within the frame or resize or rotate it.

5 Press the Esc key to select the image frame and leave it selected.

6 With the image frame selected, choose Object > Fitting > Fill Frame Proportionally to ensure that the image is filling the frame.

7 Choose File > Save Site.

Wrapping text around content

Muse allows you to wrap text around image frames, shapes (rectangles), and even other text frames. This can be a great way to insert an image into a story, which is common on news sites or blogs, or a way to create a large first letter for text, which is called a drop cap. You'll find lots of uses for wrapping text around content.

Wrapping text involves using the Wrap panel (Window > Wrap) and requires you to paste the content that the text will wrap around into the text. In this exercise, you'll wrap some text on the MENU page around a few of the images.

1 Click the MENU tab at the top of the Document window to show the page.

2 Select the Selection tool (▶) and click to select the round picture of the coffee cup again. Choose Edit > Cut.

3 Select the Text tool (**T**) and insert the cursor right in front of the text that begins "At CoffeeShop, our coffee is…."

4 Choose Edit > Paste.

> **Tip:** If you were to select the image with the Selection tool, the word "Inline" would display in the Selection Indicator on the left end of the Control panel.

Note: Where you paste an object matters. If you paste an object in the middle of a paragraph and then assign a left or right wrap, the top of the object aligns with the top of the line of text into which you pasted it.

Tip: Objects that you paste into a text frame to apply a wrap can have fills, strokes, and other effects applied.

Muse pastes the image *inline* with the text. That means that the pasted element just flows with the text. If you tried to move that image with the Selection tool right now, you could only move it vertically because it is inline. This is called *inline content*. One advantage of pasting content into a text frame instead of just placing it on top of the text frame is that if the text size increases or decreases in the browser or the frame moves, the inline content will move as well. It's also easier to manage and update text content, in the event you might need to add or delete some of the text. Wrapped text in a single text frame is easier to work with than a collection of grouped objects.

5   Choose Window > Wrap to open the Wrap panel. With the coffee cup image still selected, in the Wrap panel, click the Position Object To The Right Of Text button (🖹). I dragged the Wrap panel from the dock closer to the text to make it easier to see in context with the text.

The Wrap panel offers three options for positioning the image: inline, position left, and position right. The default position is inline, and that's what you see when you first paste the image into the text. Positioning the image to the right aligns it to the right and wraps the text along the left side of the image. Positioning the image to the left aligns it to the left and wraps the text along the right side of the image. You can try clicking each of the buttons to see the effect it has on the image and text, making sure that you click the Position Object To The Right Of Text button last.

Once you choose the desired image wrap option, you can also push the text away from the various edges of the image by using Offsets in the Wrap panel.

6   In the Wrap panel, click the Make All Offsets The Same Value button (🔘) so you can edit the offsets separately. Change Left Offset to **20**. Now change Left Offset to **−150**. A negative value may allow the text to appear over the image, which can create some interesting effects. Change Left Offset to **30**.

Note: If you attempt to select the image with the text wrap in the text frame by clicking with the Selection tool, you'll select the text frame instead. Click once more on the image to select it. You can use the Selection Indicator to determine which element is selected: "Text Frame" means the text frame is selected, and "Inline" means the image pasted in the text frame is selected. With the inline element selected, you can press the Esc key to jump up a level and select the outer text frame container.

7 With the Selection tool (▶) selected, click to select the round picture of the muffin. Choose Edit > Cut.

8 Select the Text tool and insert the cursor right in front of the text that begins "Baked on site at CoffeeShop...."

9 Choose Edit > Paste.

10 In the Wrap panel, click the Make All Offsets The Same Value button (⬚) so you can edit the offsets separately, if necessary. Click the Position Object To The Right Of Text button (⬚) and change Left Offset to **30**.

11 Choose Edit > Deselect All, and then choose File > Save Site.

Grouping and locking content

As you work, Muse lets you lock and unlock content to prevent you from inadvertently selecting and editing it. You can also combine several objects into a group so that the objects are treated as a single unit. You can then move or transform a number of objects without affecting their individual attributes or relative positions.

1 With the Selection tool (▶) selected, drag across all of the content on the page.

Tip: Another way to select multiple objects with the Selection tool is to press the Shift key and click to select each object. If multiple objects are selected, holding the Shift key while clicking one of the selected objects allows you to deselect it.

2 Choose Object > Group to group the selected content.

A dotted box appears around the group of content (an arrow is pointing to it in the previous figure). You now can move, rotate, and even resize the group as a single object.

● **Note:** To edit the objects within the group, you can also select the group and choose Object > Ungroup.

● **Note:** Resizing a group resizes the images within the group but does not change the size of text in the group.

3 With the group still selected, click on the text frame that contains the heading, "Coffee Company Food & Beverage Offerings" to select only that frame. Drag the text frame up a little to create more separation between it and the columns of text below it.

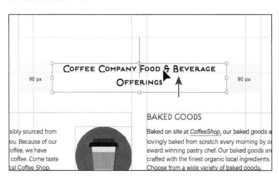

4 Press the Esc key to select the entire group again. Drag the group down on the page, aligning the top edge with the horizontal guide.

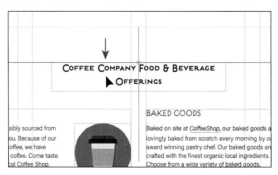

5 Choose Edit > Deselect All, and then choose File > Save Site.

Rotating content

As you've seen so far in this lesson, you can transform frames in multiple ways, including position and size. You can also rotate all types of content in Muse using several methods. When it comes to images, you can rotate the frame and image together or just the image in the frame.

1   With the MENU page still showing, choose View > Fit Page In Window, if necessary.

2   With the Selection tool (▶) selected, click the round picture of the coffee cup to select it. Notice that you select the group and not the image. Click once more on the coffee cup to select the text frame, and then click one more time to finally select the coffee cup image.

   When it comes to working with groups, if you need to select content within a group, you can either ungroup the group (Object > Ungroup) or simply click as many times on that content as necessary to select it within the group.

3   Position the pointer just off any of the corner bounding points. When you see the rotate arrow (↻), click and drag clockwise. When the measurement label shows a value of −5° (minus 5 degrees), stop dragging and release the mouse button.

▶ **Tip:** Pressing and holding the Shift key constrains the movement of content to 45 degrees as you rotate it.

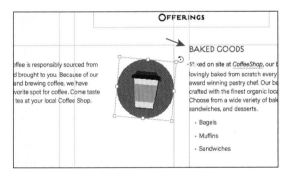

   In the Control panel, depending on your screen resolution and whether you have maximized the Muse workspace, you may see the Rotation Angle option with a value of −5°. You can change the angle of rotation by typing in a positive or negative value, or by clicking the up or down arrows. To reset the angle to its original rotation, you would set the value at 0 (zero). You can also rotate an image separate from the image frame by selecting the image within the frame.

4   Position the pointer away from the grouped content, and click to deselect.

   Now that you have the coffee cup image rotated, you'll do the same to the muffin image on the page, just using a different method.

Note: If you don't see the Rotation Angle value in the Control panel, you can also click the Transform link in the Control panel or choose Window > Transform to open the Transform panel and find it there.

5 Click three times to select the muffin image. Change the rotation angle by clicking the down arrow next to the Rotation Angle field in the Control panel above the page. Stop rotating when you see −10° in the field.

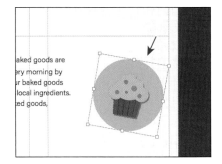

6 Drag the muffin image up a bit.

Content that has text wrap applied can be repositioned in different ways within the text frame.

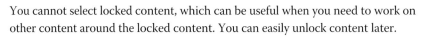

7 Choose Edit > Deselect All, then click to select the group again.

8 Choose Object > Lock.

You cannot select locked content, which can be useful when you need to work on other content around the locked content. You can easily unlock content later.

9 Choose File > Save Site.

Working with the Transform panel

The Transform panel allows you to apply transformations numerically. This can be great for making precise adjustments, for instance, when positioning content on a page. The options in the Transform panel can also be found in the Control panel, depending on screen resolution and what content is selected.

Next, you'll use the Transform panel to transform artwork.

1 Click the HOME page tab at the top of the Document window to see the page in Design mode.

2 With the Selection tool selected, click the home_1.png image on the page if it isn't still selected.

You need the image to have its left edge aligned with the left edge of the page area.

3 Change the X value to **0** in the Control panel to position the left edge of the image frame to the left edge of the page area.

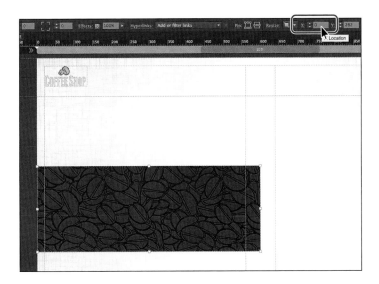

Note: If you don't see the X or Y values in the Control panel, you can also click the Transform link in the Control panel or choose Window > Transform to open the Transform panel and find them there.

Tip: To align the image to the left edge of the page, you can also click the Align link in the Control panel to reveal the Align panel (you can also choose Window > Align to open the Align panel in the workspace). Choose Align To Content Area from the Align To menu in the lower-right corner of the Align panel. Click the Align Left Edges button to align the image to the content area (page).

4   Choose Window > Transform to open the Transform panel. Change the Y value to **500** in the Transform panel.

The options you see in the Transform panel will most likely mirror what you see in the Control panel, depending on the resolution of your screen. Using the Transform panel, you can rotate, scale, and position content very precisely.

5   Click the Transform panel tab to collapse the panel again.

Aligning content

So far in the lessons you've used the Smart Guides to align content, which is an efficient way to align objects. Muse also has an Align panel (Window > Align), which is similar to other Adobe applications, that allows you to align content in different ways. Next, you'll perform a simple alignment, aligning one object to another.

1   Press Command+J (Ctrl+J) and choose Home-master from the menu, and then click OK to open the page in Design mode.

2   Choose View > Fit Page In Window, if necessary.

3   With the Selection tool, click the logo to select it, if necessary, and Shift-click the menu to select both items.

4   Click the Align link in the Control panel to reveal the Align panel (you can also choose Window > Align to open the Align panel in the workspace). Ensure that Align To Selection is chosen from the Align To menu in the lower-right corner of the Align panel (circled in the following figure). Click the Align Vertical Centers button () to align the two objects to each other.

Notice how the menu moved to align to the logo. When aligning top, right, bottom, or left, all selected objects align to the topmost, rightmost, bottommost, or leftmost object, respectively. In this case, the logo was snapped into page guides which kept it in place. The Align panel also allows you to distribute objects along the axis you specify and distribute the spacing between objects. You can use either the object edges or anchor points as the reference point, and you can align to a selection, the content area (page), or a key object.

5   Choose File > Save Site.

Aligning to a key object

Muse makes it easy to align or distribute multiple objects relative to each other, the content area (page), or a key object. A *key object* is an object that you want other objects to align to. You specify a key object by selecting all the objects you want to align, including the key object, and then clicking the key object again. When selected, the key object has a dotted outline. In this section, you'll explore a few other options for aligning objects.

1 Press Command+J (Ctrl+J) and choose HOME from the menu, and then click OK to open the page in Design mode.

2 Choose View > Fit Page In Window.

3 In the Layers panel (Window > Layers), make sure the Page layer is selected. Click the Layers panel tab to hide it.

4 Click the home_1.png image to select it, if necessary. Choose Edit > Copy, and then Edit > Paste to paste a copy of the image.

   For this design, there needs to be two images next to each other on the page. Later, you will replace one of the home_1.png images with another image.

5 With the image copy selected, click the Align link in the Control panel to reveal the Align panel. Ensure that Align To Content Area is chosen from the Align To menu in the lower-right corner of the Align panel. Click the Align Right Edges button (▣) to align the right edge of the image to the right edge of the page. Press the Escape key to hide the Align panel.

Note: You can also choose Window > Align to open the Align panel like you see in the figure. I dragged the Align panel from the dock so it was closer to the content on the page.

6 Shift-click the original image to select both images. Release the Shift key and click once more on the *original* home_1.png image on the left. Notice the bolder dotted border, indicating that the image is the key object.

7 Click the Align link in the Control panel to reveal the Align panel (or choose Window > Align). In the Align To menu, Align To Key Object will already be chosen for you. Click the Align Top Edges button (🔲) to align the copy to the original image.

Note: You can also align these images using Smart Guides, as you've been doing up to this point. It's good to understand the options in the Align panel because sometimes, when enough content is on the page, you may not be able to rely on Smart Guides for aligning.

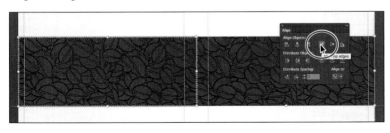

8 Choose Edit > Deselect All, and then choose File > Save Site.

Understanding the Assets panel

As you know, Muse links the images that you place (File > Place) on a page to their original image files. The Assets panel (Window > Assets) shows a list of these files as well as all the other assets used in your *entire site* regardless of which page is open in the Document window. The Assets panel also provides important information about each asset and gives you menu commands that you can use to ensure that the images are all linked properly.

1 Choose Window > Assets to show the panel.

2 With the Selection tool, click the home_1.png image *on the left* to select it.

3 Drag the left edge of the Assets panel to the left to make it wider. Look in the Assets panel to see that the selected image (home_1.png) is now highlighted.

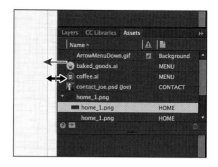

Notice "HOME" to the right of the highlighted image name in the Assets panel. This tells you that the image is on the page named HOME.

Assets listed in the Assets panel are listed alphabetically. You can click the column Name to sort them in descending rather than ascending order. Some assets listed have a disclosure triangle to the left of their name in the list, which indicates that there is more than one iteration of that asset in the pages of the site. Clicking the arrow to the left of an asset expands the list to detail every use of the image and the pages in the site where they appear. Muse calls an image on a page an *instance* of the original linked image file. Every instance links to the original image file. Right now, since you copied the home_1.png image on the HOME page, the expanded Assets panel is showing both instances. Clicking a disclosure triangle again collapses the expanded list and shows only the asset's name.

● **Note:** If the tooltip you see is simply the name of the image, home_1.png, in this case, try moving the pointer over the thumbnail of the image (to the left of the name) in the Assets panel.

4 Position the pointer over the highlighted home_1.png image name in the assets list, and Muse provides a yellow tooltip with the path to the image, among other information.

5 Scroll in the Assets panel, if necessary, and find the image named coffee.ai.

6 Right-click (Ctrl-click) the coffee.ai image in the Assets panel, and choose Go To Asset to show the image on the MENU page.

The Assets panel not only lists the assets that are linked and embedded, but it also gives you a lot of functionality found in context menus (right-clicking)—from editing images to relinking images and more.

Replacing images

After placing an image into Muse, you may sometimes need to replace that image (a different product becomes the monthly special, say) or link a different version of the original file to the instances on your pages (you recrop a photo to better highlight your office location, for example). In the Assets panel, you can choose to relink an image, which replaces that image on a page. On the HOME page, you'll replace one of the home_1.png images.

1 Click the HOME tab at the top of the Document window to return to that page.

2 With the Selection tool, right-click (Ctrl-click) the home_1.png image on the right, and choose Replace Image.

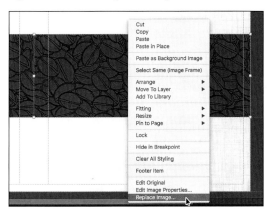

3 In the Relink dialog box, navigate to the Lessons > images folder, then select home_2.jpg, and click Open.

▶ **Tip:** If you place the same asset on multiple pages, you can easily relink every instance of the image throughout the site. To do that right-click (Ctrl-click) the parent object (with the arrow to the left of it) in the Assets panel and choose Relink All Instances Of "image name."

Note: The image *you* see may fill the frame completely and that's okay. You'll fix that next.

The new image replaces the old image in the frame, *fitting* proportionally in the frame. When you relink an image that has different dimensions, Muse *fits* the new image proportionally and centers it within the image frame. That can lead to a small image being made much larger or vice versa. It's best to replace an image with an image of the same dimensions. You can also replace the image and scale the new image using the Selection or Crop tools.

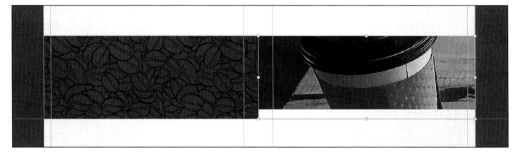

4   Right-click (Ctrl-click) the new home_2.jpg image on the page, and choose Fitting > Fill Frame Proportionally to fill the frame with the image, maintaining its proportions.

Filling the frame with this image causes the image to be larger than 100%, in this case. Look in the Assets panel and you'll see the home_2.jpg image in the list now. You'll also most likely see an icon () in the status column that indicates that the asset is being upsampled and may look pixelated. That's because you transformed the image and set it to fill the frame.

5   In the Assets panel, hover the pointer over the icon (🖼) to the right of the home_2.jpg name.

The yellow tooltip that appears tells you to resize the image to be smaller, or link to a larger asset. If you resize the image smaller, it won't fit in the frame, so you'll relink to another image that is larger.

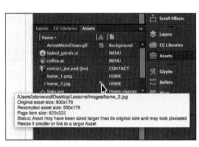

6   Click home_2.jpg in the Assets panel to highlight it. Right-click (Ctrl-click) the home_2.jpg image name and choose Relink. In the Relink dialog box, navigate to the Lessons > images folder, then select home_2_lg.jpg, and click Open.

7 Right-click (Ctrl-click) the home_2_lg.jpg image on the page, and choose Fitting > Fill Frame Proportionally to fill the frame with the image, maintaining its proportions. You may not need to do this.

● **Note:** You won't see this icon (🖼) to the right of the home_2_lg.jpg image in the Assets panel after applying the Fill Frame Proportionally command since the new image is larger in dimension than the frame.

8 File > Save Site and leave the page open.

Editing original

From within Muse, you can use the Edit Original command to open a placed image in an image-editing program like Photoshop, make changes, save the file, and return to Muse to see it updated in your design. The Edit Original command is only available for certain placed assets that are linked, and is not something you will do in this lesson.

● **Note:** The Edit Original command is not available for embedded content that was pasted from another program like Photoshop.

Fixing broken and modified links

When you place images in Muse, as mentioned previously, a link is created between the asset and the Muse site file (.muse). If the Muse site file cannot find a linked image because it has moved from its original location, the asset is considered missing. If images are missing when the site file is opened, a warning dialog box may appear. If you place an Adobe Animate CC file (.oam) or an upload asset, Muse will display a warning dialog box if the file is missing when the site is opened.

When images are placed in Muse, an optimized version of the asset is embedded in the Muse site file (.muse). Image links are important for Muse to optimize the assets when exporting or publishing or for updating the image in Muse when it has been edited in another application, such as Photoshop. If image assets are considered missing, the site can still be exported or published, but the images that are missing may not be optimized to look their best or be the smallest file size if they've been altered in Muse. For all missing assets, a missing icon (red circle with a white question mark) appears in the status column of the Assets panel next to the asset name.

You can fix missing and modified links easily in Muse, as you'll see in this exercise.

1 Choose Window > Reset Panels.

2 Choose File > Open Site. In the Open dialog box, navigate to the Lessons > Lesson05 > FixLinks folder. Select the Muse site named FixLinks.muse, and click Open.

Note: If the warning dialog box you see indicates more than one modified image, fix all of them in the Assets panel.

When you open a site that has a missing Adobe Animate CC file (.oam), missing upload asset, or other missing or modified links, a warning dialog box appears. Clicking OK instructs Muse to update any modified assets in the site. You then need to go to the Assets panel to fix the missing links. Clicking Cancel opens the site but does not fix a thing. Be careful when you click OK, because you may not know what has been modified.

3 Click *Cancel* in the warning dialog box.

4 In Plan mode, double-click the HOME page thumbnail to open the page in Design mode. Choose View > Fit Page In Window.

5 With the Assets panel showing (Window > Assets), scroll down in the panel until you see a red stop sign to the right of the DailyDrip.png listing.

6 Right-click (Ctrl-click) the name and choose Relink.

7 In the Relink dialog box, navigate to the Lessons > Lesson05 folder. Select the image named DailyDrip.png, which is in the Lesson05 folder, and click Open.

8 In the Assets panel, right-click (Ctrl-click) the image named cloud-1.png, and choose Update Asset.

Update Asset forces Muse to go look at the original linked image again and update what you see on the page to match the changes made in the linked cloud-1.png image.

9 Choose File > Close Site. You don't need to save this site.

Editing image properties

In Muse, you can add information such as alternative text and a tooltip to images. Alternative text is useful for several reasons, including for search engine optimization (SEO) purposes (depending on the search engine), for accessibility (to be read aloud by screen readers), and to show when an image link is broken or a user chooses not to display images in their browser.

Alternative text is intended to state the purpose of the image, but in addition to a sentence that describes the picture's function, you can include some relevant targeted keywords. Likewise, a tooltip is a way to provide additional information about the image to search engines and visitors. Keep tooltips relevant, short, and descriptive. The image tooltip appears as a tooltip in some browsers when a visitor hovers the cursor over the image. Setting alternative text or a tooltip is typically done on an image-by-image basis. If you have an image that appears multiple times throughout your site, it's best to add alternative text and a tooltip based on the context of the image. In this exercise, you'll add a tooltip and alternative text to the logo.

1   Back in the CoffeeShop.muse site, right-click (Ctrl-click) the logo.svg name in the Assets panel (Window > Assets). Choose Go To Asset to open the Home-master page and automatically select the logo image in the header.

2   Right-click (Ctrl-click) directly on the image, and choose Edit Image Properties.

3   In the Image Properties dialog box, enter **Coffee Shop** in the Tooltip field.

4   In the Alternative Text field, enter **Link to Coffee Shop home** and click OK.

5   Choose File > Save Site, and close all open pages.

Review questions

1 Which image file formats can you place into Muse?

2 What is SVG?

3 Briefly describe the significance of an image link.

4 What options are available when placing a layered Photoshop file?

5 What is the workflow for wrapping text around an image or rectangle?

6 What are alternative text and image tooltips used for on the web?

Review answers

1 In Muse you can place .jpg, .gif, .png, .svg, .ai (Illustrator) and .psd (Photoshop) files by choosing File > Place.

2 SVG (Scalable Vector Graphics) is an image format used on websites for vector graphics. It's great for logos, page elements, and much more, because it usually has small file sizes that compress well, you can scale it to almost any size without losing quality, it looks great on retina displays, and more. Adobe Muse allows you to place SVG (Scalable Vector Graphics) files into your Muse site or copy content from Adobe Illustrator into a Muse web page (which is converted to SVG).

3 When you place (File > Place) an image, Muse creates an image link between the instance of the image on the page and that image's original file. If you later update the original file, say in Adobe Photoshop, Muse updates all instances of that image in your website as well.

4 When you place layered Photoshop files, the Image Import Options dialog box allows you to place a composite image (all visible layers showing) or selected layers. You can also crop the placed image to the bounds of the selected layer(s) content.

5 To wrap text around content, like an image, you must either cut or copy the content from its original location, insert the cursor in the text with the Text tool, and paste the content in the text frame. Then you can use the Wrap panel to set wrapping options.

6 Alternative text is useful for several reasons, including for SEO purposes (depending on the search engine), for accessibility (to be read aloud by screen readers), and to appear when image links are broken. Adding a tooltip to an image provides additional information about the image to search engines and visitors. Alternative text and tooltips should be short, relevant, and descriptive.

6 RESPONSIVE WEB DESIGN

Lesson overview

In this lesson, you'll gain an understanding of how to work with a responsive web design in Muse. Specifically, you'll learn how to:

- Understand the different ways to design in Muse
- Understand the number of ways to start a responsive web design
- Work with breakpoints
- Pin objects
- Position, hide, and resize objects
- Format text across breakpoints
- Unlock page width
- Mix Fixed and Fluid Layouts ◼
- Work with Alternate Layouts ◼

This lesson takes approximately 60 minutes to complete. To download the project files for this lesson, log in or set up an account at peachpit.com. Enter the book's ISBN (9780134547275) or go directly to the book's product page to register. Once on the book's page, click the Register Your Product link. The book will show up in your list of registered products along with a link to the book's bonus content. Click the link to access the lesson files for the book. Store the files on your computer in a convenient location, as described in the "Getting Started" section of this book. Your Account page is also where you'll find any updates to the chapters or to the lesson files. If you are starting from scratch in this lesson, use the method described in the "Jumpstart" section in "Getting Started."

Adobe Muse provides support for creating websites that can respond to any screen size. You can use a single file in Adobe Muse to create responsive websites without any coding. In this lesson, you'll focus on learning the concept of responsive web design in Muse.

Design methods in Muse

● **Note:** If you are starting from scratch using the Jumpstart method described in the "Jumpstart" section of "Getting Started," your workspace may look different from the figures you see in this lesson.

With so many different smart phones and tablet sizes these days, it almost goes without saying that your site design will need to be optimized for different screen sizes. That means creating a site that uses responsive web design.

In Adobe Muse, there are several ways to create your site: Static, Adaptive, or Responsive. By default the sites you create in Muse will be responsive. Depending on your site design needs, you can choose any of those methods or even a combination. Here are the different methods:

- **Fixed Width layout:** A Fixed Width layout, also called a static layout usually has a layout that does *not change* in size based on the browser width. This is how sites were built in the early days of the web before responsive web design technologies came out. For example, the pages in a static design may have a fixed width of 960 pixels—meaning it won't change in size no matter what browser size or device you are looking at it in. Muse has the ability to create Fixed Width layouts.

  A fixed width site is not really used anymore for websites, but might be used if you *only* need to create a site for mobile (smart phone), for instance.

- **Alternate Layouts (a form of Adaptive layout):** Adobe Muse allows you to create alternate layouts for each page of your site. This is not responsive web design, it's a form of *adaptive* design.

  In Muse, you can start designing at mobile, tablet, or desktop size. You then create versions for other layouts. For every version you create, Adobe Muse will create another set of HTML pages. When the site is viewed on a device, the correct home page is opened, depending on the size of that device screen. Adobe Muse generates code for the site that includes detection scripts that identify which type of computer or device and which type of browser the visitor is using to access the page. This type of adaptive layout could be used if you need separate pages and content for different device sizes. An example alternate layout site can be found here: *http://spc-mobile.businesscatalyst.com/*

Desktop layout   Tablet layout   Phone layout

- **Responsive web design:** In Adobe Muse CC, you can create a single Muse site file and adapt your page layout using breakpoints to provide the optimal viewing experience on multiple devices. The pages you build are fluid, which means they scale in proportion to the browser width. This means you design a single web page that is optimized for mobiles, tablets, and desktops.

  Responsive web design is the most widely used design solution these days for websites and what you will be learning over the course of the lessons in this book. The responsive layout you will be creating can be found here: *http://musecoffeeshop.businesscatalyst.com/*

▶ **Tip:** Feel free to view the site on a mobile device as well as your desktop browser.

Responsive Web Design and this book

In the real world, as I design responsive sites in Muse, my process is usually to add the necessary design content to my pages at the largest (desktop) size, then check to see if the design works across different screen sizes. That will make more sense after you see how responsive web design works. This workflow can save you a lot of work later on as you'll learn in this and successive lessons.

Given how important responsive web design has become, it's important to integrate it into your design process, rather than treating it as an afterthought. That's why this chapter is placed earlier in this book. You will learn the bulk of the responsive web design concepts you need to know in this lesson, but in successive lessons, you will see how to incorporate specific content, such as slideshows and forms, into your responsive web design.

Responsive Web Design in Muse

In this lesson, you'll focus on understanding responsive web design in Muse. Before jumping in, let's look at the different ways to start a responsive web design in Adobe Muse. Generically, they are:

- **Using a blank layout:** In Adobe Muse you can create a site design from scratch, starting with a blank site.

- **Using starter files:** Adobe Muse offers customizable, responsive starter templates to help you get started quickly. They are fully editable and can be accessed in the Welcome Screen (Help > Welcome Screen).

- **Converting existing websites to responsive websites:** Adobe Muse allows you to migrate your existing Adobe Muse sites to responsive layouts. Change the layout of your existing Adobe Muse websites to fluid width, and tweak the layout of objects to suit different browser widths. That usually involves some work and is outside of the scope of this book.

For the purposes of learning responsive web design in Muse with this book, you created a blank site from scratch.

Mobile design considerations

Here are a few items to consider for smaller screen sizes when you're designing responsive content:

- Keep it simple: simple navigation, single vertical column design, fewer images in body content, shorter design elements vertically.

- Lead with the most important content; include action items.

- Use an image editing tool like Adobe Photoshop or Illustrator to optimize your images for mobile devices while still maintaining quality.

- Clearly define buttons and links, and add enough space to tap with a finger tip. Buttons in the lower part of the page are easier for mobile visitors to tap using their thumbs.

- Take advantage of mobile features like tapping a phone number to make a call, but also consider the limitations of mobile devices like small screen size and using finger tip or a stylus as input devices (usually). Mobile visitors can tap the screen (which is like a click), but they cannot hover over page elements, so there's no need to set the Rollover state for buttons.

Working with Breakpoints

Whatever method you choose to start your responsive site in Muse, you'll need to preview your layout in different screen sizes to make sure it looks good at the size you're previewing it at. After you add design content to a page, you can use the scrubber to preview that page layout in different screen sizes. If you need to adjust the design at a specific browser width, you can add a breakpoint and make the design change at that browser width.

Breakpoints represent the different browser widths in pixels. Breakpoints allow you to visualize your design in different browser widths, and test how the objects in a page respond to the change in browser widths. Above the scrubber is the Breakpoint bar where you can add and modify breakpoints, among other things.

Let's explore the Breakpoint bar before we begin working with breakpoints.

Note: If you have not already downloaded the project files for this lesson to your computer from your Account page, make sure to do so now. See "Getting Started" at the beginning of the book.

1   With the CoffeeShop.muse site still open, in Plan mode double-click the Home-master page thumbnail to open the page.

2   Choose View > Fit Page In Window.

3   Choose Window > Reset Panels.

In Design mode, you'll see the purple Breakpoint bar along the top of the page, below the Ruler (with rulers showing, View > Show Rulers). The Breakpoint bar shows breakpoints currently set. The scrubber, which you've worked with briefly in previous lessons, lets you resize design content. Notice that the scrubber is currently located beneath the number 1200 in the Breakpoint bar (a box is around it in the following figure). That number (1200) represents the maximum page width (Max Page Width) you set when you first created the site in an earlier lesson.

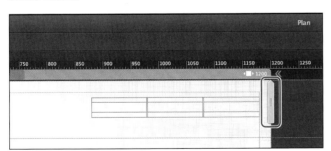

4   Begin dragging the scrubber to the left. As you drag, you'll see a browser width measurement in the gray tooltip that appears next to the pointer.

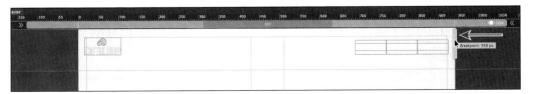

Note: What determines that a layout is "broken" is up to you. That could mean two images overlap, or an image becomes too small, or text runs off the edge of the page or wraps oddly. In other words, the design layout no longer works at a specific browser width (screen size).

One thing to remember in Muse is that in a fluid width layout, your design is fluid. That means that, by default, page objects respond to the browser width based on their default responsive behaviors. As you drag the scrubber to the left, you see what your design will look like at a specific browser width. In this case, the logo gets smaller and the menu eventually moves off of the right side of the page. When your design "breaks," you can create a new breakpoint and "fix" the layout at that size.

5 Drag the scrubber to the right, a little past the 1200 value you see in the Breakpoint bar above the page.

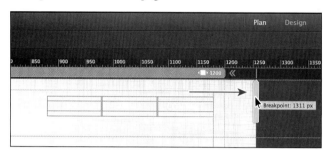

Note: If you drag too far, the page may scroll. You may need to choose View > Fit Page In Window to center the page area in the Document window again.

Notice how the content area (the page area), along with the content on the page, stops resizing and now simply centers in the Document window. That's because, when you set up the site, you set a Max Page Width (maximum width) of 1200 pixels. That means that the page cannot have a width that is wider than 1200 pixels. If the browser window is wider than 1200 pixels, the page width stops at 1200 pixels wide and the page stays centered in the browser window.

Tip: You can also click in the page (content) area to jump to the next breakpoint.

6 Click anywhere within the purple Breakpoint bar above the page.

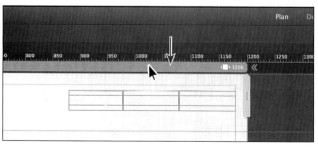

The scrubber resets to the 1200 pixel width, which makes the page 1200 pixels in width again. I said this earlier, but in Muse, you cannot add or edit content unless the page width is equal to a breakpoint width. If you absolutely must make a design change and the page width is not the same as a breakpoint width, you need to create a new breakpoint in order to make edits.

If you look in the center of the Breakpoint bar, you'll see a narrower shaded area with the value of "320." This refers to the Min Width (minimum width), in pixels, that the page can be. Pages will not shrink smaller than the minimum width and will appear cropped if the device or window is narrower than this value. The default Min Width size is 320 for a fluid width layout and can be changed if needed in the site properties, page properties, or breakpoint properties, as you'll soon see.

Tip: You can toggle the visibility of the Breakpoint bar in Muse by choosing View > Hide Breakpoints or View > Show Breakpoints.

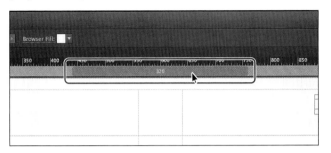

Tip: You can also edit the minimum page width value directly in the Breakpoint bar. Position the pointer on either end of the Min Width area (the darker area in the middle) and when the pointer changes (↔), drag left or right to adjust the size.

Editing the default breakpoint

When you create a new fluid width layout site in Muse, the pages start with a single breakpoint for a desktop design. The size (width) of that breakpoint is determined by the Max Page Width value you enter in the New Site dialog box (1200 pixels in this case). You can easily edit that Max Page Width value and other values. But breakpoints work like other artwork when it comes to pages and master pages. If you edit a breakpoint on a master page, any pages with that master page assigned will reflect that breakpoint change on the master page. You can add and edit breakpoints on each page, which makes sense, since each page usually has distinct content that may need to be fixed across different widths.

Let's take a look at editing the single default breakpoint that each fluid width site starts with on the Home-master page that is currently open.

1 Double-click anywhere in the Breakpoint bar to open the Breakpoint Properties dialog box.

Tip: You can also right-click (Ctrl-click) the Breakpoint bar and choose Breakpoint Properties to edit the breakpoint properties.

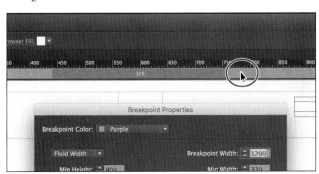

The Breakpoint Properties dialog box contains all of the editable properties for this breakpoint (currently 1200 pixels). You've already seen some of these options when you set up the site and edited the site properties (File > Site Properties).

2 In the Breakpoint Properties dialog box, change the Min Height to **900**.

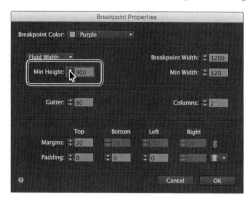

Each breakpoint has a lot of settings that you can change. These settings are unique to each breakpoint. For instance, you could set this breakpoint size to have two columns of guides. A smaller breakpoint, which might be for mobile, could then be set to have one column. This will make more sense shortly.

3 Click OK.

● **Note:** Be careful about changing the Max Page Width value with design content on the pages already. If you change the Max Page Width, the page content will not resize or move to match the new breakpoint width.

The Internal-master page updated as well since it's based on the Home-master page. If you were to open any one of the pages in the site, like the HOME or CONTACT pages, you would see that the Min-Height has been updated since both master pages were updated.

Breakpoints behind the scenes

In the code that Muse generates, for every breakpoint, Adobe Muse adds a corresponding media query declaration to your web page. Media queries is a CSS3 module that allows content rendering to adapt to different screen sizes. Most of the modern browsers can interpret the media queries corresponding to these breakpoints. When users view your web page on various devices, the most appropriate media query and the corresponding design layout is picked up by the browsers and displayed to users.

—From Muse Help

Laying out content

One of the most effective ways to work on a responsive web design in Muse is to design your pages and then use the scrubber to see how that fluid width design content works on different screen sizes. *Hint:* it probably won't. That usually means designing your pages at the maximum page width that you set initially (1200 pixels, in this case), and previewing the layout at *smaller* screen sizes. As you drag the scrubber, images, text, widgets, forms, and frames may extend beyond the page width, objects may bump into one another, or text may not be easily readable. That means that your page content may need to be repositioned, resized, or the default responsive behavior changed, at different screen sizes.

In order to "fix" the content in your design at different screen sizes, you need to learn some key concepts around responsive web design in Muse, like showing and hiding content based on a breakpoint, positioning, pinning, resizing, and more. Up to this point, you added text and images to the pages so you would have content to work with in this lesson. Now it's time to see how that content looks at smaller screen sizes.

Setting the Resize option for content

By default, in Muse, a lot of page content like images, text boxes, menu widgets, and more, are responsive. Content in a fluid width layout resizes in different ways, depending on the screen size (browser width) and the content. The following table specifies the default responsive behavior of objects in Adobe Muse.

Object	Responsive	Responsive behavior
Images, empty frames	Yes	When you view images in different browser widths, images automatically resize by width and height.
Text box, Menu widget	Yes	At different browser widths, these objects automatically resize by width. If you want these objects to span the entire browser width, you can also apply the Stretch to Browser Width setting.
Contact forms and slideshows	No	These widgets remain fixed at all breakpoints. If necessary, you can resize these objects at each breakpoint, separately.
Accordions and Tabbed Panels	Yes	Currently, you can resize these widgets separately at every breakpoint.
Social widgets	Some	YouTube, Vimeo, Facebook Comments, and Google Maps are responsive. At different breakpoints, the YouTube and Google Maps widgets automatically resize by width. If you want these widgets to span the entire browser width, you can also apply the Stretch to Browser Width setting. The other social widgets are not responsive. You can resize these widgets separately at every breakpoint.

—From Muse Help

Note: You can also begin designing at a smaller (mobile) size, and make design changes to "fix" the layout when previewing the page at larger screen sizes. The way Muse currently works, I find it easier to start at the maximum page width when designing.

Note: The ordering of features in the rest of this lesson *does not* indicate the order of importance given to these features.

Note: As of the writing of this book, frames created with the Rectangle Frame tool or Ellipse Frame tool resize by width *and* height. Frames created with the Rectangle tool or Ellipse tool resize by width *only*.

It's your job to make sure that everything you put on your pages looks good no matter what the screen size. In this section, you'll learn how to affect the sizing of responsive content and what that means.

1 Drag the scrubber to the left. As you drag, like you saw earlier, the logo eventually resizes so that it's too small.

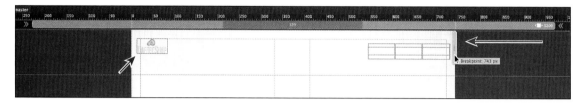

▶ **Tip:** You can also simply click and drag left or right within the Breakpoint bar to preview the page at different sizes. This has the same effect as dragging the scrubber.

By default, images in your responsive web design automatically resize by width *and* height as the web page changes in width. Sometimes this can get you in trouble, as in the case of the logo.

2 Click in the white page area when the pointer looks like this ✐₅, and "Click to jump to breakpoint" appears in a tooltip next to the pointer.

The page width jumps to the maximum width of 1200 pixels. By default, when you click in the page area to "jump to a breakpoint," the page width jumps to the next largest breakpoint so you can make a design change. Remember, to make a design change, the page width must match a set breakpoint width.

3 With the Selection tool (▶) selected, click to select the logo in the header.

4 Click the Resize button to the right of the word "Resize" in the Control panel. Choose None from the menu.

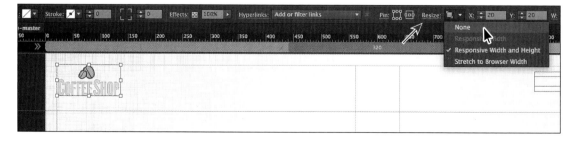

Choosing None ensures that the logo stays the same width and height across *all* screen sizes. It's small enough to begin with that it will fit nicely in the header of whatever size screen we view it at. In the Resize menu, there are four options for sizing content: None, Responsive Width, Responsive Width And Height, and Stretch To Browser Width. Here's what each of those means:

● **Note:** For objects that are not fluid (they are not responsive), the Resize options are not available.

- **None:** The object does not resize based on the screen size.

- **Responsive Width:** Only the width of the object resizes based on the screen size.

- **Responsive Width And Height:** This is the default behavior for a lot of responsive (fluid) content. The width and height of the object will resize *proportionally* based on the screen size.

- **Stretch To Browser Width:** This sets the width of the object to 100% the width of the browser window. Great for text frames, frames with background images, and more.

Next, you'll make it so the menu doesn't resize on different screen sizes either.

5 Select the menu in the header. Right-click (Ctrl-click) the menu and choose Resize > None. This is just another way to set how an object resizes.

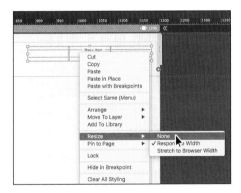

6 Start dragging the scrubber to the left. Notice that both the image and menu do not resize.

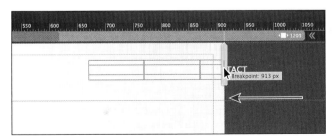

Unfortunately as the page gets narrower, the menu is hanging off the right edge of the page. You'll fix that shortly.

7 Position the pointer in the page area. When it changes appearance (✎ₒ), and a tooltip appears indicating that you need to jump to a breakpoint, click to change the page width to match the next breakpoint (1200 pixels). Leave the Home-master page open.

Setting the Resize option on the MENU page content

Next, you'll set the Resize option for a text frame on the MENU page to learn about stretching content to the browser width.

1 Choose Page > Go To Page. Choose MENU and click OK.

2 Choose Object > Unlock All On Page. The group of objects you locked in an earlier lesson should now be unlocked and selected.

3 Choose Object > Ungroup, and then choose Edit > Deselect All.

Currently in Muse, you cannot change the Resize option on objects *within* a group.

4 Right-click (Ctrl-click) on the text frame that contains the heading, "Coffee Company Food & Beverage Offerings." In the menu that appears, choose Resize > Stretch To Browser Width.

The text frame now has a width of 100% and the text will simply *flow* (not resize) inside of the text frame, if it needs to, at smaller screen sizes.

5 Start dragging the scrubber to the left. When you drag far enough to the left, the text begins to wrap within the text frame.

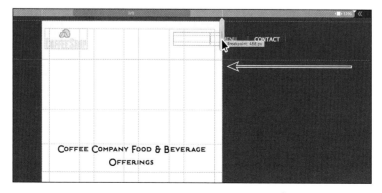

6 Position the pointer in the page area. When it changes appearance (✐), and a tooltip appears indicating that you need to jump to a breakpoint, click to change the page width to match the next breakpoint (1200 pixels).

7 Choose Edit > Deselect All, if necessary, then choose File > Save Site.

Pinning objects

In Muse, when you choose to make a fluid width layout, your design content is positioned relative to the page by default. The positioning of the objects are generally percentage (%) based in the code. That means, for instance, that the logo in the upper-left corner will be a percentage distance from the left edge of the page, so, depending on the screen size, that distance will be different at different browser widths. If you want an object to be an exact distance from the browser or page edge, no matter the screen size, you can *pin* that object either to a page or to a browser. Following is a description of each:

- **Pin objects to browser:** You can pin an object relative *to the browser* if you want the object, like a menu bar, to stay in the same place even when you scroll up or down on the page.

- **Pin objects to page:** You can pin an object to the left edge, center, or right edge of *the page or container* if you want that object to remain fixed horizontally with respect to the web page or container. For example, a company logo that always appears the same distance from the left edge of the web page no matter the page width. If the user scrolls down on the page, the pinned logo will scroll along with the rest of the content on the page.

Next, you'll focus on pinning several page objects to the *page*. In a later lesson, you will pin objects to the browser.

1 Click the Home-master page tab at the top of the Document window to open the master page.

Like you saw earlier, the menu bar eventually moves off the right edge of the page, the narrower the page gets. By default, content like the menu bar is positioned relative to the *left* edge of the page using a percentage (%). You need to make it so that the menu stays in the same position relative to the right edge of the page regardless of screen size. You can pin the menu to the page to achieve this.

Note: Remember, the page area needs to match the width of a breakpoint to make design changes (unless you make a new breakpoint at that size). If you position the pointer over the menu and a tooltip appears indicating that you need to jump to a breakpoint, click to change the page width to match the next breakpoint (1200 pixels) so you can edit the design.

2   Click to select the menu, if necessary. In the Control panel above the page, click the right box (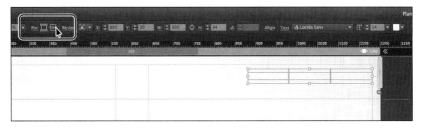) in the Pin option (called *Pin To Right*).

The Pin To Right option pins an object to the right edge of the page. The distance between the edge of the page and the right edge of the object remains *constant* no matter the width of the page. After pinning an object, you'll see a short dotted line between the object and the edge of the page. The dotted line indicates that it's pinned and how it's pinned (left, center, or right).

3   Click to select the logo. In the Control panel above the page, click the left box (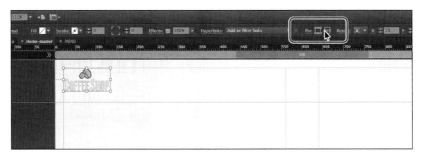) in the Pin option (called *Pin To Left*).

The Pin To Left option pins an object to the left edge of the page. The distance between the edge of the page and the left edge of the object remains constant.

4   Drag the scrubber to the left. Notice that the menu bar and logo each stay the same distance away from their respective page edges. Drag the scrubber far enough to the left, and you'll see the menu run into the logo (an arrow is pointing to it in the following figure). You'll fix that in the next section.

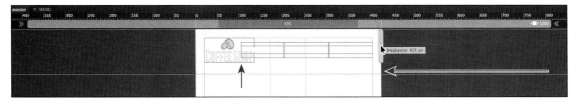

5   Click the purple Breakpoint bar to change the page width to match the breakpoint at 1200 pixels. Leave the page open for the next section.

Creating a breakpoint

You will most likely need to create more than just the default breakpoint if (and when) your design either "breaks" or you want to change columns, padding, and more, for different screen sizes. Early in the days of responsive web design, you would have actually set breakpoints to match generic device sizes like tablet and phone. These days, you create breakpoints when a design change is necessary, like when the menu runs into the logo, as in your site.

In this section, you'll learn how to create and edit a breakpoint, then make a few design changes at that breakpoint size.

1   Drag the scrubber to the left again, until you see a value of *around* 550 in the gray tooltip. Stop dragging *before* the menu runs into the logo.

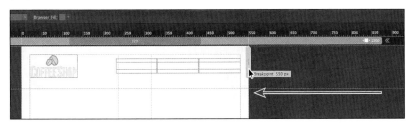

You need to set the breakpoint at a size that is a bit wider than the width at which the design content "breaks." This takes into account any variation in font size, spacing, and more between the different devices and browsers.

2   Above the scrubber, click the Create New Breakpoint icon (![icon]) that appears to create a new breakpoint.

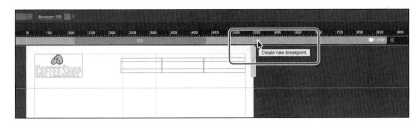

● **Note:** The figure shows just before clicking the Create New Breakpoint icon.

You should see a new color appear in the Breakpoint bar and a new width value of around 550. The original breakpoint, set at 1200 pixels, is now dimmed in the Breakpoint bar.

● **Note:** When it comes to *how many* breakpoints you should have, there is no agreed upon number. It depends on a lot of factors, including your design. I will say that you should try to keep the number of breakpoints to a minimum. Adding and editing content on a page becomes more challenging the more breakpoints there are.

Note: For the purposes of this book, I mostly have you set breakpoints at *exact* values. For instance, in this step, I have you ensure the breakpoint is 550 pixels. I'm only doing that so going forward we all have the same breakpoint sizes set and I can later refer to them easily.

Note: You may not like how the menu stretches. You could have also left the Resize value at None (or chosen Responsive Width) and clicked the Pin To Center option (⬚) in the Control panel to keep it centered. It really depends on how you want it to look and whether or not the content fits.

3 Double-click within the new (blue by default) breakpoint in the Breakpoint bar to open the Breakpoint Properties dialog box. Change the Columns to **1**, make sure the Breakpoint Width is 550, and click OK.

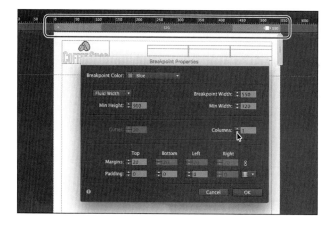

You set the columns to one since most mobile content is often a single column, as you see on smart phones. For all pages in the site, since you are making these edits on a master page, at a browser width of 550 pixels or less, there is only a single column of guides. At a browser width of 551 pixels and higher, the pages still have 2 column guides. With a new breakpoint created, next you'll change some of the design content to work better on smaller screens.

4 Click to select the menu bar on the page and choose Stretch To Browser Width from the Resize menu in the Control panel.

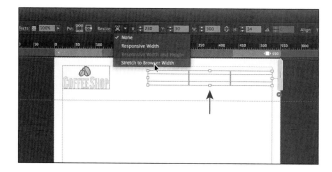

The menu itself now has a fluid width, which means it will resize based on the screen size and always stay centered. Setting this menu up this way is fine since there are only a few menu items. For a large menu, you would need to be careful that on even smaller screen sizes the menu items wouldn't run into each other, making it look bad and making it difficult for the user to tap on the right menu option. In Lesson 10, "Inserting HTML, Using CC Libraries, and Working with Widgets," you will add a separate mobile menu using a Muse widget.

5   Drag the menu so that its bottom edge snaps (aligns) with the header guide. Leave the page open for the next section.

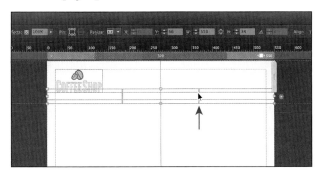

Positioning and Resizing objects on the master

You can also position objects differently and also resize objects manually in different breakpoints. For example, if you have a series of images aligned horizontally in the desktop view, you can position the images vertically at a smaller screen size. In this case, Adobe Muse remembers the position and size of objects and displays them accordingly when the screen size changes.

In this section, you'll resize and position a few design elements.

1   Make sure that the page width is still set at the breakpoint at 550 pixels. If you are unsure, you can simply click on the Breakpoint bar within the 550 pixel breakpoint (the blue area, by default).

2   On the Home-master page, click to select the logo. Drag the lower-right corner toward the image center to make it smaller. Drag until you see a width of around 100 pixels in the measurement label next to the pointer, then release the mouse button.

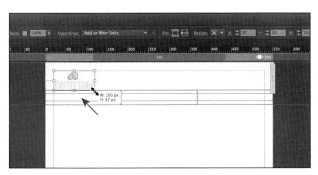

Tip: You may find the logo frame is snapping to other content on the page. You can turn off Smart Guides (View > Smart Guides) temporarily or change the logo size in the Control panel or Transform panel.

● **Note:** If you don't see a Smart Guide or it proves difficult to align the logo, you can also align the logo to center using the Align panel (Window > Align).

3 Drag the logo into the center of the page area. A Smart Guide should appear helping you align it to center.

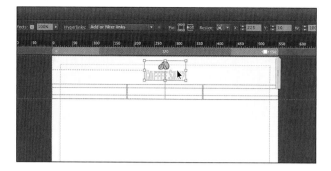

4 With the logo still selected, click the center box (⊞) in the Pin option (called Pin To Center) in the Control panel above the page. This way the logo always stays in the center of the page area when the browser width is 550 pixels or smaller.

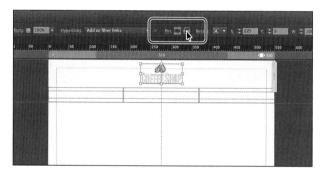

Now here comes the fun part. Seeing your responsive web design in action.

5 Click on the "1200" in the Breakpoint bar to return the page width to 1200 pixels wide. You could also click anywhere on the Breakpoint bar between 550 and 1200 to resize the page width to 1200 pixels.

6 Drag the scrubber to the left to see how the logo and menu react. Drag so that the page width is narrower than the breakpoint at 550 pixels to see the change.

Between 1200 pixels and 551 pixels, the logo and menu stay as you set them initially. Once the screen size reaches a width of 550 pixels, the new position, size, etc. are applied to the logo and menu. That new formatting overrides what was done in the previous (larger) breakpoint.

Positioning and Resizing objects on the MENU page

The MENU page also has design content that needs to be adjusted on smaller screen sizes.

1 Click the MENU page tab to show that page.

Look in the Breakpoint bar and you'll see two sets of small white triangles (a left and a right). See the following figure. Two of those triangles represent the breakpoint you set at 550 pixels on the Home-master page. As mentioned, breakpoints set on a master page appear on any pages with that master applied.

2 Position the pointer over the small white arrow in the Breakpoint bar between the numbers 1200 and 320. A tooltip appears telling you it's a master page breakpoint and that if you click, the page area will resize to 550 (in this case). Click the arrow. See the following figure.

If you wanted to add or edit design content on your page at the 550 pixel page width, you would need to add a new breakpoint. The arrows simply show breakpoints on the master page that are applied to the page. The text frames in two columns are starting to look a little too narrow. In this case, it would look better and be easier to read if the text frames were in a single column (one above the other), so that's what you'll do next.

3 Drag the scrubber to the right until the label next to the pointer shows a width of *around* 700 pixels.

When it comes to columns of text, like these, you need to determine at what page width they need to become a single column of text, rather than two. In this case, looking at the columns of text at 700 pixels, I would say that is as narrow as you want them to be. So you set a breakpoint at this width (700 pixels) and make the layout change.

Note: If you wanted the breakpoint to be an exact width value, you could double-click the new breakpoint value or bar to open the Breakpoint Properties dialog box. Make the necessary changes and click OK.

4 Click the Create New Breakpoint icon (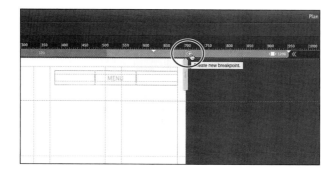) in the Breakpoint bar to create a new breakpoint.

▶ **Tip:** You can Option-click (Alt-click) the Create New Breakpoint icon (+) in the Breakpoint bar to create a new breakpoint *and* open a dialog box where you can set a few properties for the new breakpoint.

5 Choose View > Fit Page In Window.

6 With the Selection tool ( ), click the text frame in the right column that contains the "Baked Goods" heading and drag it below the text frame in the left column. Snap it to the left edge of the first column. Make the frame wider by dragging the right, middle point to the right and snap it to the right edge of the right-most column.

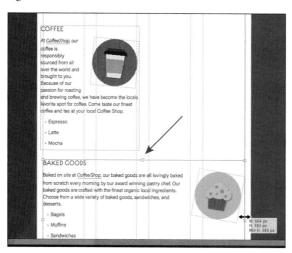

7 Drag the text frame with the "Coffee" heading so the left edge of it snaps to the left edge of the first column. Make the frame wider by dragging the right, middle point to the right and snap it to the right edge of the right-most column. Drag the bottom, middle point up to make the text frame shorter.

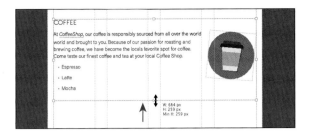

8   Click the bottom text frame that contains the "Baked Goods" heading to select it. Drag it up closer to the text frame above it, making sure it stays in the horizontal center of the page area.

● **Note:** The figure shows the aqua gap measurements, which are a great feature of Smart Guides. You may not see them or the values you see may be different, and that's okay.

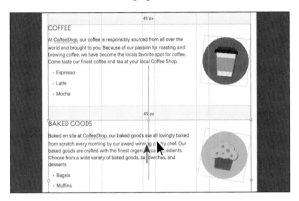

9   Drag across both text frames to select them. Click the center box (▣) in the Pin option (called Pin To Center) in the Control panel above the page.

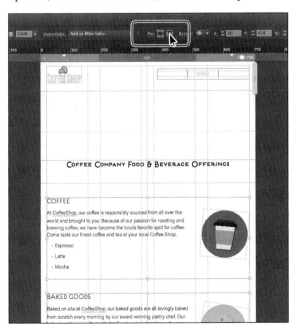

This way both text frames always stay in the center of the page area. This should work well since text frames are set to Responsive Width resizing by default. That means the width of the text frames will resize on different screen sizes and the text within will simply flow.

10 Drag the scrubber to the left and to the right to see how the design changes.

Muse remembers the position and sizing changes you made. So far you've set a few breakpoints and seen how they affect each other.

Showing or Hiding objects

At times, you may need to hide content based on a breakpoint. For instance, in the desktop design you may have a full menu. That menu may be too large for a small screen size found on a phone. You could hide the large menu on a smaller screen size and instead, show a more suitable menu that takes up less room. In this section, you'll hide one of the images on the home page at a smaller screen size.

1 Choose Page > Go To Page. Choose HOME and click OK.

2 Choose View > Fit Page In Window.

You currently have two images on the page. When the screen size is small enough, having two images next to each other, in this case, won't look good.

3 Drag the scrubber to the left until you see a breakpoint width in the measurement label next to the pointer of *around* 600 pixels. Click the Create New Breakpoint icon (⊕) in the Breakpoint bar to create a new breakpoint.

Tip: You can drag the right edge of a breakpoint in the Breakpoint bar to adjust its width.

Why 600 pixels? Because I think at that point, one of the images should be hidden. It's subjective. There is no wrong breakpoint width in this case. If you think the page can go narrower with two images next to each other, then you can set your breakpoint where you like! The previous figure shows the page *after* clicking to create a new breakpoint. The breakpoint in the figure is at *601* pixels. That's okay, it doesn't have to be exactly 600. Going forward, I will refer to this as the "breakpoint at 600 pixels."

Tip: You can show all content hidden in a selected breakpoint by choosing Object > Show All In Breakpoint.

4 Click the image on the right to select it. In this design, since these images are purely for aesthetics, you could hide either of them. Choose Object > Hide In Breakpoint to hide the image.

The image is hidden when the page width is 600 pixels and narrower (601 in *my* case since my breakpoint is set at 601 pixels).

5   Click the remaining image on the left to select it. Drag the lower-right corner of the image frame to make it larger. Snap the right edge of the frame to the right edge of the page area. See the following figure.

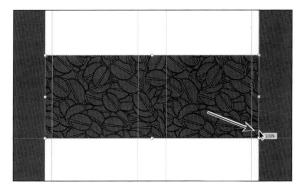

The image should now be the width of the page. When you do this, you have to be careful as always. Resizing a frame may make the image larger than 100%, which isn't good when it comes to raster image formats like .jpg, .gif, .png, or .psd. In this case, the width of the breakpoint (and page) is currently 600 pixels and the original width of this image was 700 pixels, so it's smaller.

Note: Technically the image will always be the width of the page (100%), so centering the image shouldn't be necessary, but we'll center this content to be sure.

6 With the image still selected, click the center box (⊞) in the Pin option (called Pin To Center) in the Control panel above the page.

7 Drag the scrubber to the left and to the right to see how the design changes.

8 Click in the breakpoint at 600 pixels in the Breakpoint bar.

You may see the coffee bean image move up, away from the footer guide, the smaller the screen size gets. That's because it's an image frame that has a Resize value of Responsive Width *And* Height by default. If you wanted to keep an image the same height, you could draw a rectangle with the Rectangle tool (▣) and insert the image into the frame as a background image. A frame created with either the Rectangle tool or Ellipse tool has a default Resize value of Responsive Width. That means the height does not change as the screen size changes.

▶ **Tip:** You can hide selected content in every other breakpoint except for the current breakpoint by choosing Object > Hide In Other Breakpoints.

9 In the Layers panel (Window > Layers), click the arrow to the left of the Page layer to show its contents.

You should see both images listed in the Layers panel. The image on the right that you hid is still there, it's just hiding. If you were to click in the first column of the home_2_lg.jpg image, in this case, the image would show again. A small, black dot would appear in the visibility column of the Layers panel to indicate that the object is visible in the current breakpoint view.

Understanding Multiple Breakpoints

Most of the design content in the site up to this point is looking good across the different screen sizes. In the real world, you will most likely have more content to contend with. Armed with the knowledge you've learned thus far in this lesson, you should be able to tackle most issues that arise when testing across screen sizes. Something you'll run across while previewing your pages and making design changes is formatting text and sizing across breakpoints.

1   Click the MENU page tab at the top of the Document window to show that page. Right now, on the MENU page, there are three breakpoints affecting the page content:

- The maximum page width breakpoint at 1200 pixels
- A breakpoint at 700 pixels (the breakpoint in the figures show 704)
- The breakpoint from the master page at 550 pixels

If you make a design change, like resizing an image, to any of the breakpoints, it will *not* affect that same content at the other breakpoints. This is why we try our best to get all content on the page, and then add our breakpoints.

2   Click the breakpoint at 700, if necessary, to preview the page content at the page width of 700 pixels.

3   With the Selection tool (⬧), click the coffee cup image twice to select the image.

Don't forget, the image was pasted inside of the text frame so the first click will select the text frame.

4   Open the Transform panel (Window > Transform). Click the Constrain Width And Height Proportionally button, if necessary, to change the height *and* width proportionally. Change the Width to **100** and press Enter or Return. The Height changes to 100 as well.

5   With the Selection tool, click the muffin image twice to select it.

6   In the Transform panel change the Width to **100** and press Enter or Return. The Height changes to 100 as well.

Tip: You can copy content and paste using a special command called Paste And Create Breakpoints. This command pastes not only the content but also any breakpoints on the page where the content was copied from.

Note: After clicking twice, you may wind up with the cursor in the text. If that happens, select the Selection tool and click the coffee cup image to select it.

7 Drag the scrubber to the right. The images return to their original 150 pixels in width and height when the page is wider than 700 pixels.

The page content at 700 pixels wide

The page content at 1200 pixels wide

I can't say this enough, but when you make changes to design content in one breakpoint, most of those changes do *not* affect the same design content in other breakpoints. For that reason, it is best practice in Muse to design your pages first at the largest (or smallest) size, and then preview across screen sizes.

Formatting text across breakpoints

In previous lessons, you formatted type according to how it looked on a desktop size layout. As you start previewing across screen sizes, you may find that text formatting needs to be different for various browser widths so that it's clear and readable. For instance, text placed in one breakpoint may wrap abruptly or have unwanted line breaks in another breakpoint.

To format text in responsive web design, Adobe Muse offers Text Formatting icons in the Toolbar. You can choose the Format Text Across Breakpoints option to format the same text area across *all* the breakpoints on a page. Or, if you need to format text for a specific breakpoint, you can choose the Format Text On Current Breakpoint option.

Next you'll adjust the size of the heading across breakpoints on the MENU page.

Tip: To view the next breakpoint, press Cmd+Shift+6 (Ctrl+Shift+6). To view the previous breakpoint, press Cmd+Shift+5 (Ctrl+Shift+5).

1 With the breakpoint at 1200 pixels selected (and the page previewing at 1200 pixels), and the MENU page showing, select the Text tool and drag across the heading, "Coffee Company Food & Beverage Offerings" to select it. Change the font size to 40 px in the Control panel by selecting the font size value, typing in **40**, and pressing Enter or Return.

2 Click in the breakpoint at 700 pixels in the Breakpoint bar. Notice that the text has changed to 40 in this breakpoint as well, but there may be some word wrapping that you don't want.

3 Click the Format Text On Current Breakpoint button (▣) in the Toolbar.

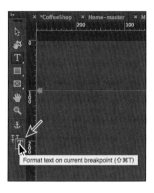

4 With the text still selected, change the Font Size to **30** in the Control panel.

▶ **Tip:** If you later change your mind, and want all of the header text, for instance, to be the same formatting, you can select the header text with the formatting you want, and choose Object > Copy Text Formatting To > All Breakpoints.

5 Click in the breakpoint at 1200 pixels in the Breakpoint bar. Notice that the text size stayed at 40 in this breakpoint.

The Format Text On Current Breakpoint does exactly what it says—it formats text on the current breakpoint only. If you are using paragraph styles, this can become a bit confusing. For this heading, you didn't have a paragraph style applied. If you did have a paragraph style applied, make any style changes that you want to affect all text to the paragraph style in the Paragraph Styles panel. If you want text in individual breakpoints to have different formatting, then set the Format Text On Current Breakpoint and make the text changes. This new formatting will override the paragraph style formatting.

6 Click Format Text Across Breakpoints to ensure that going forward text formatting you change will change on all breakpoints.

7 Choose File > Save Site.

Unlocking the page width

When you first set up a fluid width site in Muse, you chose a maximum page width for the fluid width layout. That means that your pages are responsive up to a maximum page width of 1200 pixels, in this case. On a screen size that is larger than 1200 pixels in width, the page area simply centers in the browser window. You can turn that option off, allowing the page to continue to expand beyond the original maximum page width set. This can be really useful if you are going to support larger screen sizes or you have design content like background images that lend themselves to larger screen sizes.

In this section, you'll see how to allow a page to expand beyond the maximum page width set.

1 Click the HOME page tab at the top of the Document window to open that page.

2 Choose View > Fit Page In Window, if necessary.

3 Click in the breakpoint at 1200 to preview the page at the maximum page width.

4 Drag the scrubber to the right a little and notice that the page width does not get any wider than the maximum page width set. This is something you learned about earlier in this lesson.

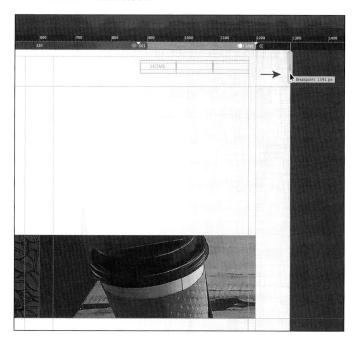

5 Click anywhere in the page area to return the preview to the max page width of 1200 pixels.

6 Position the pointer over the double-arrow to the left or right of the Breakpoint bar above the page. Click to allow the page to expand further.

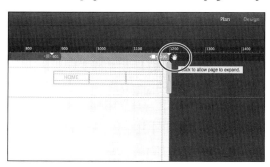

7 Drag the scrubber to the right a little and notice that the page width is now fluid, even past the maximum width set.

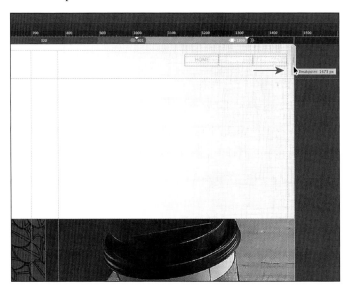

No matter the screen size, the home page will continue to expand in width. This can pose other design challenges and may require you to preview the page on larger screen sizes, making any design adjustments necessary. Also, this can only be set on a page by page basis. You currently can't set this on a master page and have it be applied to all pages with the master page applied.

8 Position the pointer over the double-arrow to the left or right of the Breakpoint bar above the page. Click to lock the page width again.

9 Choose File > Save Site.

10 Choose File > Preview Site In Browser. Explore the pages and then return to Muse. Close all open pages, leaving the site open.

Mixing Fixed Width and Fluid Width Layouts ▬◀

To learn how to mix fixed width and fluid width layouts in your site, check out the video titled "Mixing Fixed Width and Fluid Width Layouts" that is a part of the Web Edition. For more information, see the "Web Edition" section of Getting Started at the beginning of the book.

Working with Alternate Layouts ▬◀

To learn how to work with Alternate Layouts, check out the video titled "Working with Alternate Layouts" that is a part of the Web Edition. For more information, see the "Web Edition" section of Getting Started at the beginning of the book.

Review questions

1 What is responsive web design?

2 Name three main ways you can start a responsive web design in Muse.

3 What is a breakpoint?

4 What does pinning an object to a *page* do?

5 In a fluid width layout, what does unlocking the page width do?

Review answers

1 Responsive web design (RWD) in Adobe Muse CC means you can create a single Muse site file and adapt your page layout using breakpoints to provide the optimal viewing experience on multiple devices. The pages you build are fluid, which means they scale in proportion to the browser width. This means you design a single web page that is optimized for smart phones, tablets, and desktops.

2 In Muse there are three main ways you can start a responsive web design. You can start from scratch with a blank site, use a starter file (template) that comes with Adobe Muse, or convert an existing website to a responsive website.

3 Breakpoints are points at which the browser width causes the design to 'break' on different screen sizes. After you add design content to a page, you can use the scrubber to preview that layout in different screen sizes. If you need to lay out your objects differently at a specific browser width, you can first add a breakpoint.

4 Pinning an object to a *page* forces the pinned object to remain fixed to the left, center, or right, with respect to the web page. For example, this could be useful for a company logo that always appears on the right side of the web page. If the user scrolls down on the page, the logo will scroll with the rest of the page content.

5 When you set up a fluid width layout site in Muse, you choose a maximum page width. That means the pages in the site are responsive up to a maximum page width set. You can turn that option off, allowing the page to continue to expand beyond the original maximum page width set. This can be really useful if you are going to support larger screen sizes or you have design content like background images that lend themselves to larger screen sizes.

7 SHAPES, COLOR, AND EFFECTS

Lesson overview

In this lesson, you'll add more design creativity to your site and learn how to:

- Create and edit shapes
- Add content to the footer
- Create and edit color, swatches, and gradients
- Add background images to frames
- Arrange content
- Apply Bevel and Glow effects
- Work with Scroll effects
- Round the corners of content
- Make opacity (transparency) changes
- Apply effects like a shadow

This lesson takes approximately 45 minutes to complete. To download the project files for this lesson, log in or set up an account at peachpit.com. Enter the book's ISBN (9780134547275) or go directly to the book's product page to register. Once on the book's page, click the Register Your Product link. The book will show up in your list of registered products along with a link to the book's bonus content. Click the link to access the lesson files for the book. Store the files on your computer in a convenient location, as described in the "Getting Started" section of this book. Your Account page is also where you'll find any updates to the chapters or to the lesson files. If you are starting from scratch in this lesson, use the method described in the "Jumpstart" section in "Getting Started."

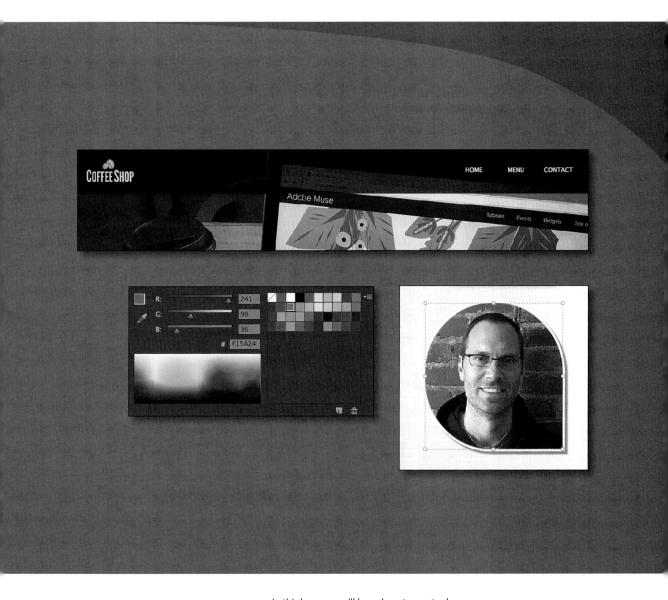

In this lesson, you'll learn how to create shapes, apply background images to frames, apply fills and strokes, and create gradients. Muse also offers many great options that add punch to your web designs, including drop shadows and other effects, rounded corners, and more.

Working with shapes

● **Note:** If you are starting from scratch using the Jumpstart method described in the "Jumpstart" section in "Getting Started," your workspace may look different than the figures you see in this lesson.

Adobe Muse comes with several shape tools in the Toolbar. To draw a shape that you can fill with a color or background image, select the Rectangle tool (■) or Ellipse tool (◉) (click and hold down on the Rectangle tool to select the Ellipse tool). These can be useful for creating colored backgrounds, buttons, graphic elements, and more.

To draw a placeholder (empty) frame that can be filled with a color, gradient, background image and/or graphic, select the Rectangle Frame tool (⊠) or Ellipse Frame tool (⊗) (click and hold down on the Rectangle Frame tool to select the Ellipse Frame tool). In Lesson 5, you worked with the Rectangle Frame tool to place Adobe Illustrator (.ai) files. In this section, you'll learn how to work with the Rectangle tool and everyday formatting options.

● **Note:** If you have not already downloaded the project files for this lesson to your computer from your Account page, make sure to do so now. See "Getting Started" at the beginning of the book.

1   With the CoffeeShop.muse site open in Plan mode, double-click the Home-master page to open the master page in Design mode.

2   Choose Window > Reset panels.

3   Choose View > Fit Page In Window, and then press Command+- (Ctrl+-) to zoom out.

    This shortcut is for the View > Zoom Out command.

4   Click the breakpoint at 1200 in the Breakpoint bar to ensure that the page is set to that breakpoint size.

5   In the Layers panel (Window > Layers), click to select the Footer layer.

    This ensures that the shape you are about to create is on the footer layer.

Drawing with the Rectangle tool

The footer for most sites contains links to other useful information, such as contact details, brief information about the site, social media, a repeat of the main navigation, and more. Corporate sites often use the footer to provide links to driving directions, telephone number, a web form (like a contact form), or at least an email. To start with, you'll draw a rectangle with the Rectangle tool that will be used as a background color behind the footer content.

1   Select the Rectangle tool (■) in the Toolbar.

2   *Above* the Footer page guide, and starting toward the left edge of the page area, click and drag to the right and down to create a rectangle that is around 150 pixels tall. You'll adjust the width and height shortly.

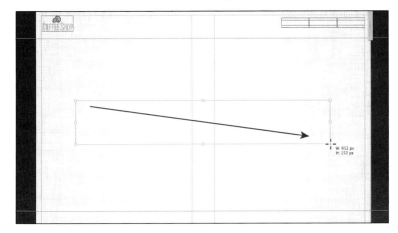

Tip: If you hold down the Shift key *before* you begin drawing with the Rectangle tool, and then release the mouse button followed by the Shift key, you can create a perfect square. If you hold down the Option (Alt) key and drag to create a rectangle, you'll draw from the center of the shape.

By default, rectangles you draw have no fill color and no stroke (border). You'll learn all about how to change the color fill and stroke of this shape in the "Working with color" section later in this lesson.

3   With the rectangle still selected, choose Stretch To Browser Width from the Resize menu in the Control panel.

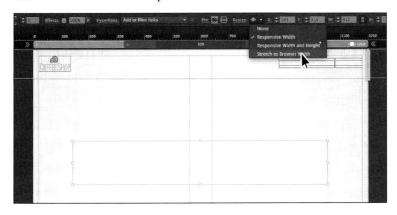

The width of the rectangle will now grow and shrink depending on the width of the screen. It will always be the width of the browser window. Since this rectangle will be a color fill for the background of the footer area, it needs to always fill the width of the browser in this design.

4 Select the Selection tool (➤) and drag the rectangle down into the footer area (below the Footer guide).

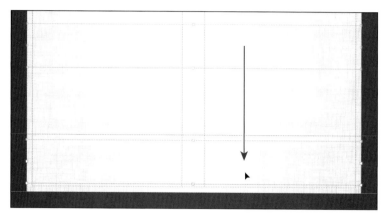

Only on master pages, can you drag content below the footer guide. You need to associate that content with the footer so it stays below the other content on the pages and is part of the footer. That's what you'll do next.

● **Note:** On the pages in your site, when you attempt to drag content below the footer guide, the height of the page area simply increases.

▶ **Tip:** You can also assign content to the footer by selecting the content on the page, right-clicking, and choosing Footer Item or by choosing Object > Footer Item.

5 With the rectangle still selected in the footer, select the Footer option in the Control panel.

This may not seem necessary, but it is. This way Muse knows to associate that content with the footer. If you don't select the Footer option for content you drag into the footer, that content may not be positioned properly on the page, especially if the page content is shorter than the browser height.

6 Drag the rectangle so the bottom edge snaps to the very bottom of the page area. A red Smart Guide appears when the bottom of the rectangle touches the bottom guide telling you the edge of the rectangle is aligned with the guide.

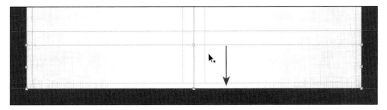

7 Drag the top, middle bounding point of the rectangle frame up until it snaps to the Footer guide. A red Smart Guide will appear when the pointer touches the guide telling you the edge of the rectangle is aligned with the guide. Leave the rectangle selected.

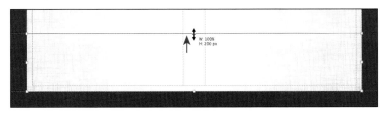

▶ **Tip:** As you saw in a previous lesson, you can also transform content in the Transform options in the Control panel or the Transform panel (Window > Transform). In the Transform panel, the X value specifies where the left edge of the selected object is relative to the left edge of the page area. The Y value indicates where the top of the selected object is relative to the top of page guide. Changing both the X and Y values of selected content positions the upper-left corner of the selected object to those coordinates.

8 Choose File > Save Site.

You can create a variety of shapes with the Rectangle tool. In fact, you can create a line in Muse several ways. The first method is to apply a stroke to a very thin rectangle or other shapes. The trick is to use a very small height for a horizontal line or a very thin width to create a vertical line. Another method is to set the left, bottom, and right stroke weights to 0, leaving only the top stroke set to 1 or higher. Then the rectangle can be any height and still display a line. Lines can be a great way to separate sidebars and other page areas from each other.

Working with color

Unlike print designs, which can use CMYK colors, Pantone color, or other color libraries, designs for the web use only the RGB color model. All colors and images that you create must be in the RGB color mode. The good news is that when you save an image in .jpg, .gif, .png, or other web format using File > Save For Web, Photoshop converts the colors to RGB mode automatically.

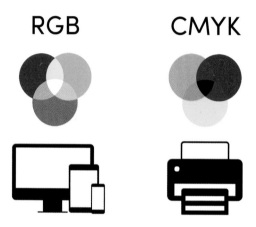

In Muse, you can describe a color with individual red, green, and blue (R, G, and B) values, HSB (Hue, Saturation, and Brightness) values, or a single, six-character hexadecimal (hex, for short) value. R, G, and B values range from 0 to 255. The values in a hex color value range from 0 to 9 and A to F. For example, the hex value AE1365 describes the same color as R: 174, G: 19, B: 101. The first two characters (AE) correlate to the red value (174), the second pair (13) to the green (19), and the third pair (65) to the blue (101).

The hex, HSB, and RGB values tell the browser which color to display, in this case a dark magenta shade. You can think of RGB, HSB, and hex values as three different numeric languages you can use to describe the same color; similar to whether you say red or rojo when you're describing the color of ketchup. Using any of those systems of values, you can transfer colors easily into Muse that you created in another application, such as Photoshop. Of course, in Muse, you also can simply create colors visually using the Color panel, Swatches panel, or Color Picker panel. Whichever method you use to specify a color, you can apply that color to a stroke and fill of a text frame, image frame, or rectangle. In this exercise, you'll begin exploring the color options available in Muse.

1   With the Selection tool, click to select the rectangle in the footer on the Home-master page (if it isn't still selected).

2   Click the Fill color option ( ) to the right of the Fill link in the Control panel to see the Color Picker panel, and take a moment to familiarize yourself with the Color Picker's features:

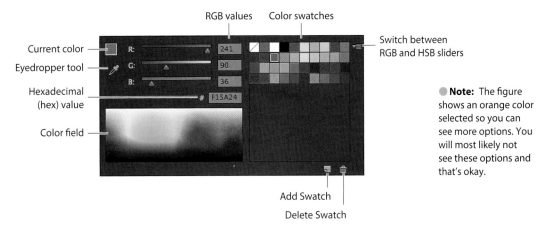

Note: The figure shows an orange color selected so you can see more options. You will most likely not see these options and that's okay.

- **Current color:** Displays the color currently selected and described by the RGB and hex values (by default).

- **Eyedropper tool:** Enables you to select colors anywhere on your screen—even outside of Muse. Click the eyedropper on the desired color to sample it.

- **Hexadecimal (hex) value:** Specifies the hexadecimal value of the current color.

- **Color field:** Enables you to sample and adjust a color.

- **RGB values:** Specifies the values of the Red, Green, and Blue channels of a color. Values range from 0 to 255.

- **Color swatches:** Contains saved colors that you can apply, create, or delete in your site.

- **Switch between RGB and HSB sliders:** Enables you to switch between RGB (Red, Green, and Blue) and HSB (Hue, Saturation, and Brightness) sliders in the Color Picker.

- **Add Swatch:** Saves a selected color in the list of color swatches.

- **Delete Swatch:** Deletes a selected color swatch in the list of color swatches.

For the remainder of the lesson, you'll experiment with color, learning how to create colors, apply color, and save color as swatches. You'll also work with color gradients to add some flair to your design.

Creating and applying a color fill

Muse offers many color options that help you easily create and save colors to reuse throughout your site. One of the most common applications is a color fill, which is color that appears inside a shape or frame. To practice, you'll create a color for the footer rectangle and then save that color so you can use it later.

1 With the rectangle in the footer still selected on the Home-master page, click the Fill color option (⬜▼) in the Control panel to show the Color Picker panel.

2 Drag in the yellow area of the color field to sample a color. As you drag, you'll see the color values change in the Color Picker. The color you sample will be applied to the selected frame.

● **Note:** You can also click away from the Color Picker panel to hide it.

3 Change the RGB values to R=**60**, G=**60**, and B=**60**. Press Enter or Return a few times, if necessary, to hide the Color Picker panel.

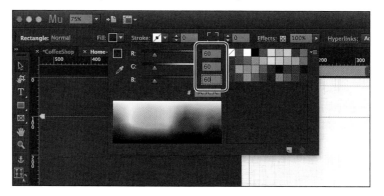

● **Note:** The figure at right shows you what the rectangle in the footer should now look like.

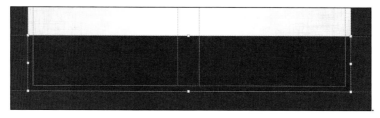

Saving and editing a swatch

Muse lets you save a color you create or a color you sample as a swatch. This makes your life easier later on if you want to reuse a color or if you decide to use a consistent set of colors throughout your site. You can find saved swatches by clicking the Fill or Stroke colors in the Control panel or in the Swatches panel.

1   With the rectangle in the footer still selected, click the Fill color option in the Control panel to show the Color Picker panel again. Click the Add Swatch button (⬜) at the bottom of the Color Picker panel (circled in the following figure).

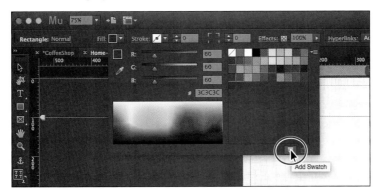

▶ **Tip:** If you delete a swatch, Muse gives you the option of replacing the swatch with another swatch or with an unnamed swatch (the color remains applied to the object, but the color won't be saved as a swatch anymore).

2   In the Swatch Options dialog box that opens, deselect Name With Color Value to add your own name. Change the Swatch Name to **FooterBG**.

In the Swatch Options dialog box, by default, you'll see a Saturation/Brightness field and a Hue column to the right of it for adjusting the selected color. You can select HSB (Hue, Saturation, Brightness), RGB, or HEX to change the color using different values.

3   Click OK.

4 Hover the pointer over the new swatch at the end of the list; a yellow tooltip appears showing the FooterBG name of the new swatch.

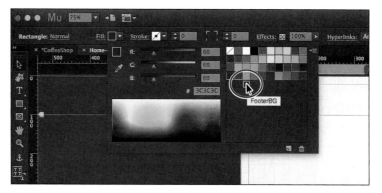

By default, the tooltip displays the RGB color values, but you changed the name of the swatch in the Swatch Options settings. Many designers prefer the tooltips to indicate what a color is to be used for, such as a heading color.

Note: Any changes that you make in the Swatch Options dialog box change the swatch as well as every object in your site to which you applied the color.

5 Press the Esc key to close the Color Picker panel, and choose File > Save Site. Leave the rectangle in the footer selected for the next section.

You can create and save as many colors as you need. Just remember that you don't have to save a color as a swatch, but doing so can be helpful, and save you time later.

Sampling color

Sampling color is a great way to either reuse a color that wasn't saved or create a new color from a color in an image on the page. You can sample color with the Eyedropper tool found in the Color Picker, Color panel, and Swatch Options dialog box when saving a swatch. Next, you'll sample a color from the logo to use later.

1 With the rectangle still selected in the footer, select the Zoom tool (🔍) in the Toolbox and drag across the logo in the upper-left corner to zoom in closely.

It's okay if you can't see the rectangle in the footer anymore. You are going to sample a color from the logo and it will be difficult to sample a color if the logo is really small.

2 Open the Swatches panel by choosing Window > Swatches.

3 Double-click the FooterBG swatch in the list. In the Swatch Options dialog box, click the Eyedropper tool () (next to Select Color:) to sample a color. Position the Eyedropper pointer over the dark brown color in one of the coffee beans in the header logo and click to sample. The logo is small, but when the pointer is over the right color, it should show in the Swatch Options dialog box. See the following figure.

▶ **Tip:** You can double-click a swatch in the list of Swatches in the Color Picker or in the Swatches panel (Window > Swatches) to edit the properties for a swatch.

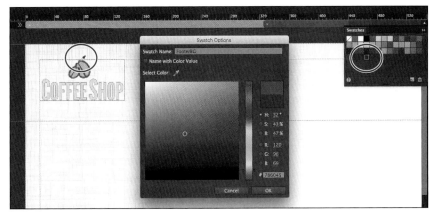

4 Click OK.

5 Choose View > Fit Page In Window.

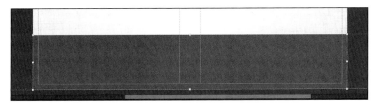

When you edit a color swatch, any content with that swatch applied in the site is updated as well. The content doesn't even have to be selected for it to update when the swatch is updated. In this case, the fill of the rectangle in the footer updated.

6 Choose File > Save Site.

Editing the stroke of an object

As in most other Adobe applications, you can control the appearance of the stroke of an object (the border), much like fills. This exercise focuses on customizing the color and size attributes for the stroke of objects. You'll also tour the Stroke Options panel, which gives you even more control over a stroke's appearance.

▶ **Tip:** If you press the Shift key and click the up or down arrows to change a field value, you will change the value by 10 instead of just 1.

1   With the rectangle frame in the footer still selected, change the Stroke Weight to **30** in the Control panel to apply a 30-pixel stroke.

Edit the Stroke of the rectangle in the footer

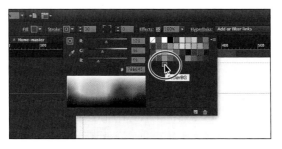

The stroke applied to the rectangle in the footer

2   Click the Stroke color (■▼) in the Control panel to reveal the stroke Color Picker panel. Click the FooterBG color swatch to apply it to the stroke.

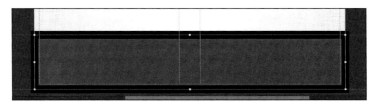

The stroke Color Picker panel is identical to the fill Color Picker panel you worked with in the previous few sections.

3 Click the Color Picker menu icon (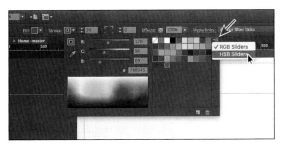) in the upper-right corner (an arrow is pointing to it in the following figure), and choose HSB Sliders.

4 Change the B (Brightness) value to **35** in the Color Picker to apply a darker version of the color to the stroke.

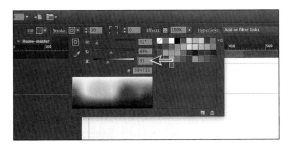

5 Click the Add Swatch button (📇) to save the color. In the Swatch Options dialog box, deselect Name With Color Value and change the name to **FooterStroke**. Click OK.

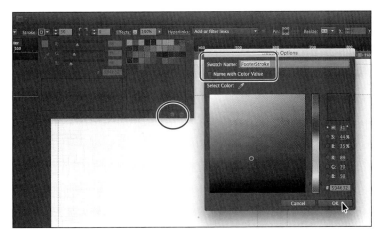

6 Press the Esc key to hide the stroke Color Picker panel.

7 Click the Stroke link in the Control panel. Click the Align Stroke To Inside button (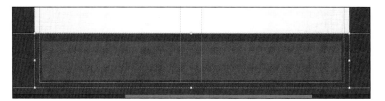) and notice that the darker stroke on the rectangle is now inside the edges of the rectangle.

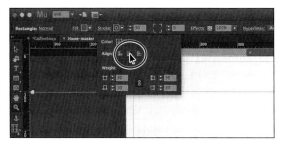

Align the stroke to inside

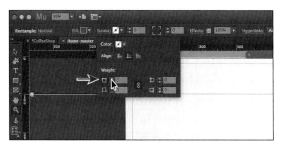

The stroke applied to the footer rectangle

The Stroke Options panel that appears shows two main options: Stroke Alignment and individual Stroke Weights. Stroke Alignment lets you align the stroke to the inside, outside, and center of the edge of a frame. The Stroke Weight options allow you to change the stroke weight for each side of a frame independently, if you want.

8 In the Stroke Options panel that's still showing, with the Make All Stroke Weight Settings The Same *on* (it should look like this [⬛]), change the Top Stroke Weight value to **0** and press Return (Enter).

9 Click the Make All Stroke Weight Settings The Same icon to turn it off (so that it looks like this [⬛]). Now you can edit each of the Stroke Weight settings independently. Change the Top Stroke Weight to **30** and press Return (Enter).

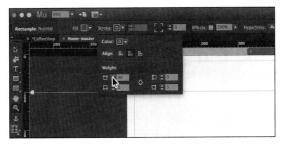

Edit the top stroke weight

The stroke applied to the top of the footer rectangle

10 Press the Esc key to hide the Stroke Options panel, if necessary, and leave the rectangle selected.

11 Choose File > Save Site.

Working with gradients

You can also apply a color fill using a gradient, which is a blend from one color to another. Muse offers many options to help you make and apply gradients to the fill of all types of frames. Next, you'll fill the footer rectangle with a gradient.

1 With the rectangle still selected in the footer, click the Fill link in the Control panel to show the Fill panel. Select Gradient in the Fill panel, and notice that the Fill panel options change and the rectangle on the page now has a gradient fill.

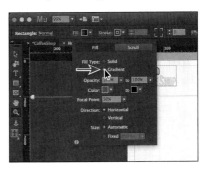

With Gradient selected, you can now specify two colors rather than one for a solid fill. When you select Gradient with a new rectangle frame selected (with no stroke and fill applied by default), Muse applies white and black as the two colors that the gradient blends between. The footer rectangle in your page already had a fill color, so the fill color is one of the colors in the gradient to start.

2 Change the Opacity value on the right to **20** and notice that the one color in the footer rectangle is now semi-transparent. Change the value back to **100**.

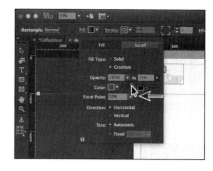

3 Click the Fill Color on the left and select the FooterBG swatch, if it isn't already selected. Click back in the Fill panel to hide the Color Picker.

● **Note:** If you don't see the HSB values in the Color Picker panel, you can choose HSB Sliders from the Color Picker panel menu (▤).

4 Click the Fill Color on the right and select the FooterBG swatch. In the Color Picker that's now showing, change the Brightness (B:) to **25**. Click back in the Fill panel to hide the Color Picker.

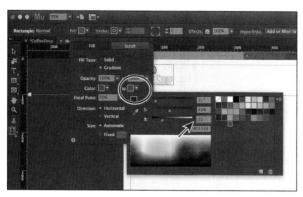

5 Click the arrow to the right of the Focal Point field and drag the slider left and right to see the effect on the gradient in the rectangle. Make sure that the value is 70 before moving on to the next step.

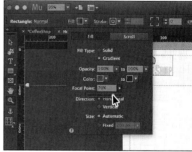

The Focal Point is where the transition between the two gradient colors occurs in the shape. For a vertical gradient, the closer the value is to 0, the closer to the top of the shape the transition appears.

6 Select Vertical to change the Direction of the gradient.

This changes the direction of the gradient from top to bottom rather than side to side.

7 Select the Fixed Size option. Change the value to the right of the selection to 50 by selecting the value and typing **50** or dragging the slider that appears after clicking the arrow to the right of the Fixed field. Notice that the distance or blend between the two colors is much shorter. Try other values to see the effect. Be sure to select Automatic when you're ready to move on.

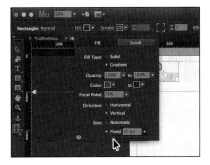

With the Automatic size option enabled, the Size setting of a gradient is automatically determined by the size of the object. By default, Muse sets each of the colors on opposite ends of the color fill to create a blend that spans the width or height of the object, depending on the Direction setting you select. If you select Fixed, you can change the size or length of the object with the gradient applied to achieve the desired effect.

8 Press the Esc key to hide the Fill color options.

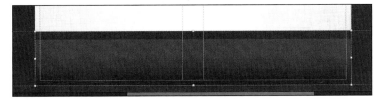

9 With the rectangle still selected, ensure that Stretch To Browser Width is still chosen for the Resize option in the Control panel. As of the writing of this book, the Resize option for rectangles may switch to Responsive Width when the rectangle height is changed.

10 Choose Edit > Copy.

11 Choose File > Save Site.

Now that you've drawn a few shapes, applied color, and worked with strokes, you'll jump into applying a background image to a frame.

Applying a background image to a frame

Text frames, frames that contain images, and any rectangles you draw can all have background images applied to them to add to your designs. Background images in frames work just like the background image for the page area and the browser fill, appearing behind the content in the frame and adding more design possibilities.

Background images can also scale within a frame if the frame is set to stretch to the browser width. This is a great way to create a responsive banner, for instance. You just have to know that at mobile size, the large image that worked well on desktop will be the same file size, only scaled down. Next, you'll add a background image to a rectangle you draw to make a header image for the Internal-master page.

1 Choose Page > Go To Page. Choose Internal-master from the menu and click OK to open the page in Design mode.

2 Choose View > Fit Page In Window.

3 Click the breakpoint at 1200 to ensure that the page is showing at the maximum page width of 1200 pixels.

Note: When you copy and paste an object with Stretch To Browser Width set for the Resize option, the pasted copy will also have Stretch To Browser Width set.

4 Select the Selection tool (↖) and choose Edit > Paste to paste a copy of the rectangle from the footer of the Home-master page.

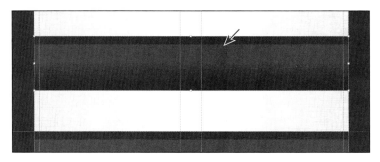

5 With the rectangle selected, deselect the Footer option in the Control panel so it's no longer associated with the footer.

6 Choose View > Hide Breakpoints to temporarily hide the Breakpoint bar. This way you can be sure to see the top of the page area.

7 Drag the rectangle up to snap its top edge to the top of the page area.

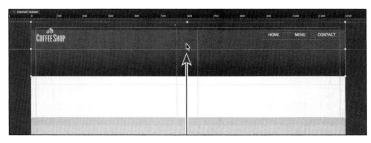

Next you'll duplicate the rectangle and paste a copy right on top of the selected rectangle now in the header. Later, you'll edit that rectangle copy to become a black transparent bar to make the menu more readable over header images you will add.

8 Choose Edit > Copy, and then Edit > Paste In Place to paste a copy on top.

9 Drag the bottom, middle point of the selected rectangle down until you see an approximate height of 230 px in the measurement label. It should snap to the horizontal guide you created in an earlier lesson.

Tip: You can press the Option (Alt) key and drag a bounding point of a frame to resize opposite sides of a frame at the same time.

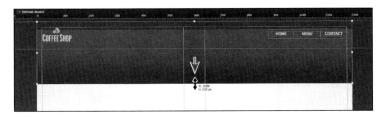

10 With the rectangle still selected, choose Object > Clear All Styling to remove the stroke and fill. The rectangle on top now has no stroke and no fill, but the other rectangle beneath it, still has the stroke and fill applied.

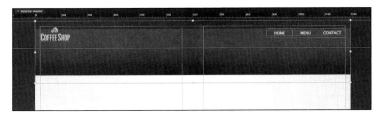

11 Click the Fill link in the Control panel. With the Fill tab selected, and the Solid Fill Type selected, click the Add Image link to select a background image. Navigate to the Lessons > images folder, choose menu_banner.jpg, and click Open.

Note: You can insert .jpg .gif, .png, .ai, .svg, or .psd files in Muse as a background image. Muse converts .ai and .psd files to an optimized format for the web when you publish or export the site.

Tip: You can also open the Fill panel by choosing Window > Fill. The Fill panel opens in the workspace and shows the same options as clicking the Fill link in the Control panel. Because it's a panel, you can leave it showing.

12 Choose View > Show Breakpoints to show the Breakpoint bar again.

13 Click the Fill link in the Control panel again. Choose Scale To Fill from the Fitting menu, and make sure that the top, center point in the position indicator (▦) is selected. Click anywhere else on the page to close the Fill menu.

14 Ensure that the rectangle still has Stretch To Browser Width selected for the Resize option in the Control panel. As of the writing of this book, the Resize option for this rectangle may switch to Responsive Width when the rectangle height is changed.

The image will always fill the rectangle regardless of the size. When you choose an image, make sure to strike a balance between that image looking good on a large screen and not being so large in file size that it loads slowly in the browser. You can best optimize images by exporting the optimized image files in the image editing program of your choice.

15 Choose File > Save Site and leave the page open.

Arranging content

As you add more content to the page, you may need to send content behind or bring it in front of other content on the same layer. This is called changing the stacking order. Right now the rectangle with the background image fill in the header is covering another rectangle. That needs to be fixed using an arrange command.

1 Open the Layers panel (Window > Layers), if necessary. With the header image still selected on the page, click the Locate Object button (▣) at the bottom of the panel to reveal the content on the Footer layer.

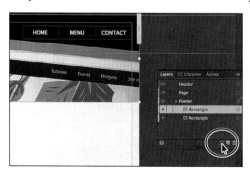

2 Click the selection column to the right of the Rectangle object at the *bottom* of the layer stack to select the original rectangle you pasted and dragged into the header at the beginning of this lesson. See the following figure for which rectangle to select.

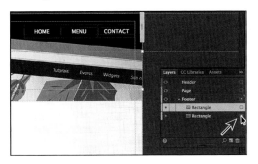

3 Choose Object > Bring To Front to bring the gradient-filled rectangle on top of all other content on the layer.

▶ **Tip:** You also could have kept the image frame selected in the header and chosen Object > Send To Back.

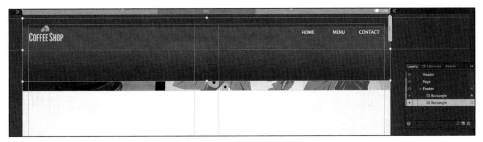

This arrange command works across all breakpoints on the page. You should see the change in the Layers panel as well.

4 Press the Shift key and click the selection column to the right of the Rectangle object at the bottom of the layer stack to select both rectangles.

▶ **Tip:** To move an object one step to the front or one step to the back of a stack of objects on a layer, select the object you want to arrange, and choose Object > Bring Forward or Object > Send Backward.

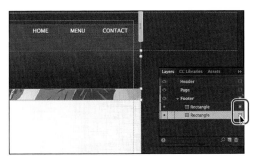

5 Choose Object > Move To Layer > Page to move both rectangles to the Page layer. Notice that they also keep the same layer stack (the brown rectangle on top of the rectangle with the header image in it).

6 Choose Edit > Deselect All.

Optimizing the background image for mobile

When it comes to background images in rectangles, the same image is downloaded across devices and machines, no matter the screen size. The background image scales nicely, but as in most responsive web sites, the background image is still the same file size, just smaller in dimension.

In this section, you'll swap out the large header image for a smaller file size image to help with lessening download time on mobile devices. This involves hiding the rectangle with the background image at the smaller breakpoint, and creating a new rectangle with a smaller background image for that smaller breakpoint.

1   Select the header rectangle with the background image on the Internal-master page. Choose Edit > Copy to copy the header rectangle. This way you don't need to create a new one.

Next you'll hide the rectangle with the background image on a new breakpoint you create at 600 pixels. You'll then paste the rectangle and swap out the image in the background for a smaller image.

2   Right-click (Ctrl-click) the Breakpoint bar and choose Add Breakpoint.

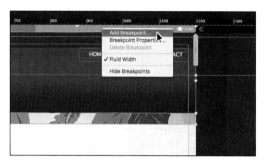

3   In the Add Breakpoint dialog, change the Breakpoint Width to **600** and click OK. A new breakpoint is created at 600 pixels and the page is previewed at that width.

4   Choose Object > Hide In Breakpoint to hide the rectangle with the background image that is still selected.

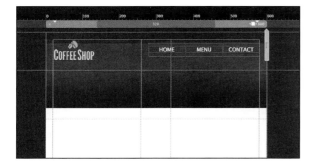

5　Choose Edit > Paste In Place to paste a copy of the rectangle on the page in the same position as the original. If necessary, drag the copy to the top of the page.

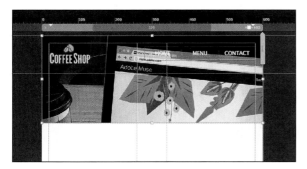

6　Choose Object > Send To Back to send it behind the brown rectangle.

7　With the rectangle selected, click the Fill link in the Control panel. With the Fill tab selected, click the menu_banner.jpg link. In the dialog box that opens, select the menu_banner_small.jpg image from the Lessons > images folder. Click Open.

The menu_banner_small.jpg image is the same image as menu_banner.jpg, only it's smaller in dimension (and ultimately file size as well). Since this breakpoint is at 600 pixels, and you don't want the image to scale past 100%, the image is large enough in dimension to fill the rectangle. When a user looks at the pages on a smaller device like a smart phone, only the content needed for that screen size (the menu_banner_small.jpg image) is downloaded from the server.

8 Choose Object > Hide In Other Breakpoints.

If it seems like nothing happened, remember this: when you add new content to a page, that content appears across all breakpoints. In this case, you have one header rectangle for the largest (maximum page width of 1200 pixels) breakpoint and another for the breakpoint at 600 pixels.

9 Drag the scrubber to the right, past the breakpoint at 600 pixels.

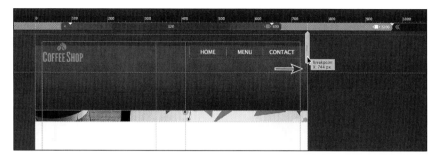

10 Click either rectangle in the header and the page width jumps to 1200 pixels.

11 Select the header rectangle with the background image and click the Fill link in the Control panel. With the Fill tab selected, you should now see a menu_banner.jpg link, indicating that on screen sizes larger than 600 pixels, the larger banner image will download and appear on the page.

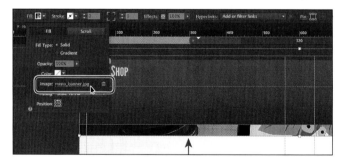

Working with rounded corners, opacity, and effects

In Adobe Muse many formatting options can help you add some real design flair to the content on your pages, aid in readability, keep up with today's design trends, and more. Those formatting options include effect settings, which consist of drop shadows, bevels, glows, rounded corners, and opacity (transparency) changes. You can apply all of these options to content from the Control panel. You'll experiment with these formatting options in the following exercises, starting with rounded corners.

Applying Bevel Effects and Glow Effects

To learn how to apply Bevel effects and Glow effects to content, check out the video titled "Applying Bevel Effects and Glow Effects" that is a part of the Web Edition. For more information, see the "Web Edition" section of Getting Started at the beginning of the book.

Working with Scroll Effects

To learn how to add Scroll Effects to your page, check out the video titled "Working with Scroll Effects" that is a part of the Web Edition. For more information, see the "Web Edition" section of Getting Started at the beginning of the book.

Rounding corners

You can round the corners on content, such as text frames, image frames, rectangles, form buttons, and more. You can also round each corner separately or round all of a frame's corners at once. Either way, you can easily adjust your initial rounding settings, as you'll see in this exercise.

1   Choose Page > Go To Page (Command+J [Ctrl+J]). Click the arrow to the right of the field and choose CONTACT. Click OK.

2   Choose View > Fit Page In Window.

3   With the Selection tool selected, click the image of Joe to select it.

4   Change the Stroke Weight to **1** in the Control panel so you can see the stroke.

5   Drag the corner of the image toward the center to make it smaller. Stop when you see roughly 40% in the measurement label.

> **Tip:** You can also begin typing the name of a page in the Go To Page dialog box to filter the names of the pages.

6 Change the Corner Radius to **100** in the Control panel.

Changing the Corner Radius changes all four corners of the frame to the same radius. The larger the radius, the more rounded the corners will become.

7 Click the lower-right Enable/Disable button (⬛) in the Control panel to disable the corner radius for just the lower-right corner.

You can adjust the radius of each corner independently for a frame to add some interesting visual effects to the content on your pages.

8 Click the lower-right Enable/Disable button (⬛) in the Control panel to enable the corner radius for the lower-right corner again.

9 Choose File > Save Site.

10 Click the Preview mode link to see the rounded corners. Click the Design mode link to return to the page and leave it open for the next section.

Adjusting opacity

Another great feature for adding design interest to your pages is the ability to change the opacity (transparency) of content. You can use opacity changes to aid in readability when placing text on an image, for instance. In this exercise, you'll change the opacity of the rectangle frame beneath the logo and menu for readability.

1 Click the Internal-master page tab at the top of the Document window to show the page.

2 Click in the breakpoint at 1200 pixels to ensure that you are previewing the page at that width.

3 Choose View > Fit Page In Window, and then choose View > Hide Breakpoints.

4 Click the brown rectangle at the top of the page. Choose Object > Clear All Styling to remove the stroke and fill.

5 Click the Fill color and select black in the Control panel.

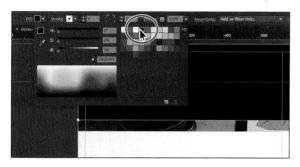

6 Change the Opacity setting to **70** in the Control panel.

Opacity changes the transparency of the selected object. If the rectangle you drew had a background image, stroke, and so on, the opacity adjustment would apply to the frame and all of its contents.

▶ **Tip:** To change the opacity, you can either click the arrow to the right of the Opacity field and drag the slider or type the value directly into the Opacity field.

7 Choose View > Show Breakpoints.

8 Click and drag the bottom, middle point of the rectangle up so that it snaps to the header guide and the rectangle is 100 pixels in height.

9 Ensure that the rectangle still has Stretch To Browser Width selected for the Resize option in the Control panel. As of the writing of this book, the Resize option for this rectangle may switch to Responsive Width when the rectangle height is changed.

10 Choose Object > Copy Size And Position To > All Breakpoints. This ensures that the height change you just made appears on all other breakpoints as well.

Always remember, making a transformation like a size change will only affect the current breakpoint!

11 Choose File > Save Site.

▶ **Tip:** You can also target a specific breakpoint to copy the size and position of content to, by choosing Object > Copy Size And Position To > [breakpoint size].

Applying a Shadow effect

The Shadow effect, or drop shadows, can add depth to your design content, so that it takes on a more 3D appearance. Next, you'll apply a shadow to the image of Joe on the CONTACT page.

1 Click the CONTACT page tab to show the page.

2 With the Selection tool selected, click to select the image of Joe, if necessary.

3 Change the Stroke Color to white and the Stroke Weight to **3** in the Control panel.

4 Click the Effects link in the Control panel to reveal the Effects menu. Making sure that the Shadow button is chosen at the top of the options, select Shadow.

   Three types of effects are listed in the Effects menu: Shadow, Bevel, and Glow, as well as the specific options for each effect.

5 Change the Shadow options to the following:

   • Color: Black (the default setting)

   • Opacity: **30**

   • Blur: **2** (specifies the "thickness" of the shadow)

   • Angle: **45** (moves the drop shadow around the object)

   • Distance: **6** (specifies the distance between the drop shadow and object)

▶ **Tip:** You can apply a shadow to text. Just make sure that the text frame is selected, not the text and that the text frame does not have a color fill.

● **Note:** Drop shadows follow the contour of an image, not the edges of the image frame. If you were to apply a color fill to the same image frame, the drop shadow would follow the contour of the color fill. If you were to apply a background image to the image frame, the drop shadow would follow the contours of the background image or image in the frame.

   Try adjusting the settings to see the effect on the shadow. Be sure to return to the settings in this step when you are ready to continue.

6 Click away from the Effects menu to hide it or press the Esc key.

7 Choose File > Save Site and close all open pages, returning to Plan mode.

Review questions

1 What must be set for content to be considered as part of the footer?

2 From what content can you sample color?

3 What does hexadecimal refer to?

4 What image types can you use as a background image in Muse?

5 Name the three main effects in the Effects menu that you can apply to content in your pages.

6 How do you apply effects to page elements?

Review answers

1 For content to be considered as part of the footer, you must ensure that the Footer option is selected for objects in the footer. This ensures that the content moves with the footer and stays at the bottom of the browser window if the "Sticky Footer" option is set in the site or page properties.

2 You can sample color from content within Muse and outside of Muse (any pixels displayed on your screen).

3 Hexadecimal values, such as 330011, are one way to tell a browser exactly which RGB (Red, Green, Blue) color you want to display.

4 In text frames, frames that contain images, and any rectangles you draw, you can insert .jpg .gif, .png, .ai, .svg, or .psd files in Muse as a background image. Muse converts .psd files to a more compact format for the web when you publish or export the site, but it's best practice to optimize the image and save it in a web format (.jpg, .gif, .svg, or .png) in a program like Illustrator or Photoshop before inserting it as a background image.

5 The three main effects you can apply to content in Muse are shadows, bevels, and glows.

6 You can apply effects to selected content by clicking the Effects link in the Control panel, choosing the tab with the desired effect, enabling the effect, and then setting the options in the Effects menu.

8 ADDING LINKS, BUTTONS, AND GRAPHIC STYLES

Lesson overview

In this lesson, you'll add links and buttons to your pages and learn how to:

- Create different types of links
- Link to a file
- Edit link properties
- Edit text link styles
- Create a button in Adobe Muse
- Work with states
- Place an Adobe Photoshop button
- Create and link to anchors
- Pin content to the browser
- Save and apply graphic styles

 This lesson takes approximately 60 minutes to complete. To download the project files for this lesson, log in or set up an account at peachpit.com. Enter the book's ISBN (9780134547275) or go directly to the book's product page to register. Once on the book's page, click the Register Your Product link. The book will show up in your list of registered products along with a link to the book's bonus content. Click the link to access the lesson files for the book. Store the files on your computer in a convenient location, as described in the "Getting Started" section of this book. Your Account page is also where you'll find any updates to the chapters or to the lesson files. If you are starting from scratch in this lesson, use the method described in the "Jumpstart" section in "Getting Started."

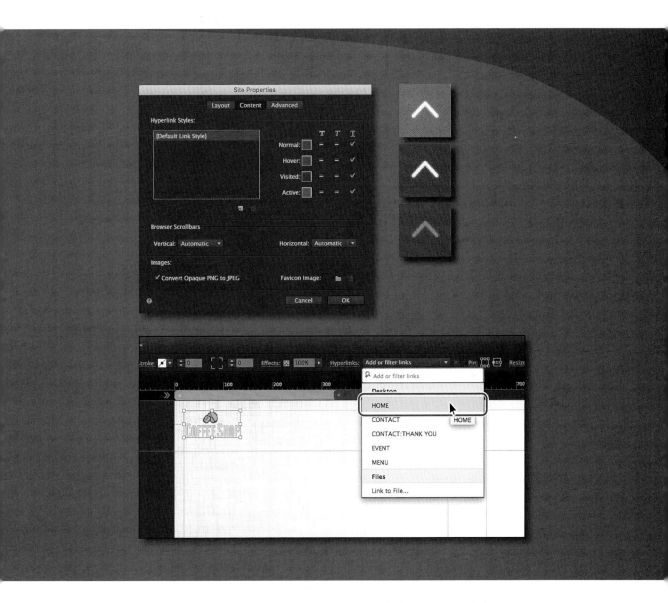

In Muse you can create and edit many types of links with ease and flexibility, and it offers some great design features. This includes linking to a website, linking to a part of the same page, or creating interactive buttons in Muse or Photoshop.

Working with links

Note: If you are starting from scratch using the Jumpstart method described in the "Jumpstart" section in "Getting Started," your workspace may look different than the figures you see in this lesson.

Note: If you have not already downloaded the project files for this lesson to your computer from your Account page, make sure to do so now. See "Getting Started" at the beginning of the book.

A hyperlink, or link, takes your users to a resource on the web or within your site. The resource can be anything that a computer can store and display: a web page, an image, a text document, a movie, a sound file, and more. With Muse you can create several types of links: internal, external, link to a file, and email links.

The simplest hyperlink is an *internal link*, which takes the visitor to another part of the same page in your Muse site, to another page in your site, to other content like a PDF stored in the site folder, or between pages in alternate layouts (desktop, mobile, or tablet). An *external link* takes the visitor to a document or resource on another website or another web host. On your site, you may want to make a file, such as a .pdf or .zip file, available for users to download. Muse includes an option to create a link on your pages to a file that you supply. The linked file will be included in the collection of files that are published or exported. An *email link* is a link to an email address that, when clicked, launches the visitor's default email program and creates a new email message configured to send to the email address you entered when you created the link in Muse.

Creating an internal link

Muse makes it easy to add different types of hyperlinks to your content. In this exercise, you'll create a link on the logo that users can click to go back to the home page.

1   With your CoffeeShop.muse site open and Plan mode showing, double-click the Home-master page thumbnail to open the page in Design mode.

2   Choose View > Fit Page In Window. If you need to, scroll up to see the logo in the header.

3   Choose Window > Reset Panels.

Tip: You can remove a link by selecting the text or object that the link is applied to and clicking the Remove Applied Link button (✖—the little x) to the right of the Add Or Filter Links menu.

4   Select the Selection tool (▶), and click the logo in the header. Click the Add Or Filter Links text to the right of the word Hyperlinks in the Control panel. Click HOME in the menu to link to the Home page.

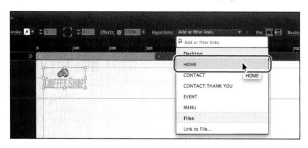

At the top of the Add Or Filter Links menu is a field for filtering your currently available links or for typing in a link. Instead of choosing an item from the menu that appears, you can also type the name of the page, for instance, to filter the list. All of the pages in that menu, except for master pages in your site, are listed and categorized by alternate layout type (Desktop, Tablet, or Phone). You won't be using alternate layouts (our site is a responsive web design instead), so the only category you'll see is Desktop.

5   Click the Preview mode link and then click the logo to visit the HOME page.

By default, when you create a link, the new page or website replaces the existing page in the same browser window or tab.

6   Choose File > Close Preview to close the Preview and return to the Home-master page.

Creating an external link

In addition to linking to pages within your site, you can also link to other websites. These links are called *external links*. Next, you'll place a few social media image icons in the footer on the Home-master page, and add links to them.

● **Note:** There are lots of ways to add social icons. This is one of the simplest methods.

1   In the Layers panel (Window > Layers), make sure the Footer layer is selected so that the new images you place appear on that layer. Click the Layers panel tab to hide it.

2   Choose File > Place. In the Import dialog box, navigate to the Lessons > images > social folder. Select the image named facebook_icon.svg to select it. Shift–click the image named twitter_icon.svg to select both images. Click Open.

3   Click below the footer guide to place the first image. Click to the right of the placed image to place the second.

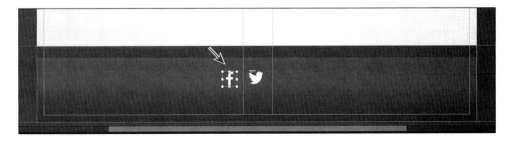

● **Note:** Your images may place in a different order and that's okay. You'll fix the ordering shortly if that is the case.

4　Select the Zoom tool () in the Toolbar and drag across the images to zoom in to them.

Note: If you place or create content below the footer guide on a master page, you do not need to select Footer in the Control panel to associate it with the footer. It is selected by default.

5　Select the Selection tool ( ), and drag the image on the right so that it's aligned horizontally with the social image to the left. Smart Guides will help you align them. If your images are placed in a different order, simply drag them like you see in the figure.

You always need to keep thinking in terms of responsive web design. By default, these two icons will scale along with the screen size. In this case, they should stay the same width no matter the size of the screen, so you'll change the default resize value for them.

6　With one of the social icons still selected, Shift-click the other to select both. Drag them into the center of the page. A vertical Smart Guide will appear when they are centered.

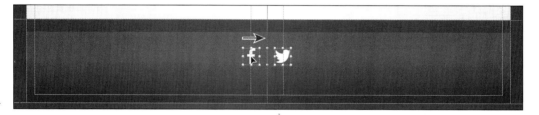

7　Choose None from the Resize menu in the Control panel. The icons will now stay the same size no matter the screen size.

8　Click the center box ( ) in the Pin option (called Pin To Center) in the Control panel above the page.

This way the icons always stay positioned relative to the center of the page, no matter the screen size.

9　Click away from the icons and other content to deselect it all. Click on the Twitter icon to select it.

10 Click the Add Or Filter Links menu to the right of the Hyperlinks link in the Control panel. With the cursor in the Add Or Filter Links field at the top of the menu, type **twitter.com/AdobeMuseCoffee**, and then press Return (Enter).

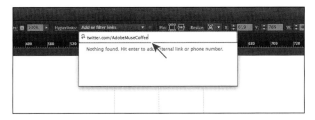

At anytime later, you can select the icon and edit the hyperlink. If you want, you can also try adding a link to the Facebook icon (Facebook.com).

11 Press Command+P (Ctrl+P) to open the page in Preview mode and see the icons in the footer of the page. You may need to scroll down.

12 Click the Twitter link to go to twitter.com/AdobeMuseCoffee.

By default, the linked website (twitter.com/AdobeMuseCoffee) replaces the original page in Preview mode. In Muse, there is no back button, but you can click the Refresh button to preview the Home-master page again (in this case).

13 Click the x on the Preview tab at the top of the Document window to close the Preview tab and return to Design mode.

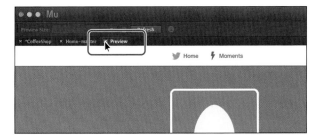

Preview appears as a tab like other pages. You can leave the Preview tab open and later, after changes have been made to the previewed page, simply refresh the page by clicking the Refresh button. You can also close the Preview tab (File > Close Preview), click another page tab, or leave the Preview tab open and simply go back to Plan or Design mode.

Creating an email link

You can create an email link exactly as you do an external link, but instead of providing a website address you type an email address or addresses.

1 With the Home-master page showing in Design mode, choose View > Fit Page In Window.

2 In the Layers panel (Window > Layers), select the Footer layer, if necessary, to ensure that the content you create is on the Footer layer.

● **Note:** You may not see the red underline under the email address you type in and that's okay.

3 With the Text tool (**T**) selected, click and drag to create a text frame below the social icons in the center of the page. Type **info@musecoffeeshop. businesscatalyst.com**.

● **Note:** You can also apply the paragraph style from the Paragraph Styles panel (Window > Paragraph Styles).

4 Drag across the text you just typed to select it. Choose Body from the Paragraph Style menu in the Control panel to apply the Body style.

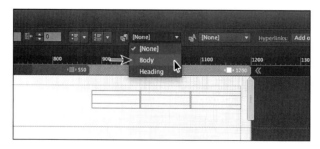

▶ **Tip:** You could have also copied the email address on the page and pasted it into the Add Or Filter Links field of the Hyperlinks menu.

5 Open the Text panel (Window > Text) and click the Align Center button (▤) to center align the selected text in the frame.

▶ **Tip:** If you want to add more email addresses, type a comma (,) after info@ musecoffeeshop. businesscatalyst. com and add another address. After every email address (except the last one), type a comma.

6 Select the Selection tool (▶) and choose Stretch To Browser Width from the Resize menu in the Control panel, so the text frame is as wide as the browser.

7 Select the Text tool and drag across the text to select it. Click the Add Or Filter Links menu to the right of the word Hyperlinks in the Control panel. With the cursor in the search field at the top of the menu, type **info@musecoffeeshop.businesscatalyst.com**. Press Return (Enter). The link will now be blue with an underline. You'll change the appearance in a later part of the lesson.

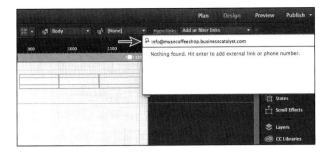

Note: The linked text on the page doesn't have to be the actual email address. You can use phrases like "Email us" or "Contact us" instead.

8 Click the Preview mode link to see the email link you just created (you may need to scroll down). Click the email link to open the default email application on your machine.

Note: If you don't have an email application installed on your machine, the link will do nothing. If you have an email application installed but it's not set up, you may be asked to set it up when the link is clicked. If the email application is installed and configured, a new message window will appear with the email address automatically entered in the To field.

9 Click the Home-master tab to return to that page.

10 Choose File > Save Site.

Linking to a file

On your site, you may want to make a file, such as a .pdf or .zip file, available for users to download. Muse includes an option to create a link on your pages to a file that you supply. The linked file will be included in the collection of files that are published or exported. Next, you'll add a .pdf file of the food menu that users can download from the MENU page.

1 Press Command+J (Ctrl+J) and type **menu** in the Go To Page dialog box. When MENU appears in the Page field, click OK.

2 Choose View > Fit Page In Window.

> **Tip:** After typing in the page name, you can also press Enter or Return to close the dialog box and go to the page.

Note: You may need to click in the 1200 pixel breakpoint in the Breakpoint bar to resize the page to the maximum page width.

3 With the Text tool selected, in the column with the "BAKED GOODS" heading, insert the cursor in the frame after the last item in the bullet list ("Sandwiches") and press Return (Enter) three times to create a new paragraph that is no longer a part of the list. Type **Download our menu (PDF-1MB)**. Select the text you just typed in.

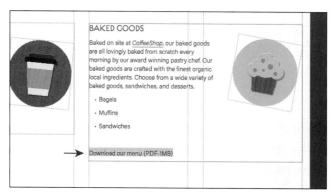

4 With the text selected, click the Add Or Filter Links menu to the right of the word Hyperlinks in the Control panel. Choose Link To File from the Files section at the bottom of the Hyperlinks menu.

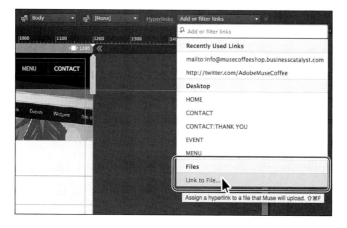

Tip: In the next section, "Editing Link Properties," you'll learn about setting a link to open in a new window or tab. In the case of this link, it may be a good idea to set it to open in a new window or tab.

5 In the Import dialog box that opens, select the menu.pdf file from the Lessons > Lesson08 folder and click Open.

The link is created, and the linked text is blue and underlined. You'll change the appearance later in this lesson.

6 Open the Assets panel (Window > Assets) to see the menu.pdf file listed.

The PDF file will be uploaded to the server when the site is published or added to the folder of files when the site is exported. You can drag the left edge of the panel to the left to make it wider if you need.

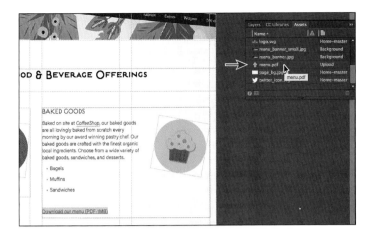

An arrow appears to the left of the name in the Assets panel, and the word Upload appears in the Page column, indicating that the file will be uploaded when the site is published or added to the folder of files when the site is exported.

Editing link properties

By default, links you create open the linked page or site in the same window or tab, replacing the current page. You can change this setting to make external links open in another browser window or tab so that your site remains open in the existing browser window, encouraging visitors to remain on your site.

1   Click the Home-master page tab at the top of the Document window to open that page in Design mode.

2   Select the Selection tool (🔪), and click to select the Twitter icon in the footer.

3   Click the word Hyperlinks in the Control panel to see the Hyperlinks options.

● **Note:** To make changes to linked text, you must use the Text tool to select all of the text that is linked. The Hyperlinks menu and Hyperlinks options are dimmed if you simply insert the cursor in the linked text.

4   In the Hyperlinks Options menu, select Open The Link In A New Window Or Tab.

5   In the Tooltip field, type **View the CoffeeShop Twitter Timeline**.

A tooltip can be beneficial in several ways: It displays as a tooltip in some browsers when the cursor is over the text link on the page, and it can be read aloud by some screen readers, among other things. The tooltip provides information about where the link will send the user and can contain keywords and other relevant information.

6 Press the Esc key to hide the Hyperlinks options.

7 Choose File > Save Site.

Styling text links

When you create text links, you'll likely want to change their appearance to better match your design and to differentiate the various types of links with unique styling. For instance, in this site, the links in the footer will need to be white, or a lighter color, to be readable in the footer, but links in the page area will need to be a darker color to be readable. Of course, all of your links should still give the appearance of being a link and clickable.

In this exercise, you'll edit the default appearance of the links, called *link styles*, and create styling for different types of links.

1 Choose File > Site Properties and click the Content tab.

▶ **Tip:** With the text selected, the cursor in text, or a text frame selected, you can also click the word Hyperlinks in the Control panel, and then click the Edit Link Styles button in the Hyperlinks options to open the Site Properties dialog box.

Every site in Muse has default formatting for the text links, which is blue and underlined. That default style is called [Default Link Style] and is listed in the Site Properties dialog box. You can change the appearance of the default link style, and all text links in your site will change to match. Link styles also have four states: normal, hover, visited, and active. See the sidebar "About link states" to learn more about states. For each state, you can change the color, add bold or italic, and remove or retain the underline.

2 Click the color box to the right of Normal, and in the Color Picker that appears, make sure the RGB sliders are showing. If they aren't, choose RGB Sliders from the panel menu ( ). Change the hex color value to **#369bc8** (a blue). Click away from the Color Picker panel to hide it and return to the Site Properties dialog box. Click the checkmark in the Underline column as many times as necessary until the box is empty (see the following figure).

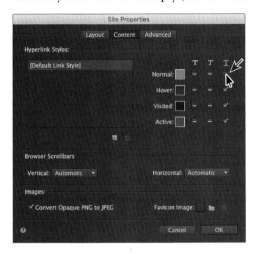

Note: If you want to edit the bold, italic, or underline attributes, you can click several times on one of the boxes in the Bold, Italic, or Underline columns. As you click, you'll see three selection options: a check mark, a blank box, and a box with a filled box inside. A check mark indicates that the formatting is applied to the link; for instance, a check mark in the Underline column tells the browser to underline the link and write that in the code. A blank box tells Muse to write the code for underline but set it at the default of no underline. A box with a filled box inside tells Muse not to write anything in the code for underline—leaving the formatting at the default (no underline).

About link states

You can create different styling for each state of a link: normal, hover, visited, and active. These states are similar to the functionality of the states found in the States panel in Muse.

- **Normal:** This is the first state that visitors will see. When a page is opened and the text links appear, the normal state is what a link looks like when a visitor hasn't interacted with it yet.

- **Hover:** When a visitor rolls over a link on your web page, you can change the appearance of the link.

- **Visited:** After a visitor clicks a text link and then returns to the same page, you can change the appearance of the link to indicate that the link was clicked previously.

- **Active:** The active state can change the appearance of the link between the time the visitor presses the mouse button and releases it.

3 Click the color box to the right of Hover and change the color to the 50% Grey swatch (you can try another color if you like), and leave the rest of the options for Hover at the defaults.

The Hover state appearance can be very important. It can give users an indication that they are about to click on a link.

4 Change the color for Visited to **#369bc8**, and leave the rest of the options at their defaults.

The appearance of visited links are often overlooked, but they can be helpful for users, especially on larger websites. When someone returns to a page, they can tell which links they've clicked on previously. In this case, the visited links will be the same blue as the Normal state, but have an underline.

5 Leave the Active state options at their defaults. You can always experiment later. Leave the dialog box open for the next steps.

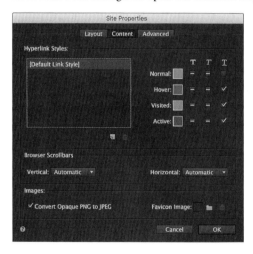

6 Click the New Link Style button (▣) below the Hyperlink Styles section of the Site Properties dialog box. Rename the new style to **Footer Links**.

Muse creates a new link style in the Site Properties dialog box that is an exact copy of the default link style. The default link style applies to every link by default, but you can apply your new style to text links that you want to look and behave differently. This new link style will be available for use on every page within the current site only.

7 In the Normal state, change the color to white and make sure the Underline option does not have a checkmark in the box (it is empty). Feel free to experiment with the remaining states. Click OK.

● **Note:** Later, you can change the appearance of the link styles or create more in the Site Properties dialog box. The Delete Link Style button enables you to remove any link styles that you don't want to keep. You can use these link styles throughout your site.

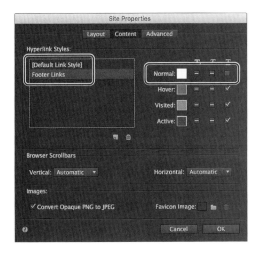

8   Click the Home-master page tab at the top of the Document window to open that page in Design mode, if necessary. You should be able to see the email link in the footer. Choose View > Fit Page In Window, if necessary to see it.

9   With the Text tool, select the info@musecoffeeshop.businesscatalyst.com text.

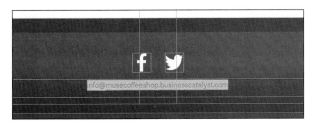

▶ **Tip:** You can also apply link styles in the Text panel (Window > Text).

● **Note:** You may see the visited link appearance on some of the links when you test the page. That's because your browser has cached those links (you've visited them previously). You can clear the browser's cache.

10 Click the word Hyperlinks in the Control panel and select the style named "Footer Links" from the Text Link Style menu.

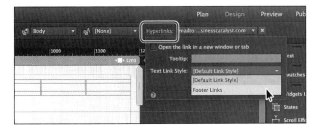

11 Choose Edit > Deselect All.

12 Choose File > Save Site, and close all open pages, returning to Plan mode.

Working with buttons

▶ **Tip:** Muse also has a built-in button in the Widgets Library panel called a State Button. You'll learn about working with widgets in Lesson 9, "Working With Widgets."

On the web, designers use buttons as well as links to link to other content, other pages, or other websites. A button is usually styled to look more three dimensional so it resembles a physical button that you can press. Buttons tend to appear on a web page less frequently than text links. Site designers use them primarily to encourage users to do something or as a call to action on a website, giving them action names like Buy, Sign Up, Search, or View My Portfolio.

Creating a button in Muse

You can create a button from almost any object in your design—text frames, image frames, and rectangle shapes. Muse lets you change the appearance of the button object with states, a background color and image, strokes, effects like drop shadows, rounded corners, and much more. In this exercise, you'll create a button that you'll insert to the right of the menu in the header.

1   In Plan mode, double-click the Home-master page thumbnail to open the page in Design mode.

2   Choose View > Fit Page In Window.

3   Click in the 1200 breakpoint in the Breakpoint bar to resize the page to the maximum page width, if necessary.

4   In the Layers panel (Window > Layers), select the Header layer.

▶ **Tip:** Don't forget; you can type the text in lowercase and choose Edit > Change Case > UPPERCASE to make it uppercase.

5   With the Text tool selected, toward the top of the page, click and drag to create a text frame and type **COFFEE CLUB**.

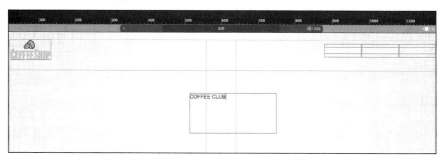

● **Note:** Don't worry if the frame isn't positioned to match the figure exactly. Later, you'll move it into its final position.

6   Select the text. In the Control panel, change the following options:

•   Font: Acumin Pro Semibold (or another font)

•   Font Size: **17**

•   Text Color: FooterStroke

•   Click the Align Center button (▤)

7   Select the Selection tool, and Muse selects the text frame, not the text. Click the Fill Color in the Control panel and select the white swatch to fill the background of the text frame.

8   Change the Corner Radius to **5** in the Control panel.

9   Resize the text frame to make it closer to the text. As you drag, you'll see the measurement label. Make sure the height is 40 pixels and the width is approximately 150 pixels. See the following figure.

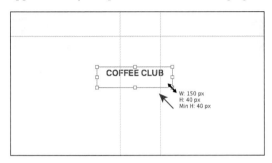

▶ **Tip:** If you wanted to add an icon to the button, like an arrow, you could click the Fill link in the Control panel, and click the Add Image link to select a background image you've already created in another program like Photoshop, for the text frame. You could set the Fitting menu to Original Size and try different Position options.

Next, you'll work with the Spacing panel to add spacing between the edges of the text frame and the text inside.

10 Choose Window > Spacing to open the Spacing panel on the right side of the workspace. Make sure that the Make All Padding Settings The Same button is on (⬜). Change the top (T:) Padding value to **10**, this changes all values together.

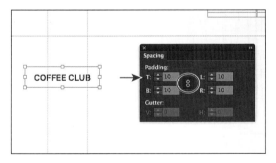

● **Note:** I dragged the Spacing panel closer to the content in the page.

● **Note:** If you chose a different font for the button text, you may want to experiment with the Spacing values to try and "center" the text in the button.

11 Click the Preview mode link and check out the new button you've started. Click the Design mode link to return to the page in Design mode, leaving the text frame selected.

12 Choose File > Save Site.

Using the States panel to add button states

Muse allows you to add states to your button. As you've learned previously, states are useful for changing the appearance of content when visitors interact with it. A state can be used to indicate that the button will perform an action. You don't have to add states to a button, but as you'll see, sometimes it can be beneficial to alert visitors that something will happen when the button is clicked.

1   With the COFFEE CLUB text frame still selected, click the Normal link in the Selection Indicator at the left end of the Control panel to show the States panel. Click the Rollover state to edit its appearance.

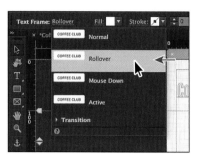

Any appearance changes you make now will affect the rollover state of the selected button.

> **Note:** You must have the frame selected, not the text, in order to edit the states using the States panel because states can't be applied to selected text.

2   Click the Fill color option in the Control panel to show the Color Picker panel. Change the RGB color values to R=**230**, G=**205**, B=**174** (a light tan).

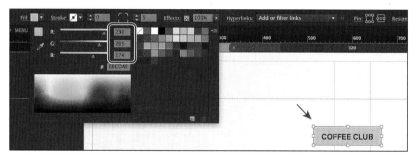

This is a very simple rollover appearance change. You could apply any number of changes to the text frame or text. When a user interacts with an object, like your button, you can also add a smooth transition between states, which is what you'll do next.

3 Click the Rollover link to show the States panel again. Click the arrow to the left of Transition. In the options that appear, select Fade, and choose Ease In/Out from the Speed menu.

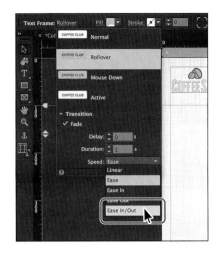

Now when the user hovers the pointer over the button, the appearance from the normal state to the rollover state will have a smooth transition. So, the background color will *fade* from one color to another. In the States menu, you'll also see that the Mouse Down state looks the same as the Rollover state. You could change the appearance of the Mouse Down or Active state if you like, but in this case it's not necessary.

4 Click the Preview mode link to test the button. Hover over the button, and you'll see the rollover state and fade transition. Move the cursor off of the button and you'll see it change to white with *no fade transition*.

5 Click the Design mode link to return to the Home-master page in Design mode.

● **Note:** When you clicked the Preview mode link to test the page, Muse selected the Normal state for the button.

6 Click the Normal link on the left end of the Control panel. With the Normal state selected, click the arrow to the left of Transition, if necessary. Select Fade, and choose Ease In/Out from the Speed menu.

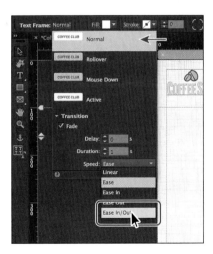

7 Click the Preview mode link to test the button. Hover over the button, and you'll see the rollover state and fade transition. Move the cursor off of the button and you'll see it change to white now with a fade transition.

8 Click the Design mode link to return to the Home-master page in Design mode.

9 Choose File > Save Site.

Adding a link to a button

Adding a link to a button typically involves selecting the button (frame), not the contents, before adding the link. By adding a link to a frame, the pointer will become a hand when you hover over the button, which is what you usually see when it comes to buttons.

1   With the text frame still selected, click the Add Or Filter Links menu to the right of the word Hyperlinks in the Control panel. Choose CONTACT from the Desktop category in the menu.

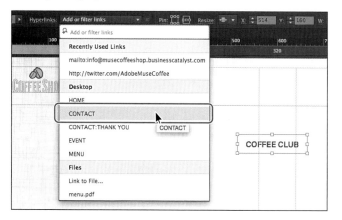

Now that the button is done, you can put it in the header where it belongs.

2   With the button still selected, choose None from the Resize menu in the Control panel.

This way, the button won't resize and the text shouldn't wrap in the button (since the button is text, you can't account for what all browsers will do to the sizing).

3   Click the menu in the header to select it. Begin dragging it to the left. As you drag, press the Shift key to constrain the movement to horizontal (in this case). Drag it far enough to the left to fit the button to the right of it. When it's in position, release the mouse button and then the key.

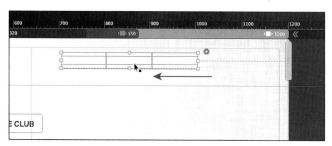

4 Drag the button up to the right of the menu. It may be a little tricky, but Smart Guides will help you align the button to the top edge of the menu.

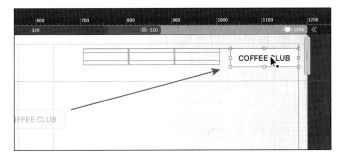

5 Select the Zoom tool () and drag across the menu and button to zoom in.

6 Select the Selection tool (▶) and drag the button so that it's *vertically* aligned with the menu. A Smart Guide will appear to show you when it's aligned.

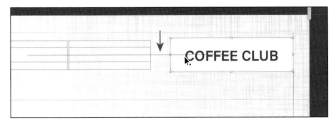

To align the menu and button vertically to each other you could have used the Align options in the Align panel. Zooming in will give you more precision when you drag objects.

7 Click the right box (▦) in the Pin option (called Pin To Right) in the Control panel above the page.

This way the button always stays positioned relative to the right edge of the page, no matter the screen size.

Testing the button in different screen sizes

Now it's time to make sure that the button and menu design changes you made "work" across the smaller screen sizes.

1 Choose View > Fit Page In Window.

2 Drag the scrubber to the left. If you drag the scrubber far enough to the left, eventually the menu will run into the logo before the breakpoint at 550. That's because the menu is now positioned further to the left than it was initially.

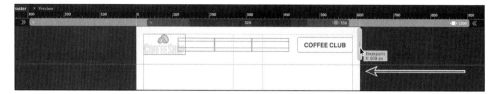

This is one instance where trying to preview the fluid width design at different screen sizes and applying fixes before *all* of the design content is in place can cause you to apply "fixes" to your design content more than once.

In this particular design, it has been decided that the COFFEE CLUB button will be hidden in the header at a smaller screen size. Next, you'll create a breakpoint *before* the menu runs into the logo and hide the button.

3 Drag the scrubber until the menu no longer overlaps the logo (at around 700 pixels). Make sure there is some room between the two to account for browser rendering differences (see the following figure). Click the Create New Breakpoint icon (⊕) in the Breakpoint bar to create a new breakpoint.

I also chose 700 because it's smaller than most tablets and for this design, the button isn't necessary on device sizes smaller than that. You need to hide the button in all of the breakpoints *except* for the breakpoint at 1200. Instead of going to each breakpoint to hide it, you can go back to the breakpoint at 1200 where you need the button to show, and choose Hide In Other Breakpoints.

4 Click in the breakpoint at 1200 in the Breakpoint bar to preview the page at that size. Click the "COFFEE CLUB" button to select it. Choose Object > Hide In Other Breakpoints.

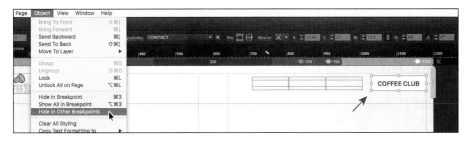

5 Click in the breakpoint at 700 to preview the page at that size.

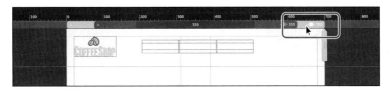

The button is hiding, but the menu is still in the same relative position as it was (with a gap between it and the right edge of the page where the button was).

6 Click the menu in the header to select it. Begin dragging it to the right. As you drag, press the Shift key to constrain the movement to horizontal (in this case). Drag the menu until the right edge snaps to the right margin guide. Release the mouse button and then the key.

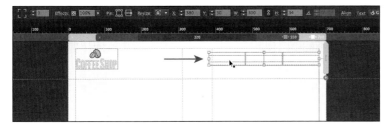

7 Choose File > Save Site.

Placing a Photoshop button

You can place a button created in Photoshop into Muse by choosing File > Place Photoshop Button. When you place a Photoshop button (.psd file) in Muse, you can select a single layer for each state that you want the button to have. For any states that you don't want to use in Muse, don't include a layer with the name of that state in the Photoshop file. Also, ensure that any layers you want to display in Muse have content on them.

⬤ **Note:** When naming the layers in Photoshop to match a Muse state name like Normal, the names are not case sensitive. For example, in Photoshop you could name a layer normal, Normal, NORMAL, or any combination of uppercase and lowercase letters. Muse would still recognize it and assign it to the Normal state. Also, you don't have to name the Photoshop layers the same as the states. You can name them whatever you like and simply choose them from the menus in the Photoshop Import Options dialog box.

Setting up a button in Photoshop

Although you can create buttons in Muse, you also have the option of creating a button in a program like Photoshop, which gives you even greater design flexibility. You can then place the layered .psd file on your page by choosing File > Place Photoshop Button.

If you name the layers in Photoshop the same as the typical states found in the States panel—Normal, Rollover, Mouse Down, and Active—Muse automatically assigns the content on those named layers to the state with the same name in the States panel. The figure here shows the Layers panel in Photoshop displaying the named layers of a sample button.

Next, you'll place a Photoshop button that users can click to scroll back to the top of the page.

1 Press Command+J (Ctrl+J) and type **home** in the Go To Page dialog box. When HOME appears in the Page field, click OK.

2 Choose View > Fit Page In Window.

3 Choose Window > Reset Panels.

4 In the Layers panel (Window > Layers), make sure the Header layer is selected so that the new image you place will appear on that layer. Click the Layers panel tab to hide it.

5 Choose File > Place Photoshop Button. Navigate to the Lessons > images folder, and select the image named backtotop_button.psd. Click Open.

In the Photoshop Import Options dialog box, Muse assigns layers in the Photoshop file to a state of the same name, if those layers are present. For each state of the button in Muse, you can choose a different layer in the Photoshop file. Notice that each state has the layer of the same name from the Photoshop file selected automatically.

● **Note:** Placing a Photoshop button creates a link to the original .psd file and adds it to the list in the Assets panel. As with other assets listed in the Assets panel, you can relink the button to another Photoshop file, embed the link, and more.

6 Click the Normal State menu, and you'll see the Photoshop layers in the file listed as well as a Composite option. Leave the normal layer selected and click OK.

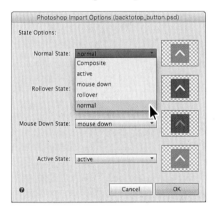

Selecting the Composite option for the Normal state would show all of the layer content visible in Photoshop when the file was last saved.

7 Click to place the button on the right edge of the page, towards the bottom *above* the footer.

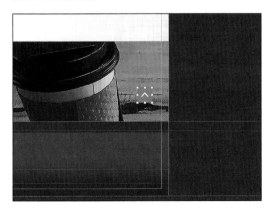

▶ **Tip:** Because the layers in a group in your .psd file will appear in the Photoshop Import Options but the groupings will be ignored, you're better off creating Smart Objects from your layers with multiple layers of content in each Smart Object layer. Smart Objects are layers that can contain image data from raster or vector images, such as Adobe Photoshop or Adobe Illustrator files.

● **Note:** Any layers in the Photoshop file that are empty will not appear in the state menus in the Photoshop Import Options dialog box.

8 Open the States panel by choosing Window > States. Click the Rollover state in the States panel.

Muse is using the layer named "rollover" from Photoshop as the rollover state. Muse also uses the rollover layer as the Mouse Down state for this button if no layer named "Mouse Down" is in the Photoshop file. The normal layer from Photoshop is used as the Active state if no layer named "Active" is in the Photoshop file.

You can select each state and apply different effects, like adding a drop shadow or even rounded corners. When you publish or export the site, Muse will save the states as separate images.

9 With the button still selected, choose None from the Resize menu so it won't resize on different screen sizes. Don't worry about the position for now.

With the Photoshop button now on the page, you need to add some interactivity to it. In this case, you'll add a link that will scroll to the top of the page.

Editing a Photoshop button

Just as you can do with other assets listed in the Assets panel, you can edit a button's original .psd file in Photoshop and update it in Muse. With the button selected on the page, you can open the Assets panel (Window > Assets), right-click the name of the .psd file, and choose Edit Original. Edit the image in Photoshop, save it, and return to Muse to see the updates. This command allows you to edit each of the layers in the Photoshop file.

If you delete a layer in Photoshop that is named after a state in Muse, the corresponding state will revert to the Normal state content. On the flip side, if you add a layer to the Photoshop button file that is named after a Muse state, when you save the Photoshop file and return to Muse, the new layer will become the content for the corresponding state.

Working with anchors

Long pages with a lot of vertical content to scroll through can be cumbersome for visitors to navigate. You can alleviate this issue in Muse by creating internal links that make the page jump to a specified section when a visitor clicks the link. The commonly used "Back to Top" link, which quickly scrolls to the top of the page when clicked, is a good example of this type of internal link.

To link to a part of a page, you need to insert an anchor at the desired spot and then link to that anchor. The anchors are invisible to visitors but allow you to create internal links to different parts of a page. You can create multiple anchors on a single page; however, each anchor must have a unique name.

Linking to anchors

The first step toward aiding visitors in scrolling long pages is to insert the anchors that you'll create links to later on. Next you'll start by inserting an anchor.

1 With the HOME page still showing in Design mode, choose View > Hide Breakpoints.

2 Choose View > Fit Page In Window, if necessary.

3 Click the Anchor button (⚓) in the Toolbar. The pointer will change to a Place Gun (⚓). Position the Place Gun just above the page below the ruler and on the left edge of the header (you may need to scroll up). Click to insert an anchor and open the Rename An Anchor dialog box.

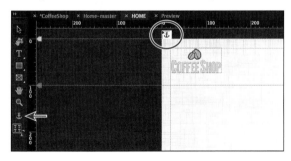

4 In the Rename An Anchor dialog box, change the name to **top** and click OK.

You should now see the anchor icon above the page with the word "top" to the right. With the Selection tool you can move the anchor, or you can select it and press Delete (Backspace) to remove it. If you need to rename the anchor, right-click the anchor icon and choose Rename Anchor. Now that the anchor is in place, you can create a link to it. You'll apply the link to the Photoshop button you placed previously.

● **Note:** You can name anchors anything you want, just keep it simple. Anchor names cannot start with a number, and Muse will warn you if you use an illegal character.

▶ **Tip:** You can also choose Object > Insert Link Anchor to insert an anchor. If you click multiple times on the Anchor button in the Toolbar, the number of times you click is the number of anchors you can place. The Place Gun cursor shows a number next to the anchor icon, indicating the number of anchors you can create. Clicking the Anchor button twice loads two anchors into the Place Gun that you can then place.

▶ **Tip:** You can also cut or copy and paste an anchor on the page when it's selected, or press Option (Alt) while you drag the anchor with the Selection tool to create a copy, and then rename it.

5 With the Selection tool selected, click the Photoshop button on the right side of the page above the footer to select it.

6 Click the arrow to the right of the Hyperlinks field in the Control panel. In the menu that appears, choose "top" below the HOME page in the Desktop category.

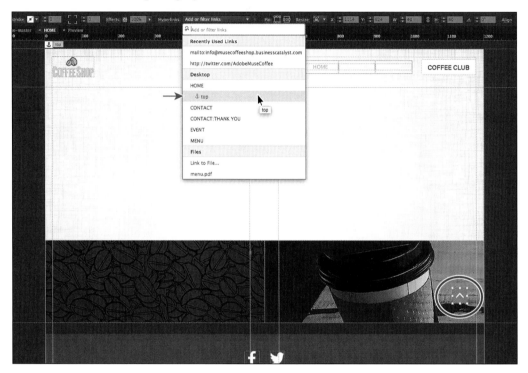

Note: If your screen resolution is too large, and the page content fits within the Document window, scrolling may not work. You can return to Design mode and, with the HOME page showing, choose File > Preview Page In Browser. You can resize the browser window to make it smaller, then test the scrolling.

7 Click the Preview mode link and scroll down the page, if necessary, making sure you can see the button. Click the button to return to the top of the page.

Notice that the page scrolls up smoothly. Also, notice that the button moves with the rest of the page content.

8 Click the Design mode link to return to the HOME page.

9 With the HOME page still showing in Design mode, choose View > Show Breakpoints.

Next, you'll "pin" that same button in place so that it stays in the same relative position in the browser window as the page content scrolls beneath it.

Pinning content

In Lesson 6, "Responsive Web Design," you learned about pinning an object to the page so that it remains fixed with respect to the web page (horizontally), regardless of screen size. But how do you make something always stay visible when you scroll up and down in the browser window? If a page is long (contains a lot of vertical content), visitors can no longer see content from the top of the page when they scroll down. What if you wanted a Twitter follow button, menu, or just an image to always be visible as the rest of the content scrolls? You need to pin the content *to the browser*. The Control panel makes pinning content easy. You simply set the pinned content, such as an image, to a specific location in relation to the edge of the browser window. It always stays in one spot regardless of other scrolling page elements.

The pinned element will move to maintain its pinned position in relation to the browser if the visitor resizes the browser window, but the pinned element will not move if the visitor scrolls the page content horizontally or vertically.

Next, you'll pin the Photoshop button you previously placed.

1 On the HOME page, choose View > Fit Page In Window.

2 Click in the breakpoint at 1200 to switch to that breakpoint, if necessary.

3 Select the button on the page, if necessary, and drag it so that the right edge of the button aligns with the margin guide.

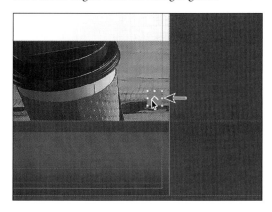

4 Click the bottom-right position of the six possible options in the Pin tool located in the Control panel.

Note: You may want to consider hiding the back to top button on smaller screens. It's up to you and your design as to whether or not it is useful at smaller screen sizes or simply covers up too much content.

A dotted line will appear between the bottom of the button and the bottom of the page as well as between the right edge of the button and the right edge of the page, telling you it's been pinned.

5 Click the Preview mode link and decrease and increase the width of the Preview window by dragging the bottom-right resize handle. Scroll down the page to see that the button is stuck in position vertically and horizontally to the browser window.

Note: If you can't drag the bottom-right resize handle, you can return to Design mode, and with the HOME page showing, choose File > Preview Page In Browser. You can resize the browser window to make it smaller, then test the scrolling.

6 Click the Design mode link to return to the HOME page.

Like everything else you add to your pages in a fluid width layout, you want to drag the scrubber and check the button across different screen sizes to make sure it is positioned where you want it.

7 Choose File > Close Page to close the page and return to Plan mode.

Working with graphic styles

Just as you use paragraph and character styles to quickly format text, you can also use graphic styles to quickly format graphics and apply attributes to frames. Graphic styles include settings for stroke, fill color, effects, wrap, and more, but do not contain text formatting. If you work in Adobe InDesign, you may be familiar with Object styles. Object styles in InDesign are very similar in basic functionality to graphic styles in Muse.

In Muse, graphic styles are often used for formatting submenus, image frames, tooltips, and much more. Let's start by exploring the Graphic Styles panel.

1 In Plan mode, double-click the CONTACT page thumbnail to open the page.

2 Choose View > Fit Page In Window.

3 Choose Window > Reset Panels.

4 Choose Window > Graphic Styles to open the Graphic Styles panel.

Take a minute to familiarize yourself with the options in the Graphic Styles panel. As you progress through this exercise, you'll learn about each of these options.

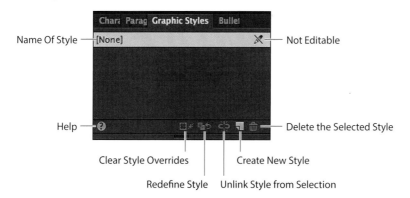

Creating and applying a graphic style

Next, you'll create a graphic style from content on the CONTACT page.

1 On the CONTACT page, with the Selection tool selected, click to select the picture of Joe.

With the image frame selected, you'll save the frame formatting you applied in a previous lesson (rounded corners, shadow, and stroke) as a graphic style that you can then apply to another image.

2 With the image selected, zoom in by pressing Command+= (Ctrl+=) a few times.

3 With the Graphic Styles panel still visible (Window > Graphic Styles) and the image still selected, click the Create A New Style button (🔲) at the bottom of the panel to create a new graphic style based on the image formatting.

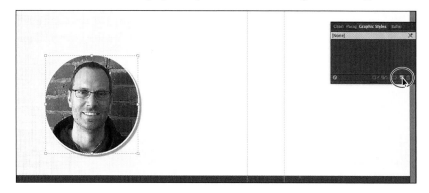

● **Note:** The order of the attributes listed in the Style Setting section of the figure might be different than those listed in your Graphic Style Options dialog box, and that's OK.

4 Double-click the new graphic style named "Style." Change the Style Name to **Headshot**, and notice all of the formatting that was captured in the Style Setting area of the Graphic Style Options dialog box. Click OK.

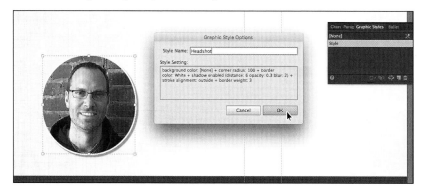

Graphic styles cannot contain formatting like sizes of objects (width and height), text formatting, and more. Now you'll apply the graphic style to another image you place.

5 Choose File > Place. In the Import dialog box, navigate to the Lessons > images folder. Select the image named contact_marie.jpg to select it and click Open.

6 Click to place the image to the right of the image of Joe.

7   With the Selection tool, drag the upper-right corner of the selected image of Marie, toward the center to make it smaller. Stop dragging when you see 40% in the measurement label.

8   In the Graphic Styles panel, click the Headshot style name to apply it to the image of Marie.

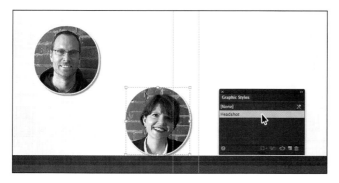

9   With the image of Marie selected, choose None from the Resize menu so that the image stays the same dimensions no matter what size the screen is.

Note: I dragged the Graphic Styles panel into the workspace to bring it closer to the image. You don't have to do that.

Note: Be careful not to click a graphic style in the Graphic Styles panel with nothing selected. The graphic style will apply to the page area. If you accidentally do this, you can select the graphic style named [None] to remove the formatting.

Clearing overrides and editing a graphic style

In Muse, updating a graphic style is accomplished by *redefining* that style. To redefine a style, you edit the formatting for an object on the page that has that graphic style applied. Then you redefine the style based on the changes. This makes the graphic style match the new settings, and all other objects with that style applied automatically update to match.

1   On the CONTACT page, with the image of Marie still selected, change the stroke color to a red in the Control panel.

    In the Graphic Styles panel, notice that the Headshot style now displays a plus (+) to the right of the name.

2   Position the pointer over the Headshot style name. In the tooltip that appears below the dotted line you'll see the local formatting options (in this case, it is the "border color" that is applied to the selected content that differs from the existing attributes of the graphic style).

3   Click the Clear Style Overrides button (⬛✱) at the bottom of the Graphic Styles panel to remove the red border (stroke) color override.

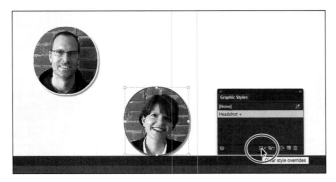

    Being able to clear any extra formatting from an object can be a real time saver if you want to make sure multiple objects have consistent formatting. Next, you'll redefine the graphic style formatting.

4 With the image of Marie still selected, click the Effects link. With the Shadow option selected at the top of the Effects panel, change the following:

- Opacity: **50**
- Blur: **7**
- Angle: **0** (zero)
- Distance: **0** (zero)

In the Graphic Styles panel, the Headshot style displays a plus (+) to the right of the name again. This time you'll update the graphic style to reflect the changes you just made by redefining the style.

5 Click the Redefine Style button (⊞) at the bottom of the Graphic Styles panel.

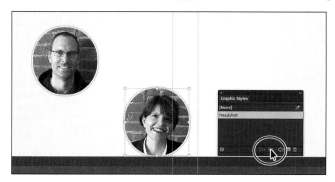

As a result of redefining a style, two things happen:

- The plus sign (+) next to the graphic style's name disappears in the Graphic Styles panel.
- All other elements that have the style applied are updated to use the new style attributes.

This workflow is especially helpful when you want to make changes that affect many different elements in a site. You can redefine the applied style to update them all at once.

6 Choose File > Save Site.

In a later lesson, you will arrange the images of Joe and Marie when you add some more content.

7 Close all open pages and return to Plan mode.

Graphic style options

Graphic styles have many of the same options that paragraph and character styles have, including deleting, duplicating, and unlinking. To access most of these options, in the Graphic Styles panel you can right-click on a style name and make a selection in the context menu that appears, or just click the corresponding buttons at the bottom of the Graphic Styles panel.

Deleting a graphic style removes it from the list. If the style has been applied to content in your site, a dialog box will appear asking you to replace the graphic style with another.

Duplicating a graphic style makes an exact copy of the style. Rename the duplicate style after creating it. Then you can make subtle changes to make it different from the original style.

Unlinking a graphic style from selected content is useful if you want to create a style similar to another style. Unlinking a graphic style can also be useful if you want to apply a style but don't want the formatting of that content to change in the event that you decide to update the graphic style later. You can unlink selected content from a graphic style by clicking the Unlink Style From Selection button (⬚) at the bottom of the Graphic Styles panel or by right-clicking on a style's name and then choosing the Unlink Style option from the context menu that appears.

Review questions

1 Name and describe the four generic types of links.

2 How can you apply a link to text without changing the appearance of that text?

3 What is the benefit of placing a .psd file using File > Place Photoshop Button?

4 What is the purpose of adding anchors?

5 What is meant by pinning content?

6 Name a benefit of using a graphic style.

Review answers

1 The four generic types of links that you can create in Muse are internal, external, link to a file, and email links. The simplest hyperlink is an *internal link*, which takes the visitor to another part of the same page in your Muse site, to another page in your site, to other content like a PDF stored in the site folder, or between pages in alternate layouts (desktop, mobile, or tablet). An *external link* takes the visitor to a document or resource on another website or another web host. Muse includes an option to create a link on your pages to a file that you supply. The linked file will be included in the collection of files that are published or exported. An *email link* is a link to an email address that, when clicked, launches the visitor's default email program and creates a new email message configured to send to the email address you entered when you created the link in Muse.

2 If you select the *text frame* but not the text, and then apply a link, the appearance of the text within the frame isn't changed.

3 Placing a layered Photoshop file using the File > Place Photoshop Button command opens the Photoshop Import Options dialog box. In this dialog box you can assign layers in the Photoshop file to the states in the button.

4 An anchor allows you to link to a part of a page. Anchors are invisible to visitors. They add code that enables you to create links that jump to a specific section of a longer or wider page.

5 Pinned content is set to a specific location in relation to the browser window or page regardless of other scrolling page elements or a browser window being resized.

6 Just as you use paragraph and character styles to quickly format and update text, you can use graphic styles to quickly format graphics, image frames, and text frames. Graphic styles include settings for stroke, fill color, effects, wrap, and more.

9 WORKING WITH WIDGETS

Lesson overview

In this lesson, you'll add customizable widgets to your pages and learn how to:

- Work with Button widgets
- Insert and edit a Composition widget
- Add and edit a form
- Edit the States of your Submit Button ▆
- Edit the Form widget states ▆
- Create a copy of the form for the footer ▆
- Insert a Social widget
- Insert and edit a Slideshow widget
- Add an Accordion Panel widget ▆

This lesson takes approximately 75 minutes to complete. To download the project files for this lesson, log in or set up an account at peachpit.com. Enter the book's ISBN (9780134547275) or go directly to the book's product page to register. Once on the book's page, click the Register Your Product link. The book will show up in your list of registered products along with a link to the book's bonus content. Click the link to access the lesson files for the book. Store the files on your computer in a convenient location, as described in the "Getting Started" section of this book. Your Account page is also where you'll find any updates to the chapters or to the lesson files. If you are starting from scratch in this lesson, use the method described in the "Jumpstart" section in "Getting Started."

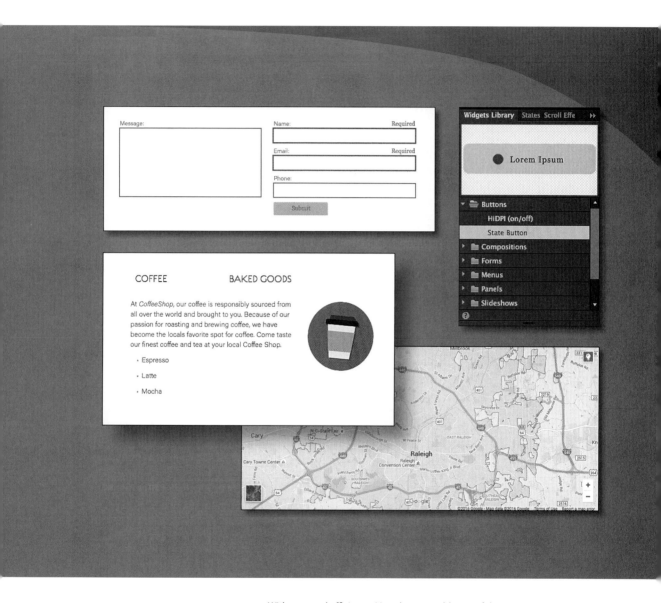

With ease and efficiency, Muse lets you add powerful interactivity to your pages in the form of widgets. In this lesson, you'll explore various widget types and see how simple it is to customize them.

About widgets

● **Note:** If you are starting from scratch using the Jumpstart method described in the "Jumpstart" section of "Getting Started," your workspace may look different from the figures you see in this lesson.

On the web these days, you see all sorts of cool, interactive content like slideshows that cycle through larger images, and much more. You may have even heard of jQuery, one of the behind-the-scenes technologies that power these advanced features. Adobe Muse provides much of the same interactive functionality in the form of widgets. *Widgets* are reusable building blocks of interactivity and behavior that are completely customizable. By simply dragging them onto your pages, you can take advantage of the power they offer without writing your own code.

Muse groups widgets into seven categories in the Widgets Library panel (Window > Widgets Library): Buttons, Compositions, Forms, Menus, Panels, Slideshows, and Social. Each provides an easy way of adding different types of interactivity to your web pages. Because Muse has multiple widget types in each of the widget categories, in this lesson you'll explore several of the more popular widgets. Since you will most likely be designing your site using a fluid grid layout (responsive web design), you'll need to remember to check the widget content you add to your pages across breakpoints to ensure that they look good at the different screen sizes.

The following table specifies the responsive behavior of each widget in Adobe Muse, as of the writing of this book.

Object	Responsive	Responsive behavior
Menu widget	Yes	At different browser widths, these objects automatically resize by width. If you want these objects to span the entire browser width, you can also apply the Stretch to Browser Width setting.
Composition widgets, Contact forms, and slideshows	No	These widgets remain fixed at all breakpoints. If necessary, you can resize these objects at each breakpoint, separately.
Accordions and Tabbed Panels	Yes	You can resize these widgets separately at every breakpoint.
Social widgets	Some	YouTube, Vimeo, Facebook Comments, and Google Maps are responsive. At different breakpoints, the YouTube and Google Maps widgets automatically resize by width. If you want these widgets to span the entire browser width, you can also apply the Stretch to Browser Width setting. The other social widgets are not responsive. You can resize these widgets separately at every breakpoint.

—From Muse Help

Understanding Button widgets

The first category of widgets to discover, called *Buttons*, offers two types of buttons that you can use in your design: a HiDPI button and a State button. Each type of button has prebuilt button states that you can edit and style to match your design.

● **Note:** If you have not already downloaded the project files for this lesson to your computer from your Account page, make sure to do so now. See "Getting Started" at the beginning of the book.

● **Note:** HiDPI (High Dots Per Inch), also referred to as a Retina display, is a name for screens with a relatively high resolution.

1 With the CoffeeShop.muse site open, in Plan mode double-click the MENU page thumbnail to open the page in Design mode.

2 Choose View > Fit Page In Window.

3 Choose Window > Widgets Library to open the Widgets Library panel. In the panel, click the folder icon or arrow to the left of the Buttons category to display that category's widgets. Click the State Button to select it.

Using a State Button can be a faster way to create a button with states. It is also another way to create buttons other than the method you learned in Lesson 8.

The HiDPI (on/off) button requires that the Resolution setting in the site properties (File > Site Properties) be set at HiDPI (2x) rather than standard resolution. For sites with HiDPI assets, this button offers visitors the ability to toggle between HiDPI and normal resolution assets. If the site isn't viewed on a HiDPI screen, the button will show the HiDPI Unavailable button state and be grayed out (the option isn't available).

Working with Composition widgets

Composition widgets allow you to interact with an area on the web page in order to change the content shown in another area. A fade or sliding animation occurs on change. This can be a great way to show other content without forcing the visitor to go to another page or to reload the same page.

Tip: Check out the Composition widget you will add in this section, by visiting: http://musecoffeeshop. businesscatalyst.com/ menu.html. Hover over the "COFFEE" and "BAKED GOODS" headings to see how it works.

An example of a Composition widget

For example, you could have a listing of work projects you've done that you'd like to show in a small space. When the visitor clicks text like "Web Design Project" (called the "trigger"), for example, an image with text and even a video could appear on the page, providing more information and samples of the project, replacing content that was showing by default.

The Widgets Library panel offers five Composition widgets: Blank, Featured News, Lightbox Display, Presentation, and Tooltip. Each has the same widget options available, but each has different options set by default. In Composition widgets, you can move the larger content areas independently of each other. You can stack them on one another so only one at a time is visible, as in an image slideshow (the default for all but one of the Composition widgets), or you can scatter them around the page so you can see more than one at a time, as in a Tooltip Composition widget that displays target content when the visitor interacts with the trigger area on a page.

Inserting a Composition widget and editing the options

Note: As of the writing of this book, Composition widgets are not responsive, so you'll manually adjust the widget content across different breakpoints.

Tip: You can also insert a Composition widget by choosing Object > Insert Widget > Composition > [specific widget you need].

Similar to other Composition widgets, the Featured News widget can show and hide text, images, and more. In this exercise, you'll insert a Featured News widget and edit its appearance and contents. You'll insert the text already on the page into the widget because sometimes you may change your mind when designing.

1 In the Layers panel (Window > Layers), make sure that the Page layer is selected.

2 In the Widgets Library panel, click the folder icon or arrow to the left of the Compositions category to display that category's widgets. Click Featured News to see a preview at the top of the panel. Drag the widget from the Widgets Library panel into the page *beneath* the columns of text. The Composition Options menu will appear to the right of the widget.

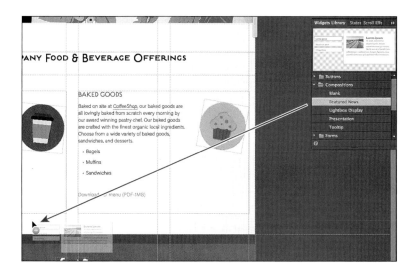

After inserting any widget, you can edit its options, including turning on and off widget features, as well as customizing the widget's actions. All Composition widgets offer the same group of options for you to edit, but each option is set slightly differently by default, to suit the widget's specific purpose. However, these settings are simply a starting point. You can further customize a Composition widget's function as well as its content and appearance to suit your needs.

Note: The bounding box of the selected Composition widget has eight points around it, which in Muse usually means that you can resize something. That's not the case for Composition or Slideshow widgets. Here, the eight points have no function, hence the X in place of each bounding point.

3   Choose Edit > Deselect All, and then click the widget to select it. You may need to zoom out for the next steps. Click the blue arrow button (circled in the following figure), and in the Composition Options menu that appears, change Transition Speed to **0.3**. Leave all of the other options at their default settings.

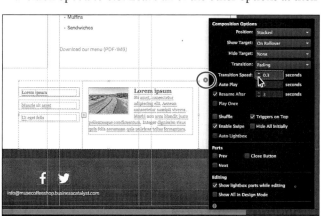

4   Press the Esc key to hide the Composition Options menu for the widget.

5   Click the Preview mode link to test the widget. Roll over one of the triggers to see the target container change. Click the Design mode link to return to the MENU page.

Adding or deleting a trigger

When you drag a Featured News Composition widget onto your page, it includes three triggers (the small boxes with text) that, when clicked in Design mode, show one of three large target containers (areas). Each trigger can contain text, images, and more. The larger target containers are stacked on top of each other by default, making it look like there's only one. Next, you'll add and remove triggers. When you add or remove a trigger, its associated target container is also added or removed (along with the content in it).

1 With the Selection tool, click the small triggers one at a time to see each associated target container and its content. You may want to zoom in a bit to see the widget on the page.

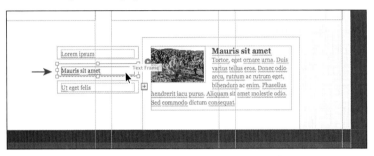

In Design mode, you can interact with triggers to access the different target containers and edit their contents.

2 Click away from the widget, in a blank area of the page to deselect it. Click once on the widget to select the entire widget again.

● **Note:** The placeholder images you see in this lesson may be different than what you see in Muse and that's okay.

3 Click the plus (+) icon that appears to the right of the lowest trigger element to add another trigger and blank target container set.

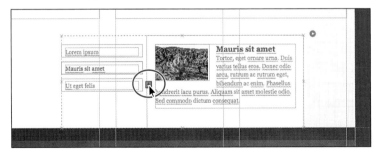

You can add a series of triggers and their associated targets, depending on your design needs. In this design, you only need two triggers, so you'll remove a few of the triggers and targets.

4 Click the newly added trigger to select it, and press Delete (or Backspace) to remove the trigger and the associated target container.

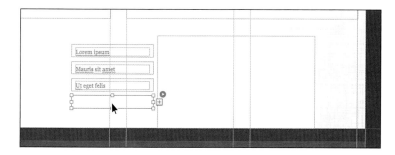

Note: The figure shows the widget *before* deleting the fourth trigger.

5 Click the third trigger from the top to select it (the one that contains the placeholder text "Ut eget felis"). The word "Trigger" will appear in the Selection Indicator in the Control panel. Press Delete (Backspace) to remove the trigger and the associated target. Two triggers remain.

Note: The figure shows the widget *after* deleting the third trigger.

6 With the Selection tool, click away from the Composition widget to deselect it.

Each trigger and target container can contain content and have formatting applied. In the following sections, you'll edit the trigger and target containers. If you had more than one trigger and target container, you would repeat the steps for each, even creating graphic styles and text styles to make it easier to ensure consistent design formatting.

Editing the trigger content

The triggers in a Composition widget can contain backgrounds, text, images, effects, and more. Each trigger is a container that can hold other content. The appearance and states for each trigger and target are independent. That means, if you want to apply the same formatting to two triggers, you either need to apply the formatting to each or you can create and apply a graphic style. In Lesson 8, "Adding Links, Buttons, and Graphic Styles," you learned how to create a graphic style to save time, maintain consistency, and update content easily.

Next, you'll edit the content for each of the triggers.

1 Click on the Composition widget to select it. Drag it into the horizontal center of the page.

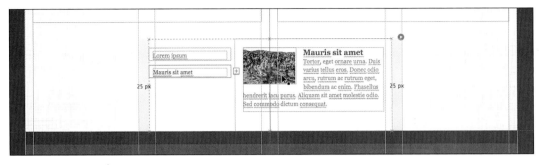

● **Note:** If you select the wrong part of the Composition widget, just click away from the widget to deselect it and then try again.

2 Position the pointer over the larger target container. You'll see a tooltip next to the pointer change to "Target." Click to select the target. "Target" also appears in the Selection Indicator in the Control panel.

3 Drag the target beneath the two trigger areas.

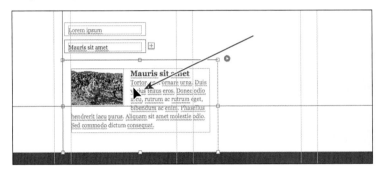

4 Click the bottom trigger to select it (both triggers are now above the target container). The word "Trigger" appears in the Selection Indicator in the Control panel. Drag the selected trigger to the right of the other trigger, using the Smart Guides that appear to ensure that the centers of the triggers are aligned with each other (a blue line appears in the center when they are aligned horizontally).

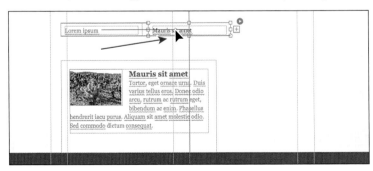

5 Select the Text tool (**T**) in the Toolbar. Triple-click to select the text, "COFFEE" in the left text column. Choose Edit > Cut. Select all of the text in the leftmost trigger and choose Edit > Paste to replace it.

● **Note:** You triple-clicked in order to select the *entire* paragraph. This way, the text formatting came with the text. Otherwise, if you select and copy just the word "COFFEE," in this case, when you paste it, the COFFEE text would most likely take on the formatting of the text you are pasting into.

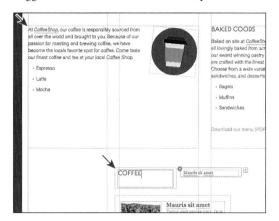

6 After pasting the text "COFFEE" into the trigger, there most likely will be a paragraph return after the word COFFEE. If that is the case, insert the cursor on the line below the COFFEE text and press Backspace or Delete to remove the paragraph return.

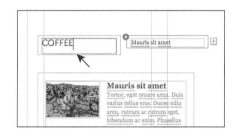

7 Triple-click to select the text, "BAKED GOODS" in the right text column to select it. Choose Edit > Cut. Select the text in the rightmost trigger and choose Edit > Paste to replace it.

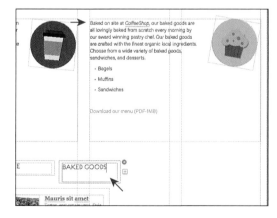

After pasting the BAKED GOODS text, you'll probably notice that its text color is different from the COFFEE text. This has to do with default text formatting applied to the trigger states.

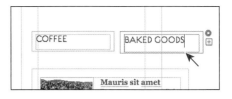

Note: The COFFEE and BAKED GOODS triggers may be different heights. Don't worry, we'll fix that shortly.

8 After pasting the text "BAKED GOODS," there most likely will be a paragraph return after the words BAKED GOODS. If so, insert the cursor on the line *below* the BAKED GOODS text and press Backspace or Delete to remove the paragraph return.

Editing trigger states

Triggers, like buttons, menus, and more, can change appearance when a visitor interacts with them. Next, you'll change the appearance of the different trigger states in the States panel.

1 Select the Selection tool (![icon]) and click to select the trigger that contains the "COFFEE" text. Open the States panel (Window > States). I dragged the States panel closer to the widget.

Every trigger has its own set of states and each state in a trigger has a fill and a stroke. You can select each state, like you've done in previous lessons, and edit the appearance of a trigger by changing the fill color, adding a text frame, inserting a background image that changes with each state, dragging a button in, and more.

2 Choose Edit > Select Same (Trigger) to select both triggers.

So that you don't have to apply the same formatting to each trigger separately, you've selected both triggers. Next you will change the formatting of both together.

Tip: With both triggers selected, you could also choose Object > Clear All Styling to remove the appearance formatting.

3 Select the Normal state in the States panel, if necessary. Change the Stroke Weight to **0** in the Control panel. Click the Fill color and select the [None] swatch to remove the fill in the Control panel.

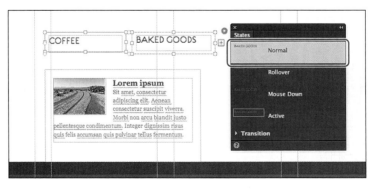

Note: The Height value may be blank, indicating that the two triggers have different heights to begin with.

4 Deselect the Constrain Width And Height Proportionally button (![icon]) in the Control panel (or Transform panel). Change the Height to **45** in the Control panel (or Transform panel).

5 Click the Rollover state in the States panel, and click the Reset To Default button (🗑) at the bottom of the States panel.

The Reset To Default button, in this case, makes the Rollover state (and Mouse Down state) have the same general appearance attributes as the Normal state.

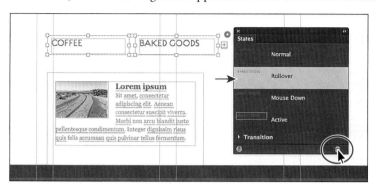

▶ **Tip:** With the Rollover state selected, you could select the text with the Text tool and make any changes you wanted. For this exercise, you'll leave the text appearance alone.

6 Select the Active State in the States panel and click the Reset To Default button (🗑) at the bottom of the States panel. This sets the appearance to be the same as the Normal state.

7 With the Selection tool, click the "COFFEE" text to select the text frame.

"Text Frame" will appear in the Selection Indicator on the left end of the Control panel. The text frame that is contained within the trigger can also change appearance using states. That's what you'll do next.

8 Select the Normal state in the States panel.

9 Ensure that the Leading is 120 and change the Space After to **0** in the Text panel.

● **Note:** As of the writing of the book, it is advised that you do not add strokes to each of the triggers when they are aligned horizontally as in this lesson. Unexpected results may occur.

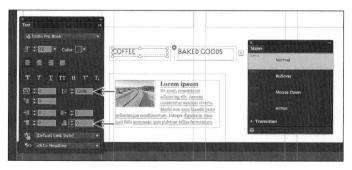

● **Note:** You may notice the Min-Height dotted line appear in the trigger. If you find that the trigger text is hidden in any browsers (it shouldn't be), you could resize the height of the text frame in each trigger to remove the Min-Height.

10 Click the Rollover state in the States panel. Click the Reset To Default button (🗑) at the bottom of the panel to give the text the same appearance as the Normal state.

11 Click the Active state in the States panel. Click the Reset To Default button (🗑) at the bottom of the States panel to give the text the same appearance as the Normal state.

Note: You are applying a really subtle state change to the text. You could add more formatting to the text (bold, etc.) if you think it works well in the design.

12 Change the Text color to Black in the Text panel.

13 With the Selection tool, click twice on the "BAKED GOODS" text to select the text frame. Repeat steps 8–12 to apply the same formatting to that trigger text.

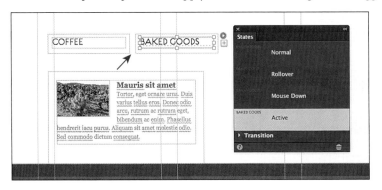

Adding content to the target containers

Note: When you click away from content in the page area, you deselect that content but wind up selecting the page. Be careful when making changes at that point because they will affect the page area. If that happens, choose Edit > Undo.

Now that the triggers are ready, you can focus on the larger target containers (content area) for each trigger. A target container is where the main content appears. You can add text, images, or any other type of content using Muse's design features by drawing frames or rectangles within the bounds of the content area, inserting embedded HTML, or dragging content into the area.

1 Click away from the widget on the page to deselect it, if necessary. Click the "COFFEE" trigger text a few times until the target content for that trigger shows (it may already be showing).

2 Click the larger target container to select it.

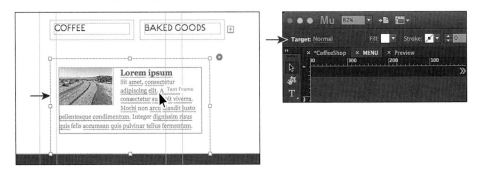

The word "Target" appears in the Selection Indicator on the left end of the Control panel (see the previous figure). Next, you'll remove the default content and replace it.

3 Click the text frame in the target to select it, and press Delete (Backspace) to delete it. This removes the default content in the target. Leave the target selected.

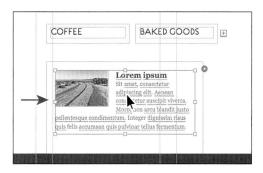

You can now create, paste, place, or drag other content into that area. By default, pasted content is pasted within the bounds of the selected target.

4   Select the text frame in the left column that starts with "At CoffeeShop, our coffee is..." Choose Edit > Cut.

5   Click on the larger target container in the widget until you select it (twice). Choose Edit > Paste to paste the text frame within the target container.

Tip: You can also drag content into a target container. If you drag content, when the pointer is within the bounds of the target container and a thicker border appears around the target container, release the mouse button.

Note: As of the writing of this book, the target container might not resize to fit around the content you paste in. It should, but it might not.

6   Click the "BAKED GOODS" trigger text to show the target content. Click the content in the larger target container twice to select it. Press Delete (Backspace) to delete it. Leave the target selected.

7   Select the text frame in the right column that starts with "Baked on site at CoffeeShop..." Choose Edit > Cut. Click on the larger target container until you select it (twice). Choose Edit > Paste to paste the text frame within the target container.

Tip: At anytime you can resize the Target area, change the background, apply rounded corners, effects, and more.

Note: The larger of the text frames you pasted into the target dictates the height of the target container.

8 Press the Esc key to select the target container. *If the target container does not fit around the content*, drag the corner of the target container to make it a little larger than the content you pasted in.

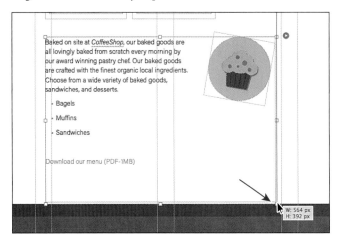

At this point you could click again on the pasted text frame to edit the content if necessary. You could also create more content in the larger target container or drag/paste other content in as well.

9 Choose Edit > Deselect All.

Editing target states

Target areas can also change appearance when a visitor interacts with them. Next, you'll change the appearance of the different target container states in the States panel.

1 With the Selection tool (![pointer]) selected, click twice on the trigger that contains the "COFFEE" text to select the trigger and to ensure that the target for COFFEE is showing.

2 Click to select the target container beneath the trigger. In the States panel (Window > States) select the Normal state, if necessary. Click the Fill color and select the [None] swatch to remove the fill in the Control panel.

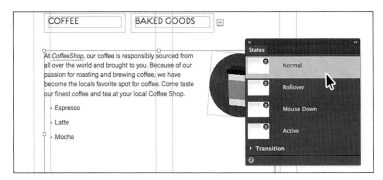

3 In the States panel select the Active state and click the Reset To Default button (🗑) at the bottom of the States panel to ensure that the Active state has the same appearance as the Normal state.

4 Click on the trigger that contains the "BAKED GOODS" text to select it.

5 Click to select the target container. In the States panel select the Normal state. Click the Fill color and select the [None] swatch to remove the fill in the Control panel.

⬤ **Note:** As you've seen, every trigger has a target container. Each target container has its own formatting and states.

6 In the States panel select the Active state and click the Reset To Default button (🗑) at the bottom of the States panel to ensure that the Active state has the same appearance as the Normal state.

7 With the target for "BAKED GOODS" still selected, drag it so its left edge is aligned with the left edge of the COFFEE trigger on the page and it's a little closer to the triggers. A Smart Guide will show to help with alignment.

8 Press the Esc key until the Composition widget is selected and "Composition" displays in the Selection Indicator in the Control panel. Drag the composition so it's centered on the page and just below the heading above it on the page. A Smart Guide will show to help align it to center. Leave it selected.

9 Click the Preview mode link to test the widget. Hover over each trigger to see the corresponding target content appear.

10 Click the Design mode link to return to the MENU page.

Checking the Composition widget across screen sizes

As of the writing of this book, Composition widgets are *not* responsive, so you need to check and make sure it works across all screen sizes. That's what you'll do next.

1 With the Composition widget still selected, click the center box (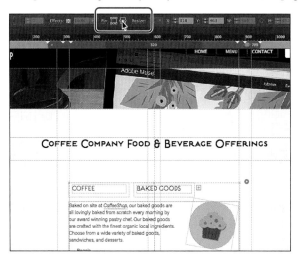) in the Pin option (called Pin To Center) in the Control panel above the page. This way the composition widget always stays in the center of the page.

2 Choose Object > Copy Size And Position To > All Breakpoints.

Note: You also could have deleted the breakpoint at 700 pixels to remove the resizing and repositioning you applied to the text frames, but you would also remove the text sizing you did to the "Coffee Company Food & Beverage Offerings" heading.

In a previous lesson you added the columns of text and also repositioned and resized them in a smaller breakpoint (700 pixels), making them one column instead of two. Since the text frames are now inside of the Composition widget, you are copying the size and position of the Composition widget to override all changes you made to the text frames at the different breakpoints. This is a case where it would have been easier to start with the Composition widget and add the text directly, but once again, we all change our minds from time to time.

3 Click in the breakpoint at 700 pixels in the Breakpoint bar.

The Composition widget should still be in the center of the page area and the same size (since it's not responsive, as of the writing of this book). To keep things simple and not add yet another breakpoint, you'll change the size of the widget so it fits on smaller screens in the breakpoint at 700 pixels.

4 With the Composition widget still selected, click the COFFEE text in the trigger to show the target container, if it's not already showing. Click twice on the text frame in the *target* container (below the trigger) to select it. Making sure the Constrain Width And Height Proportionally is off (), change the Width to **350** pixels in the Control panel or Transform panel.

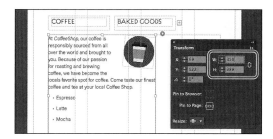

The target container of a Composition widget is as wide and tall as the widest and tallest content within. In order to resize the Target, you first need to resize the content within.

5 With the Composition widget still selected, click the BAKED GOODS text in the trigger to show the target container. Click twice on the text frame in the target container to select it. Change the Width to **350** pixels in the Control panel or Transform panel.

6 Press the Escape key to select the Target. Change the Width to **350** pixels in the Control panel or Transform panel.

Note: It is difficult to tell in the figure but the Target is selected. You can tell it is selected, and not the text frame within, because "Target" appears in the Selection Indicator on the left end of the Control panel.

7 Drag the Target area into the horizontal center of the page area.

8 Drag the COFFEE and BAKED GOODS triggers, one at a time, into the center of the page area, one on top of the other. See the figure.

Note: You may want to check the positioning of all of the page content across screen sizes. At a smaller screen size, there may be a gap above the heading. To fix it, you can add a new breakpoint and drag the content up.

9 Choose File > Save Site.

Adding a form

▶ **Tip:** Check out the form you will create in this section by visiting: http://musecoffeeshop. businesscatalyst.com/ contact.html. You may need to scroll down on the page to see the form.

Muse includes a long and short contact form that you can drag and drop onto the page and edit as you see fit. You can add and remove fields, and style the form as you would other Adobe Muse elements. You can independently style the various states of the form and form fields to provide a compelling user experience with visual cues for Error states, Empty states, and more.

In Adobe Muse CC, the supplied contact forms found in the Widgets Library work with most web hosts. When you export or publish by choosing File > Upload To FTP Host, PHP files are uploaded along with your site content. Those PHP files make the forms work behind the scenes.

● **Note:** Your web host must support PHP, and the PHP mail service must be properly configured to send email messages. If you use the FTP Upload feature within Muse, Muse will attempt to warn you if it detects that your web host does not meet these requirements. If you host your site on a non-Adobe host server and your contact forms are not working, contact your hosting provider to learn more about configuring your hosting account to process forms.

Inserting a form and editing options

The first step in the process of adding a form is to add one of the form widgets to a page, and that's what you'll do next.

1 Press Command+J (Ctrl+J) and type **contact** in the Go To Page dialog box. When CONTACT appears in the Page field, click OK.

2 Choose View > Fit Page In Window.

3 In the Layers panel (Window > Layers), make sure that the Page layer is selected.

● **Note:** The two contact forms are identical except that the Detailed Contact form shows more fields; those fields can easily be added to the Simple Contact form as well.

4 In the Widgets Library panel, click the arrow or folder to the left of the Forms category. Two forms are available to choose from: Detailed Contact and Simple Contact. Drag the Simple Contact Form widget into a blank area of the page.

After inserting the Form widget into your page, you need to edit the main form options that appear automatically, and then edit the individual form field options as well.

5 Ensure that the following options are set accordingly in the Options menu:

- Form Name: **Main Contact**

- Email To: *your email address* (the default setting, which references the Adobe ID used to install Adobe Muse).

▶ **Tip:** You can insert multiple email addresses by separating them with a semicolon like this: brian@website.com; jane@website.com.

- After Sending: **CONTACT:THANK YOU**

- Standard Fields: Select **Cell Phone Number** and ensure that both **Name** and **Email** are selected. The Standard Fields area contains an array of fields that you can add to your form.

- Add Custom Fields: The **Single Line Text** field adds a generic single-line text field to the form. The generic **Multiline Text** field adds a multiple-line field. You can add or remove form fields at anytime.

- Edit Together: **Selected** (the default setting, which means any style attributes you apply to one field will affect all of the fields).

Note: If you don't see the Options menu, select the widget and click the blue arrow button in the upper-right corner of the widget.

Note: I didn't have you put anything on the THANK YOU page. You might want to add some text to that page thanking users for filling out the form, some social media contact information, links to other relevant content, and more.

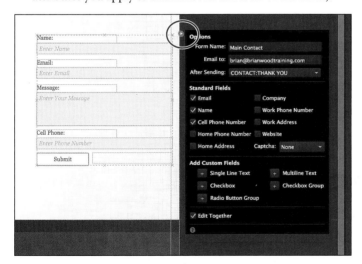

6 Press the Esc key to hide the Options menu, and click in a blank area of the page to deselect the form.

7 Choose File > Save Site.

Editing form field options

With the form in place and the options set, you can begin to edit the individual options for each field.

1 With the Selection tool, click the form to select it. Position the pointer over the Name field. A tooltip with the words "Form Field" appears. Click once to select both the form field and the "Name" text.

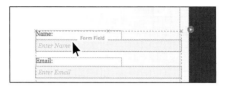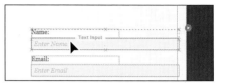

Notice that "Form Field" appears in the Selection Indicator in the Control panel. A form field is typically composed of a label (the text "Name:") and the field (called *Text Input* in this case).

2 Click the blue arrow button to show the Name Field Options menu. Ensure that the following options are set accordingly:

- Require Entry: **Selected** (the default setting)

  Certain fields are "optional" in a Muse form, but the Email form fields are required by default. This means that the user is required to fill out the field in order to submit the data.

- Show Prompt Text When Empty: **Deselected**

  The prompt text is the text "Enter Name," which appears in the field initially. This text can be very helpful to display details like a date format, for instance.

- Label: **Selected** (the default setting)

- Message Text: **Selected**

  The Message text is a text frame that shows the editable text "Required," by default. You can change the position, content, and other formatting properties.

● **Note:** The prompt text may not initially disappear from the field in Design mode, and that's OK. When you preview the page, it will be gone.

3 With the Text tool (**T**) selected, select the text "Enter Name" in the Name *field* and change it to **Your Name Here**.

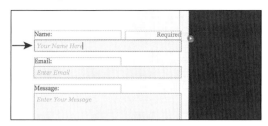

By default, that text will appear in the field. This is called prompt text and can be very useful for users if you decide not to show the label text above each field. If you don't want the prompt text, you could either delete it or deselect Show Prompt Text When Empty, as you'll see next.

4 With the Text tool selected, insert the cursor into the "Cell Phone:" text. Change the text to **Phone:**.

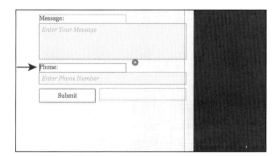

5 Select the Selection tool (![selection tool]) and the Label for the Phone field will be selected. Click the blue arrow button to show the Cell Phone Number Field Options menu and change the following options:

- Require Entry: **Deselected**
- Show Prompt Text When Empty: **Deselected**
- Label: **Selected** (the default setting)
- Message Text: **Deselected** (the default setting)

Note: You can have either the Label or the field (Text Input in this case) selected to change the options for the field.

Note: If you select multiple fields, clicking the blue arrow button shows the options that pertain to the entire form, not the individual field options.

6 Click the Email field to select it. Click the blue arrow button to show the Email Field Options menu and change the following options:

  • Require Entry: **Selected** (the default setting)
  • Show Prompt Text When Empty: **Deselected**
  • Label: **Selected** (the default setting)
  • Message Text: **Selected**

7 Click the Message field to select it. Click the blue arrow button to show the Multiline Text Field Options menu and change the following options:

  • Require Entry: **Deselected** (the default setting)
  • Show Prompt Text When Empty: **Deselected**
  • Label: **Selected** (the default setting)
  • Message Text: **Deselected** (the default setting)

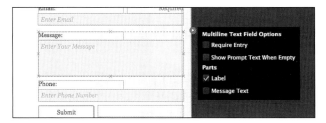

8 Click the Preview mode link to preview the form.

   When you preview the forms in Muse or in a browser, you typically get an error message when you click Submit. Although you can see the form's appearance when previewing, you'll need to wait until you've published the trial site to test form functionality.

9 Click the Design mode link to return to the CONTACT page in Design mode.

Moving and resizing form fields

Now that the form has form fields, as well as options set, you can edit the position of fields and their labels.

1 With the Selection tool selected (➤), click away from the form to deselect it. Click twice, slowly, on the Message field to select the form field and label. Drag the form field to the left of the existing fields and align the Message label with the top of the Name label. See the following figure.

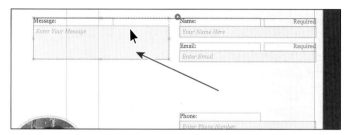

2 Click the Phone field to select it. Begin dragging the field up to beneath the Email field. Blue Smart Guides are temporarily displayed as you drag the element to help keep the field aligned with the center of the others. When aqua gap measurements show the same value (14 px) above and below the Email field, release the mouse button. Leave the field selected.

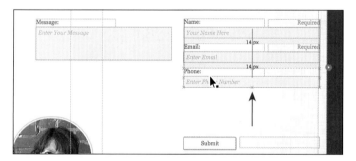

● **Note:** Aqua gap measurements are a great feature of Smart Guides. They appear when Smart Guides are on (View > Smart Guides) and you drag content on your page. They appear if the distance between the object you're dragging and another object (or guide) matches the distance between that other object (or guide) and at least one other object.

3 Click the Submit button and Shift-click the form message field to the right of the button (the empty frame). Drag both objects up, closer to the Phone field.

4 With the Selection tool, click twice on the Message field label (the text "Message:" above the field). Drag the label to the left side of the field.

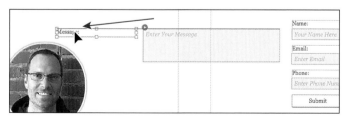

▶ **Tip:** You can also move selected field(s) by pressing the arrow keys. Pressing Shift+arrow key will move the field(s) 10 pixels with every key press.

▶ **Tip:** To move all the labels at once, select one label (like you did) and then choose Edit > Select Same (Label).

You can change the size of the label, the position of the label, text formatting (like alignment), and much more. A good, simple, rule of thumb to keep in mind is that when the data being collected is familiar (like a simple contact form), labels should be stacked vertically on top of fields or not shown at all (with prompt text indicating what the user should enter into the field). When the data being collected is unfamiliar or complex, labels should be placed to the left of the field.

5 Choose Edit > Undo Move Item to return the label to its original position.

6 Click away from the form in a blank area of the page to deselect the form. Click to select the form again and drag it into horizontal center of the page beneath the images of Joe and Marie. A Smart Guide will appear, helping you align it to center.

7 With the form still selected, click the center box (⊞) in the Pin option (called Pin To Center) in the Control panel above the page. This way the form always stays in the center of the page.

8 With the Selection tool, click the Message field (not the label) twice to select just the field. The words "Multiline Text Input" will appear in the Selection Indicator in the Control panel. Click and drag the bottom, middle bounding point down until it's about as tall as all of the fields to its right. See the following figure.

Tip: If you change the height or width of one of the single-line input fields (name, email, or phone), the rest of them will change as well. The reason is that the Edit Together option is selected in the form options.

Tip: You can also set the width and height of fields using the Transform options in the Control panel or the Transform panel.

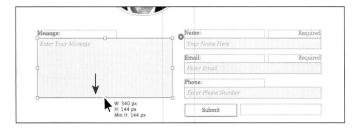

9 Press the Esc key until the entire Form object is selected. Leave the form selected for the next section.

When it comes to sizing fields, keep the visual design of the entire form in mind. Some very simple forms, such as a login form (username and password), use the same size fields. It may confuse visitors to create longer, more complex forms with a series of fields of varying widths.

Editing the appearance of the form fields

You may find that you want to modify the formatting options of the form fields and labels to change colors, borders, and more. That's what you'll do next.

1   With the form still selected, click twice on the Name field (not the label) to select it. The words "Text Input" appear in the Selection Indicator in the Control panel.

2   Click the Fill color and select the [None] swatch to remove the fill in the Control panel. Change the Stroke Weight to **2** and the Stroke Color to **#555555**.

Tip: When styling form elements, treat each form field like a rectangle you drew. You can change the stroke and fill, add effects, as well as change the opacity and more. For instance, you could set the fill color to None and the stroke weight to 0 for a form field, and then place an image behind the entire form or each field to make the field take on a different appearance.

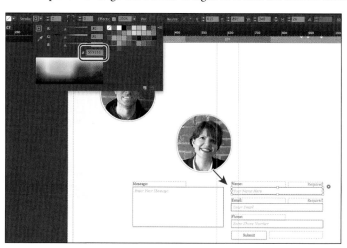

Notice that all of the form fields changed appearance because Edit Together is selected in the form Options menu. Next, you'll edit the text formatting of the labels and the fields. By editing one label, all of the labels will change in appearance.

3   With the Selection tool, click the Name: label to select it. The word "Label" will appear in the Selection Indicator in the Control panel. Change the font to Acumin Pro Light (or another) in the Text panel.

4   Click the Name field once to select it.

If you want to change the appearance of the field messages (that contain the text "Required"), you can select one and make text formatting changes and the other field messages will change as well. Now that the font is set for the field labels, you'll add some padding between the message text and the edge of the fields using the Spacing panel.

5 Choose Window > Spacing to open the Spacing panel. Making sure that the Make All Padding Settings The Same button (⬛) is on, change the Top Padding (T:) to **8** so that all of the values change together.

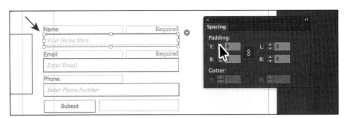

6 Make the Height a few pixels taller in the Control panel or Transform panel so that the Min-Height dotted line disappears from the field. I made the Height of mine **31**, but yours may be a bit different. This will change the height for the Name, Email, and Phone fields.

After adding padding to all of the fields, the fields are too close together. You'll fix that next.

7 With the Name field still selected, press the Esc key to select the Form Field (the label and the field). "Form Field" will appear in the Selection Indicator in the Control panel. Shift-click the Email field and then Phone field to select the Email and Phone fields as well.

● **Note:** I dragged the Align panel closer to the content so it would be easier to see.

8 Click the Align link in the Control panel or open the Align panel (Window > Align) and choose Align To Key Object from the Align To menu. One of the fields will have a bold highlight around it. Change the Distribute Spacing value to **10**, and click the Vertical Distribute Space button (⬛) to make the spacing the same between the fields.

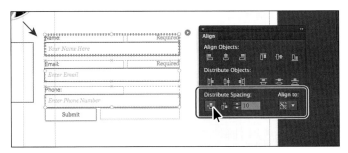

You might want to reposition the Submit button so it isn't as close to the fields and make the Message field taller to match the other fields like I did.

9 Choose File > Save Site and then Edit > Deselect All.

Editing the states of your form fields

When visitors fill out the form, all required fields are checked by code created by Muse when you preview, publish, or export the site to ensure that they are filled out. If one or more fields are not filled out properly, errors will appear in the form after the visitor clicks the Submit button, indicating which form fields are required. This is generically referred to as *form validation*.

Five states of form fields can be edited (see the sidebar "Field states explained"). In this part of the lesson, you'll focus only on the Error state.

1   With the Selection tool, click the form on the page. Click once more on the Name field to select the label and field ("Form Field" will appear in the Selection Indicator).

2   Click the link named "Empty" to the right of the text "Form Field" in the Selection Indicator in the Control panel. Select the Error state.

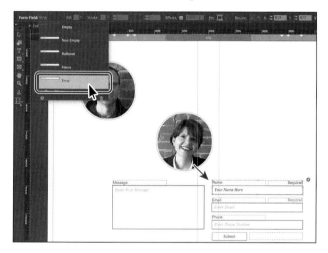

Tip: You can also select states in the States panel (Window > States).

Tip: You can also change the appearance of the other form fields states if you like, including the Rollover and Non Empty states.

When a visitor clicks the Submit button, all text in the Name field, label, and message text of required fields will turn red if the fields are empty or not filled out properly (in the case of the Name field, for instance). With the Error state selected, you could select the field, label, or message text and change the appearance.

3 Press the Esc key to hide the States menu in the Control panel. With the Selection tool, click the Name field to select it. Change the Stroke Weight to **3** in the Control panel. The Error state for *all* required fields will now be updated.

Field states explained

Each state is defined as follows:

- **Empty:** The appearance of a field when the field has yet to be clicked.
- **Non Empty:** The appearance of a field when a visitor has typed content into the field, but it is not the field in focus.
- **Rollover:** The appearance of a field when the visitor hovers over the field.
- **Focus:** The appearance of a field when the field is in focus (the Tab key has been pressed to insert the cursor in a field or the visitor has clicked into the field).
- **Error:** The appearance of the field when the field has not been properly filled out and the Submit button is pressed.

● **Note:** You'll most likely see a dialog box when submitting a form on a page that hasn't been published. The dialog box will indicate that the form won't work in Preview mode. You'll need to publish the form in order to test it. Click OK.

4 Click the Preview mode link. Test the form by simply clicking the Submit button. The errors should appear on the Name and Email fields. Fill out all of the fields in the form and click Submit again.

5 Click the Design mode link to return to the CONTACT page, and then choose File > Save Site.

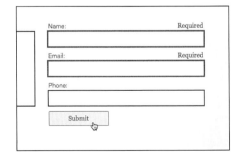

Editing the appearance of the Submit button

Next, you'll change the appearance of the Submit button.

1   With the Selection tool, click to select the Submit button.

2   Click the Fill color in the Control panel, and change the fill to a yellow/orange color with the values R=**231**, G=**168**, B=**0**.

Tip: You could also add a background image to the button to create some interesting effects.

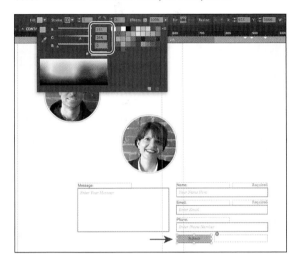

3   Change the Stroke Weight to **0** in the Control panel. Leave the Submit button selected for the next section.

> **Tip:** When it comes to the Submit button, like other form fields, you could change the formatting of the text as well. You can also change the text on the Submit button from Submit to anything you like by selecting the "Submit" text with the Text tool and changing it. If the text is too wide, you may need to resize the button using the Selection tool.

Checking the form across screen sizes

Since Form widgets are *not* responsive as of the writing of this book, you need to preview the form across different screen sizes and make adjustments, which is what you'll do next.

1   With the Selection tool selected, drag the scrubber to the left to preview the page and contents at a smaller screen size. At a certain point, around 700 pixels, you'll see that the form is wider than the page.

2   Click the plus (+) above the scrubber to add a new breakpoint. Double-click the new breakpoint value in the Breakpoint bar and change the Breakpoint Width in the Breakpoint Properties dialog box to **800**. Click OK.

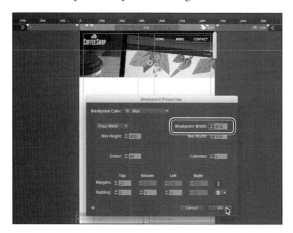

3   With the Selection tool selected, click the form to select it. Click again on
    the Submit button to select it, then Shift-click the Form Message to the
    right of the Submit button to select both. Drag them down to make room for
    the Message field. Make sure they stay aligned with the fields above them. Smart
    Guides will appear to help you align them.

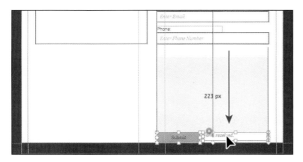

4   Click to select the Message field and drag it down between the Phone field
    and the Submit button. Change the spacing if you need by dragging the form
    objects around.

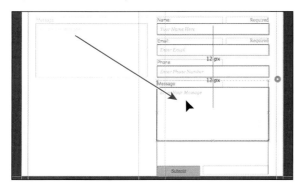

5   Click the Submit button to select it, then Shift-click the Form Message to
    the right of the Submit button to select both. Drag them up closer to the
    Message field, if necessary.

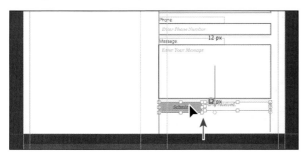

6 Press the Esc key to select the entire form. Drag the form into the center of the page area. Smart Guides will help you align the form to center.

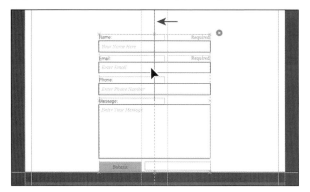

7 Drag the scrubber further to the left to ensure that the form looks good at even smaller screen sizes.

8 Click in the breakpoint at 1200 to return the page to that preview size.

9 Choose File > Save Site.

Editing the states of your Submit button ▬◀

To learn how to edit the states of your submit button, check out the video titled "Editing Submit Button States" that is a part of the Web Edition. For more information, see the "Web Edition" section of Getting Started at the beginning of the book.

Editing the Form widget states ▬◀

To learn how to edit form widget states, check out the video titled "Editing Form Widget States" that is a part of the Web Edition. For more information, see the "Web Edition" section of Getting Started at the beginning of the book.

Creating a copy of the form for the footer ▬◀

To learn how to create a copy of the form in the footer, check out the video titled "Create a Copy of the Form" that is a part of the Web Edition. For more information, see the "Web Edition" section of Getting Started at the beginning of the book.

Adding Social widgets

Adobe Muse has a category of widgets in the Widgets Library panel called Social widgets that allow you to add social media content—such as Google Maps, Twitter widgets, YouTube videos, and much more—to your pages. In a fluid width layout (responsive web design), it's important to know that YouTube, Vimeo, Facebook Comments, and Google Maps are responsive. As a result, at different breakpoints, the YouTube and Google Maps widgets automatically resize by width. The rest of the social widgets are currently not responsive.

You'll work with the Google Maps widget next to give you an idea of how Social widgets work.

Adding the Google Maps widget

The Google Maps widget allows you to embed a Google map into a page. If you don't have an Internet connection, the preview for the map will not be generated, but you can still add a map to the page.

1   With the CONTACT page still open, choose View > Fit Page In Window.

2   In the Layers panel (Window > Layers), make sure the Page content layer is selected.

Note: If you don't see the Options menu, select the widget and click the blue arrow button off the upper-right corner of the widget.

3   In the Widgets Library panel (Window > Widgets Library), click the folder or arrow to the left of the Social category to show the widgets in that category. Drag the Google Maps widget onto the page, above the form.

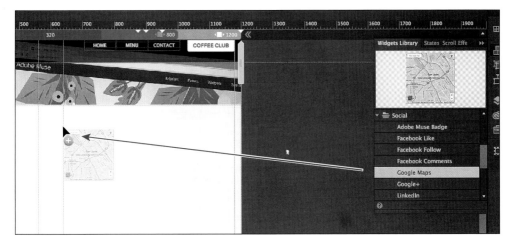

As soon as you drop the widget onto the page, the Google Maps Options menu appears. Each of the Social widgets has different options that you can set. By now, the process of dragging widgets from the Widgets Library panel should be familiar to you.

4 In the Google Maps Options menu, change the following options:

- Address: **Raleigh, NC**
- Map Kind: **Roadmap** (the default setting)
- Expand Pin Info: **Selected** (the default setting)
- Zoom Level: **12** (the default setting)

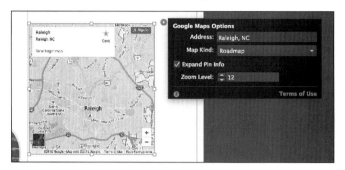

5 Drag the map *below* the form. The footer content will most likely move down and the page height will expand to fit the new content.

6 With the map selected, make sure the Constrain Width And Height Proportionally option is not selected (▣) in the Control panel (or Transform panel). Change the width to **900** and the height to **400** pixels in the Control panel (or Transform panel). See the figure for sizing help. The map preview will refresh to fill the area (if you have an Internet connection).

7 Drag the map into the center of the page. Smart Guides will appear to help you align it.

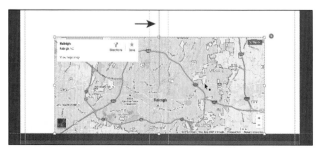

8   With the map still selected, click the center box () in the Pin option (called Pin To Center) in the Control panel above the page. This way the map always stays in the center of the page.

9   Choose File > Save Site.

Checking the map across screen sizes

The Google map widget is responsive, but you still need to check and make sure it sizes and is positioned where you want it. That's what you'll do next.

1   Drag the scrubber to the left. Notice that the Google map is responsive. At a certain point, the map may be too narrow to be useful.

2   Click the breakpoint at 800 you set in the previous section to preview the design at that screen size. The map may overlap the form above it. Drag the map down if it is overlapping the form.

3   Choose Stretch To Browser Width from the Resize menu. The map is now the width of the page at screen sizes of 800 pixels or less.

Note: Choosing Stretch To Browser Width overrides the Pin To Center option set at the 1200 pixel breakpoint.

To me, having the map be the width of the page on smaller devices looks great. You do need to be careful with touch devices like a smart phone or tablet, for instance. If the map covers the page width, users will find it difficult to scroll the page near the map since the map will zoom instead. It's a good idea to publish a temporary site, which you'll learn about in Lesson 11, and test it on mobile devices.

4   Click on the breakpoint at 1200 to reset the page width.

5   Choose File > Save Site.

Working with slideshows

Slideshow widgets are a great way to add robust image slideshows to your pages. They are also what you typically see on the web these days.

Muse offers five Slideshow widgets: Basic, Blank, Fullscreen, Lightbox, and Thumbnails. Each has different preset options enabled to create a specialized configuration, but all have the same options available. You can explore each slideshow configuration to discover which slideshow works best for your project. Slideshow widgets are not responsive and remain fixed at all breakpoints. If necessary, you can resize these objects individually at each breakpoint.

Slideshow widgets are different from Composition widgets in that they can contain only images, and they can include a caption, first and last buttons, and thumbnails that can be shown or hidden for each larger image. The larger content areas must be stacked, displaying one at a time (unlike Composition widgets).

In this section, you'll insert a Blank Slideshow widget that is 100% width.

Adding and configuring a Slideshow widget

A Blank Slideshow widget is one of the simplest slideshows. By default, previous and next arrows are displayed to help the visitor cycle between the images.

1   Press Command+J (Ctrl+J) and type **home** in the Go To Page dialog box. When HOME appears in the Page field, click OK.

2   Choose View > Fit Page In Window.

3   In the Layers panel, select the Page layer.

● **Note:** You may need to click in the 1200 pixel breakpoint in the Breakpoint bar to resize the page to the maximum page width.

4   In the Widgets Library panel, click the folder or arrow to the left of the Slideshows category to show the Slideshow widgets. You may need to scroll down in the panel. Drag the Blank Slideshow widget into the middle of the page. Leave the widget selected and the Slideshow Options menu showing; you'll reposition it later in the lesson.

Next, you'll add some images to the slideshow. One important detail to be aware of is that the images you add will use the Fitting option set in the New Hero and New Thumbnail options in the Options menu. If you don't want to apply the default option Fill Frame Proportionally to the images and instead want them to Fit Frame Proportionally, you need to set these options before adding images.

5 In the Slideshow Options menu, click the Add Images folder icon (see the following figure). Open the Lessons > images > slideshow folder. Click the image named home_slide1.jpg, Shift-click the image named home_slide3.jpg to select all three images. Click Open. All of the images are loaded into the slideshow, but you'll only see one on the page since the images are stacked on each other.

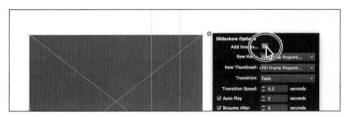

6 If the Slideshow Options menu is not still showing, click the blue arrow button just off the upper-right corner of the widget to show the menu, and ensure the following options are set accordingly:

- New Hero: **Fill Frame Proportionally** (the default setting; images you add to the slideshow will fill the larger content area, ensuring that there are no gaps and that a portion of the image is cropped. If the image frame is resized later, the image will always fill the frame proportionally. The Hero is the image in the larger content area.)

- New Thumbnail: **Fill Frame Proportionally** (the default setting)

- Transition: **Horizontal**

- Transition Speed: **0.4**

- Auto Play: **Selected** (the default setting)

- Auto Play: **3** (the default setting)

- Resume After: **Selected** (the default setting)

- Resume After: **3** (the default setting)
- Play Once: **Deselected** (the default setting)
- Shuffle: **Deselected** (the default setting)
- Enable Swipe: **Selected** (the default setting)
- Lightbox: **Deselected** (the default setting)

  Selecting the Lightbox option would hide the larger content areas initially, as with the Composition Lightbox widget.

- Full Screen: **Deselected** (the default setting)

  Selecting the Full Screen option would scale the content of the slideshow to fill the entire browser window for the computer or device screen.

- Free Form Thumbnails: **Deselected** (the default setting)
- Prev, Next, Captions: **Selected** (the default setting)
- First, Last, Counter, Close Button: **Deselected**
- Thumbnails: **Deselected** (the default setting)
- Show Lightbox Parts While Editing: **Selected** (the default setting)
- Edit Together: **Selected** (the default setting)

  This configuration will hide all of the slideshow parts except for the larger content areas, arrows, and the captions.

7 Press the Esc key to hide the Slideshow Options menu.

Editing the appearance of the Blank Slideshow widget

You can apply all sorts of formatting options to the triggers and the larger content areas (targets) of Slideshow widgets, just like the other widgets. In this exercise, you'll resize the larger images, and then edit and style the captions.

1 Choose View > Hide Breakpoints.

2 Choose View > Fit Page In Window.

3 With the slideshow selected on the page and the Selection tool selected, click the Hero Image (the large image in the slideshow). The words "Hero Image" will show in the Selection Indicator in the Control panel.

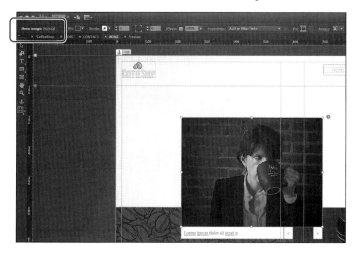

4 Drag the Hero Image up until it snaps to the top of the page area.

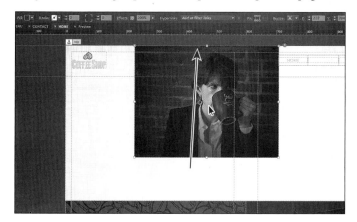

Note: If you decide to apply Stretch To Browser Width, you need to make sure that the images you use in the slideshow are large enough in dimension. The images will fill the frame, which means they will scale, no matter how large the frame becomes.

5   Choose Stretch To Browser Width from the Resize menu in the Control panel.

The slideshow hero images will now have a width of 100%. You'll set the height next.

6   In the Control panel, make sure that the Constrain Width And Height Proportionally option is off (⬚). Change the Height to **600** in the Control panel or Transform panel.

Each image will fill the image frame automatically, with no distortion. Next you'll move the two images that were already on the HOME page to make more room for the slideshow and other content.

7   Choose View > Zoom Out.

You'll find that working with fluid width layouts, you wind up having to move content down the page at times to accommodate new content above it. In Muse, you can select an object and drag the Vertical Move Handle up or down. Any content *below* the selected object will be moved up or down as well.

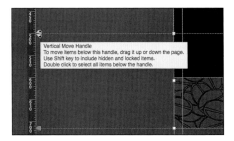

8 With the Selection tool, click to select the smaller image on the left (the image of the coffee beans). Drag the Vertical Move Handle down so there is a gap between the hero image of the slideshow and that image of the coffee beans. You will probably drag far enough for the footer content to move down and the page to be taller. See the following figure.

▶ **Tip:** You can press the Shift key and drag the Vertical Move Handle to drag locked and hidden items as well. If you double-click the Vertical Move Handle, all items below the handle will be selected.

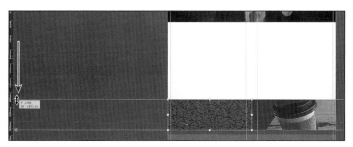

● **Note:** Changing the position of the images will only affect their position in the current breakpoint. In the next lesson, you will need to fix the spacing between the images and the slideshow at smaller screen sizes.

9 Select the Zoom tool (🔍) in the Toolbar and click twice in the center of the slideshow image to zoom in.

10 Select the Selection tool (▶) and click twice to select the slideshow caption. Drag it so that it snaps into the left edge of the first column, just above the bottom of the slideshow image.

11 Select the Text tool (**T**) and select the text in the caption. Change the caption text to **Coffee Shop**.

▶ **Tip:** You can change the formatting of the caption text and text frame, including background fill, stroke, rounded corners, effects, and more. Changing the appearance of one caption changes them all.

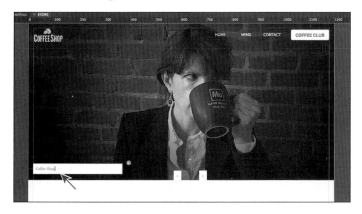

12 Select the Selection tool and click the previous arrow to show another hero image and caption (circled in the following figure).

● **Note:** There is one more image in the slideshow that you can change the caption for.

13 Double-click the text in the caption to switch to the Text tool. Select the caption text and change it to **Morning Coffee**.

▶ **Tip:** The Prev and Next arrows are actually text frames. The arrow in each is a character that you can change and format.

14 With the cursor still in the caption, click the blue arrow button to show the Slideshow Options menu and deselect the Prev and Next options to hide the arrows.

Later, if you want to edit the hero images or the caption for a specific image, you can show either the Prev and Next arrows or the thumbnails in the Slideshow Options menu, use them to cycle through the images, and then hide them again.

15 Click the Preview mode link to test the slideshow in Preview mode. Click the Design mode link to return to the HOME page.

16 Choose File > Save Site.

Checking the slideshow across screen sizes

As previously mentioned, slideshows are not responsive by default in Muse, as of the writing of this book. That's why you made the hero images stretch to the browser width. You still do need to test in different screen sizes so you can check the screenshow parts like the caption, and that's what you'll do next.

1 On the HOME page, choose View > Show Breakpoints.

2 Choose Edit > Deselect All.

3 Choose View > Fit Page In Window.

4 Drag the scrubber to the left to see how the slideshow looks on smaller screen sizes.

   The hero image stays the same size, but is cropped on the left and right as the screen gets smaller, until the scrubber reaches the breakpoint at 600 pixels. At 600 pixels, the hero image is the original height of 360 pixels. The height change you made to the hero image was only applied to the breakpoint at 1200 pixels. The caption is also now too far down on the page.

5 Click the small arrow in the Breakpoint bar at 700 pixels. This is a master page breakpoint that you need to use so you can fix the slideshow hero images. Click the plus (+) on the breakpoint bar to add a new breakpoint at 700.

6 With the Selection tool, click twice on the slideshow hero image to select it. Change the Height to **350** in the Control panel.

7 Click the slideshow caption and drag it straight up onto the hero image.

Note: At this point, you could change the font size or width of the caption to make it a bit smaller. Remember, if you want to change the font size, you should select Format Text On Current Breakpoint in the Toolbar so it only affects that breakpoint.

Unfortunately, there is a smaller breakpoint at 600 on this page, which means the sizing and positioning of the slideshow parts you just made won't change on that breakpoint. You'll fix that next.

8 Click in the breakpoint at 600 pixels to preview the page at that size.

9 Adjust the height of the hero image making it shorter and drag the caption on top of the hero image. You can also resize the caption to make it a bit smaller. In this case, the size changes will only affect screen sizes that are 600 pixels and smaller.

Note: Check the back to top button you added to your HOME page at this breakpoint and make sure it is still sitting above the footer, against the right margin guide.

10 Click the Preview mode link to test the pages. Click the Design mode link to return to the page.

11 Close all open pages and Preview mode, and return to Plan mode.

12 Choose File > Save Site.

Adding an Accordion Panel Widget ▣

To learn how to add an Accordion Panel widget to your pages, check out the video titled "Adding an Accordion Panel widget" that is a part of the Web Edition. For more information, see the "Web Edition" section of Getting Started at the beginning of the book.

Review questions

1 What are Muse widgets?

2 What are the seven categories of widgets available in Muse?

3 Describe what a trigger and target are in a Muse widget.

4 Name a benefit of using a Tabbed Panel widget in your page.

5 Name the major difference between Composition and Slideshow widgets.

Review answers

1 Widgets are reusable site features that offer configurable interactivity and behaviors. Widgets allow visitors to click or hover (or auto-run) to show and hide page content. They are completely customizable and can be styled to fit your design. Widgets provide an easy way of adding interactivity to your web page.

2 The seven categories of widgets available in Muse are: Buttons, Compositions, Forms, Menus, Panels, Slideshows, and Social. Each of these categories contains multiple widgets, each customized for a specific purpose.

3 Most, but not all, widgets in Muse are composed of at least one small container (the trigger) that acts like a button to display content in a larger container (the target) in response to user interaction. Triggers can be hidden in certain widgets that are set to auto-play.

4 Tabbed Panel widgets are helpful for displaying more elements within a smaller screen area. Visitors can click the tabs of these types of widgets to reveal the contents of each container. Both Tabbed Panel widgets and Accordion widgets add interactivity to pages by enabling visitors to choose the content they want to show.

5 Slideshow widgets are different from Composition widgets in that they can contain only images, and they can have a caption and first and last buttons, as well as thumbnails that can be shown or hidden that correspond to each larger image. The larger content areas in Slideshow widgets must be stacked, displaying one at a time (unlike Composition widgets), because their targets can be scattered on a page.

10 INSERTING HTML, USING CC LIBRARIES, AND WORKING WITH WIDGETS

Lesson overview

In this lesson, you'll learn how to:

- Embed and edit HTML from other sites
- Work with the CC Libraries panel
- Work with the Library panel widgets

 This lesson takes approximately 30 minutes to complete. To download the project files for this lesson, log in or set up an account at peachpit.com. Enter the book's ISBN (9780134547275) or go directly to the book's product page to register. Once on the book's page, click the Register Your Product link. The book will show up in your list of registered products along with a link to the book's bonus content. Click the link to access the lesson files for the book. Store the files on your computer in a convenient location, as described in the "Getting Started" section of this book. Your Account page is also where you'll find any updates to the chapters or to the lesson files. If you are starting from scratch in this lesson, use the method described in the "Jumpstart" section in "Getting Started."

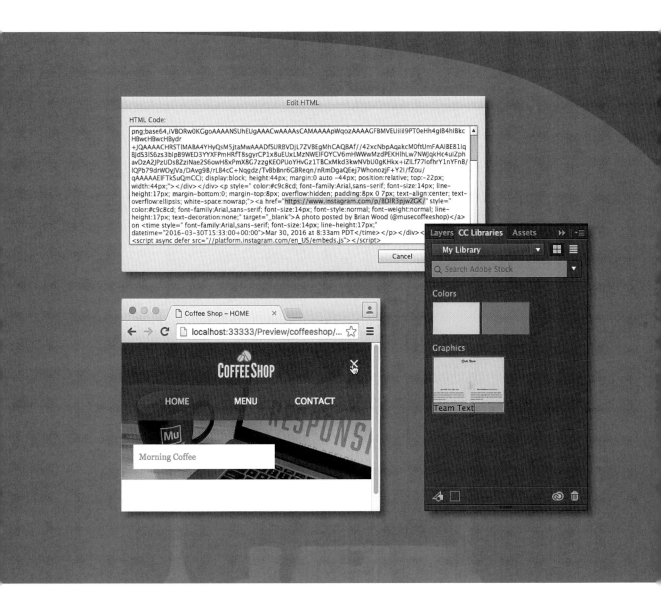

Extending the capabilities of Adobe Muse is easy with the ability to insert HTML from other sources, share content across sites and with others using the CC Libraries panel within Muse, and add widgets to your Muse site.

Embedding HTML

Note: If you are starting from scratch using the Jumpstart method described in the "Jumpstart" section of "Getting Started," your workspace may look different from the figures you see in this lesson.

In Adobe Muse, you can incorporate source code content generated by a number of different websites, such as a Google map, a Tumblr blog, Flickr content, or a form. You simply copy and paste the code from those sites, and then embed that HTML into your pages. Embedding HTML into a Muse page is like putting a window inside a page on your site that displays the content of a third-party site.

Embedded HTML is a great way for you to add complex information (such as maps, contact forms, and weather forecasts) as well as rich media (like videos, slideshows, and audio files) quickly and easily to your Muse site. If you want to insert social content, like Twitter Follow buttons or YouTube videos, for instance, don't forget that Muse has built-in Social widgets in the Widgets Library panel (Window > Widgets Library).

Although embedding HTML has limitless uses, in this lesson you'll focus on one that is related to the coffee shop website you're working on.

Inserting HTML

To practice inserting HTML content into your pages, in this exercise you'll insert an Instagram post into a page. So that you can see the Instagram post in your page, you'll need an Internet connection.

1   With the CoffeeShop.muse site open in Muse and Plan mode showing, double-click the HOME page thumbnail to open the page in Design mode.

2   Choose Window > Reset Panels.

3   In the Layers panel, select the Page layer. Click the Layers panel tab to collapse it.

4   Click in the breakpoint at 1200 to ensure that the page is previewing at that size, if necessary.

5   Choose View > Fit Page In Window.

Note: You may not see as much white space above the images and that's okay.

6   Drag across the coffee bean image and the coffee cup image just above the footer to select both. Choose Object > Group.

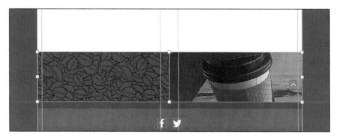

Grouping content ensures that all of the grouped content stays together and moves as a single object if the page content above it grows or shrinks in size.

7 Choose File > Place. Navigate to the Lessons > Text folder and select the Instagram.txt (or Instagram) file. Click Open. Click to place the text *off the right side of the page* in the gray area.

Next, you'll copy the HTML from the text you just placed, then you'll insert the HTML into the HOME page using the Insert HTML command (Object > Insert HTML). You can also paste the HTML content directly into the page in Design mode. In most cases, Muse detects HTML source tags and will automatically paste the code as HTML into the page.

8 Select the Text tool and insert the cursor into the placed text. Press Cmd+A (Ctrl+A) to select all of the text. Choose Edit > Copy.

9 Choose Object > Insert HTML. In the Edit HTML dialog box, delete the sentence "Insert your HTML here." Right-click in the Edit HTML dialog box and choose Paste.

When you insert HTML into Muse, the live content will appear in Design mode in most cases, but it typically won't be interactive until you preview the page.

10 Click OK. The Instagram post appears on the page.

11 With the Selection tool (🔧), drag the Instagram post content so the left edge snaps into the left edge of the righthand column. See the following figure.

When you hover over embedded HTML content that isn't selected, the words "Embedded HTML" appear in a tooltip next to your cursor. If the embedded HTML is selected, "Embedded HTML" appears in the Selection Indicator in the Control panel.

Note: The code you are using was copied from an Instagram post. There are a lot of ways to get Instagram content and other social content like this into your pages, including using 3rd party Muse widgets found here: http://resources.muse.adobe.com/collections/widgets.

Note: Your Instagram content may look a bit different and that's okay. The post on the Instagram site may be updated after this book is published.

▶ **Tip:** Embedded HTML can also be dragged or pasted into widgets like a Composition widget or Accordion widget, for instance.

12 With the Embedded HTML content selected, press and hold the Shift key, then drag the lower right bounding point down and to the right to make the Embedded HTML content bigger. Drag until you see a width of approximately 345 pixels. Release the mouse button and then the key.

Editing the embedded HTML

After you embed the HTML content, you can either delete the object on the page to delete the HTML content, or you can edit the HTML if you want to make changes or replace it. You'll make some changes to the embedded HTML next.

► **Tip:** You can right-click in the HTML Code dialog box and choose commands like Select All or Paste.

1 Right-click the Embedded HTML content on the page, and choose Edit HTML. You will change the Instagram post by editing a little bit of the code. Find this code toward the end of the code: "https://www.instagram.com/p/ **BDlRPjwQZFE**/" Replace it with this code: "https://www.instagram.com/p/ **BDlR3pjwZGK**/"

► **Tip:** If you are comfortable editing code, you can also change embedded HTML objects by editing the source code in the HTML dialog box. Some changes, like updating the height or width of the embedded HTML object, might be achieved by simply making the change in the HTML dialog box.

2 Click OK.

After a few seconds, the embedded HTML should update to show a new Instagram post. If the Instagram content doesn't show again, possibly because of an error, simply copy all of the code off the right edge of the page again, right-click the Instagram content on the page and choose Edit HTML. Replace the code in the dialog and click OK.

3 With the Selection tool (⬆), select the text you placed off the right edge of the page and delete it.

Up to this point, you've been checking the design content you add across the screen sizes once it is in place at the breakpoint at 1200. In this case, you are going to add more content to the HOME page in the next section, so you'll wait until all content is in place to preview it across screen sizes (this is best practice). That way, with all content in place, you can see how it interacts at different screen sizes.

4 Choose File > Save Site.

Note: If the Instagram content overlaps the images beneath it, you can select one of the images beneath the Instagram content and drag the Vertical Move Handle down so it no longer overlaps.

Working with Creative Cloud Libraries

Creative Cloud Libraries are an easy way to create and share stored content such as graphics, colors, Adobe Stock assets, Creative Cloud Market assets, and more between Adobe Muse, Adobe Photoshop CC, Adobe Illustrator CC, Adobe InDesign CC, and certain Adobe mobile apps.

Creative Cloud Libraries connect to your Creative Profile, putting the creative assets you have saved at your fingertips. When you create content in Muse or other Creative Cloud apps, and save it to a Library, that asset is available to use in any Muse site. Those assets are automatically synced and up to date and can be shared with any Creative Cloud account.

Note: In order to use Creative Cloud Libraries, you will need to be signed in with your Adobe ID and have an Internet connection.

In this section, you'll explore Creative Cloud Libraries in Muse.

Saving color to Creative Cloud Libraries

The first thing you'll learn about is how to work with the CC Libraries panel (Window > CC Libraries) in Muse and add assets to it. This is a great way to capture content you can reuse repeatedly across any site.

1 With the HOME page still open, choose View > Fit Page In Window.

Next, you'll open another site that contains design content that you will capture to use in the CoffeeShop.muse site.

2 Choose File > Open Site. Navigate to the Lessons > Lesson10 folder and select the Library_Content.muse site file. Click Open.

Note: If you see a warning dialog, click OK to update the asset.

3 Double-click the Home page thumbnail in Plan mode to open the Home page in Design mode.

4 Choose View > Fit Page In Window.

Note: The content you see in your CC Libraries panel may be different and that's okay.

5 Choose Window > CC Libraries to open the CC Libraries panel. Drag the bottom edge of the panel down so you can see more of the panel contents.

By default, you have one library to work with called "My Library." You can add your design assets to the default library, or you can create an unlimited number of Libraries—maybe to save assets according to clients or projects.

6 Click to select the orange shape at the top of the page, in the header.

▶ **Tip:** You can double-click a saved color in the CC Libraries panel to edit it using the Color Picker dialog box.

7 In the CC Libraries panel, click the Add Fill Color button to save the color.

If artwork has a fill, including selected text, the Add Fill Color option at the bottom of the CC Libraries panel will reflect the fill color of the selection.

Note: The colors you capture in the CC Libraries panel will be available no matter what site is open. As a matter of fact, if you open the CC Libraries panel in InDesign, the Libraries panel in Illustrator, or the Libraries panel in Photoshop, you will be able to apply this same color to artwork in those applications.

8 Click the yellow shape in the background and click the Add Fill Color button at the bottom of the CC Libraries panel to add that color to the library as well.

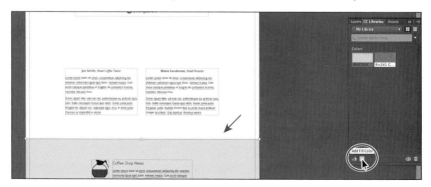

Saving graphics to Creative Cloud Libraries

You can create graphic assets in Muse or other Creative Cloud apps, save those assets in a Creative Cloud Library, and use these graphics while creating websites in Adobe Muse. If you place graphics in Muse that were saved from Illustrator or Photoshop into a Creative Cloud Library, and those assets are then modified in the application in which they were created, Adobe Muse indicates that you need to synchronize the outdated assets. You can view the out-of-sync assets, and update them through the Assets panel in Adobe Muse.

Next you'll save a placed graphic and text in a library in the CC Libraries panel.

1   Click to select the "Our Team" text. A group of objects will be selected. Drag the selected artwork into the CC Libraries panel. When a plus sign (+) and a name (such as "Artwork 1") appears, release the mouse button to add the graphic.

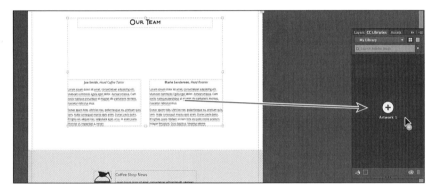

You can also select artwork and click the Add Graphic button () at the bottom of the CC Libraries panel. The assets you store as a graphic in a Creative Cloud Library retain their original form, whether that's text, raster or vector. So the group you just dragged into the CC Libraries panel is still a group of text frames that can later be edited when you drag them onto a page.

As you save assets in the CC Libraries panel, notice how they are organized by asset type. You can change the appearance of the items (icons or list) by clicking the buttons in the upper-right corner of the CC Libraries panel.

2   Position the pointer over the new asset in the CC Libraries panel, most likely named "Artwork 1." Double-click the "Artwork 1" name, and change it to **Team Text**. Press Enter or Return to accept the name change.

3 Click to select the coffee pot icon on the page, which is a placed and linked SVG file. The icon is grouped with a text frame. Click the Add Graphic button (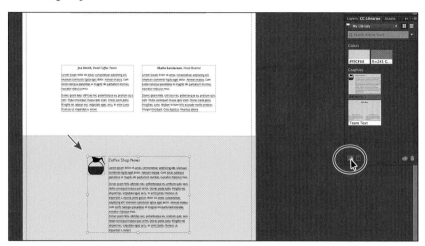) at the bottom of the CC Libraries panel to add the graphic and text that is a part of the same group.

▶ **Tip:** You can share your Library with others by choosing the Library you want to share in the CC Libraries panel and then choosing Share Link from the panel menu (≡).

4 Position the pointer over the new asset in the CC Libraries panel, most likely named "Artwork 1." Double-click the "Artwork 1" name, and change it to **Home Text**. Press Enter or Return to accept the name change.

5 Choose File > Close Site to close the Library_Content.muse site file and return to the HOME page of the CoffeeShop.muse site. Don't save the file if asked.

Notice that the CC Libraries panel still shows the assets in the default library named "My Library." The Libraries and their assets are available no matter which document is open in Muse.

Using Library assets

Now that you have some assets in the CC Libraries panel, once synced, those assets will be available to other Adobe applications and apps that support Libraries, as long as you are signed in with the same Creative Cloud account. Next, you'll use those assets in a few pages of the CoffeeShop.muse site.

1 With the HOME page in the CoffeeShop.muse site showing, make sure the Page layer is selected in the Layers panel.

2 Drag the "Home Text" asset from the CC Libraries panel onto an empty area of the page.

▶ **Tip:** You can also place a library graphic on a page by right-clicking the library item in the CC Libraries panel and choosing Place Copy and then clicking in the page.

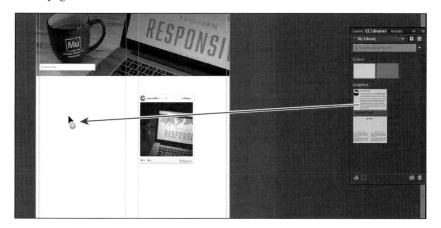

3 Once on the page, drag the group into the left column. Align its top edge with the Instagram content on the page. A horizontal Smart Guide will appear, helping you align the content. Leave the group selected.

4 Click once more on the text frame within the group to select it. Drag the right, middle point to the right so it snaps to the right edge of the column.

5 Open the Paragraph Styles panel (Window > Paragraph Styles) and select the Body style to apply it to the text.

● **Note:** If a plus (+) appears next to the Body style name in the Paragraph Styles panel, click the Clear Style Overrides button (⬛) to remove local formatting.

6 Press Command+J (Ctrl+J) and type **contact** in the Go To Page dialog box. When CONTACT appears in the Page field, click OK.

7 With the CONTACT page showing, make sure the Page layer is selected in the Layers panel.

8 Choose View > Fit Page In Window.

9 Click in the breakpoint at 1200 to ensure that the page is previewing at that size, if necessary.

● **Note:** The ΔY means the *change* in the Y value (the distance from the top edge of the page area).

10 Click the form on the page to select it. Drag the Vertical Move Handle down to move the form and the Google map down to make room for some text you are about to add to the page above that content. Stop dragging when you see a ΔY value of approximately 200 pixels in the measurement label next to the pointer.

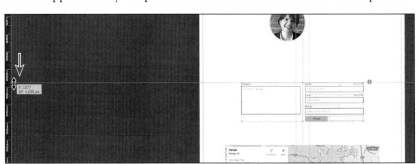

● **Note:** To apply a color in the CC Libraries panel to content, select content on a page in Muse and click the color in the CC Libraries panel.

11 Open the CC Libraries panel and drag the "Team Text" asset from the CC Libraries panel onto an empty area of the page.

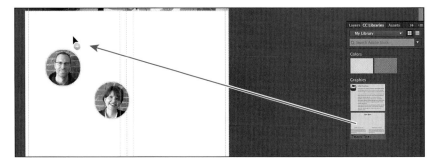

12 With the library content on the page, choose Object > Send To Back to place it behind everything on the Page layer.

The group you dragged from the CC Libraries panel is still editable text. You could apply the Body style to the body text and change the other text to match text already found in your pages.

13 Drag *all* of the content around on the page to arrange it like the figure. You may need to select the form and drag the Vertical Move Handle down to move the form and all content beneath it down further to make more room.

14 Click to select the Our Team text group, if necessary. Choose Object > Ungroup.

15 Choose File > Save Site.

Checking the CONTACT page content across screen sizes

Like everything else you place on your fluid width pages in Muse, there is no guarantee that it will look good across all screen sizes. That is why you need to preview the content in Muse across screen sizes. In the previous lesson, on the CONTACT page you already set a breakpoint at 800 pixels and repositioned the form and map. That content will most likely need to be fixed again, as you'll see.

● **Note:** I'm having you fix the layout of previous content on purpose. If there's one thing to remember about responsive web design in Muse, it's this: it's easier to get all of the content on the page, and THEN check the page content across different screen sizes. I did it this way because sometimes you'll add content to a page later that you never planned for. That's why it's often best to see a situation like this in a learning environment first.

1 With the CONTACT page showing, ensure that the page is previewing at 1200 pixels by clicking the breakpoint at 1200, if necessary.

2 Choose View > Fit Page In Window, if necessary.

3 Click away from the content in a blank area to deselect all.

4 With the Selection tool, click the text frame with the "Our Team" text in it. Choose Stretch To Browser Width from the Resize menu in the Control panel.

● **Note:** I chose to stretch this object because it is already centered and there is not a lot of text. The text will fit nicely on almost any size screen.

5   Drag across the two images *and* the text frames below the "Our Team" heading to select all four objects. Click the center box (⊡) in the Pin option (called Pin To Center) in the Control panel above the page. This way the content always stays pinned to the center of the page. Leave this content selected.

It will take a little time to figure out how content that needs to be pinned should be initially pinned (left, center, or right). It's a good idea to try a pin setting and preview the pinned content in other screen sizes.

6   With the content (images and text) still selected, choose Object > Copy Size And Position To > All Breakpoints.

The Copy Size And Position To command is really important when it comes to fluid width layouts. Remember that changes you make to content after the fact will only affect the breakpoint you are viewing the page in.

7   Click in the breakpoint at 800 pixels and you'll see that the layout needs to be fixed. Select the form, which is probably overlapping the text and images above it. Drag the Vertical Move Handle down to make more space.

8 Select the two text frames *below* the images of Joe and Marie by dragging across them. Making sure the Constrain Width And Height Proportionally is off (⬚), change the Width in the Control panel or Transform panel (Window > Transform) to **300** pixels.

9 Deselect everything by choosing Edit > Deselect All. Drag the text frames and images (Joe and Marie) as in the following figure. Align each image (Joe and Marie) and the text beneath into the middle of the column it's in. Smart Guides will help you align objects to each other and the columns.

Note: As you drag content, you may find that with all of the content on the page, the content is attempting to snap to everything. You can temporarily disable Smart Guides (View > Smart Guides) and use the Align panel (Window > Align) to align everything.

Right now, at this page width, the text and images look good. When you view this page in a smaller screen size the text will eventually need to be in one column instead of two columns.

10 Click the arrow in the Breakpoint bar to the left of the breakpoint at 800 to jump to that breakpoint. Remember, that arrow represents a master page breakpoint. Click the plus (+) in the Breakpoint bar to add a new breakpoint at 700 pixels.

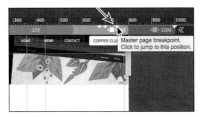 

Note: You will most likely need to move the form and Google map down the page again using the Vertical Move Handle. This is ultimately good practice to see how you need to adjust your layout across the different screen sizes.

11 Drag the content in the page as in the following figure. You'll want to make the text frames wider so they look a bit better as well.

Checking the HOME page content across screen sizes

Next, you'll fix the design content on the HOME page.

1 Click the HOME page tab at the top of the Document window to show the HOME page again. Ensure that the page is previewing at 1200 pixels by clicking in the breakpoint at 1200, if necessary.

2 Choose View > Fit Page In Window, if necessary.

3 Click to select the Instagram content on the page. Choose Object > Hide In Other Breakpoints.

The Instagram content will show on the page with a width greater than 700 pixels. At 700 pixels and narrower, the Instagram content will be hidden.

4 Drag the scrubber to the left to preview the content on the page. When you drag the scrubber far enough (at around the 700 pixel breakpoint), the content will become too narrow and a large area of white space my appear above.

You should see that the coffee pot icon and text group, as well as the Instagram content, are simply resizing in place. You didn't pin it so that it could do this.

5 Click in the breakpoint at 700 pixels in the Breakpoint bar to preview the page at that width.

6 Drag all of the content into position as in the following figure (including the images you previously grouped together). You may want to resize the text frame that is grouped with the coffee pot icon. Don't forget, you can click twice on the text frame to select the group first, and then select the text frame.

● **Note:** Make sure the back to top button is still above the footer guide. I had to reposition it again, you may not have to.

Your page most likely will have a large gap between the coffee pot icon group and the images you previously grouped above the footer. Most of the time this is because of the content resizing and shifting on different breakpoints.

7 Click in the breakpoint at 600 to preview the page at that size. Once again, you will most likely need to reposition and possibly resize content to look good.

Your content may look different from what you see in the following figure. That's okay. As long as you adjust the layout to look good.

● **Note:** Make sure to drag the scrubber further to the left. You may need to drag the coffee bean image down further at the 600 pixel breakpoint to allow for the text frame to expand vertically.

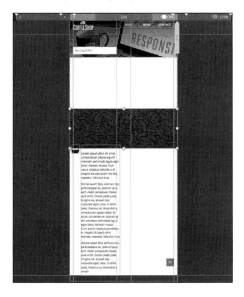

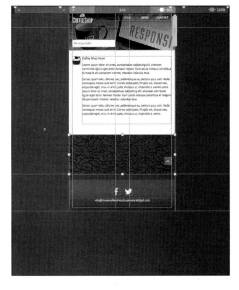

Working with the Library panel

The Library panel (Window > Library) in Muse offers a convenient way to store and manage common page elements. You can add items to the Library so that you can quickly access them and add the content to pages in your site. The Library can contain many types of elements, including logos, site images, color swatches, guides, customized widgets, embedded HTML, and paragraph, character, and graphic styles. The Library panel is different from the CC Libraries panel in that the content stored within the Library panel is not synced using CreativeSync and is not accessible in other Adobe applications and apps.

Accessing Muse widgets

From the Library panel, you can access a growing library of widgets found on the Adobe Muse Widget Directory website (http://resources.muse.adobe.com/collections/widgets). On that site, you can search for, discover, and download content to use in your Muse projects. Widgets you store in the Library panel can be used as a way to extend Muse and add other functionality. You can even upload your own libraries to either share for free or sell on the site.

In this section, you will download a Muse mobile menu widget. You will then add it to the Home-master page, in place of the existing menu.

1   Press Command+J (Ctrl+J) and type **home-master** in the Go To Page dialog box. When Home-master appears in the Page field, click OK.

2   Choose View > Fit Page In Window.

3   Click in the breakpoint at 1200 to ensure that the page is previewing at that size, if necessary.

4   Open the Library panel by choosing Window > Library.

● **Note:** We are simply using the Library panel as a way to access the http://resources.muse.adobe.com/collections/widgets website.

5   Click the word "online" in the text, "Find more library items online" that appears at the top of the panel to visit the Adobe Muse Widget Directory website in your default browser.

6   With the resources.muse.adobe.com website open in a browser, find the widget called "Mobile Menus" and click on it.

● **Note:** If you do not have an internet connection, the menu file you need to complete this part of the lesson is called "Mu_Resp_Menus.muse" and is located in the Lessons > Lesson10 folder.

If you are having trouble finding it, you can search the site for "mobile menu" to find the widget.

7   On the next page, click Get This Widget to download the .muse file you will need in this section. Close the browser, if you like, and return to Muse.

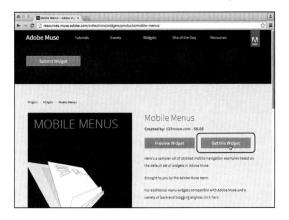

Note: The file you download may be a .zip file or similar. If that is the case, then unzip the file you download and open the .muse file in Muse. You you can also just open the "Mu_Resp_Menus.muse" site file in the Lessons > Lesson10 folder.

8   Back in Muse, choose File > Open Site. Locate the Mu_Resp_Menus.muse file that you downloaded to your machine and click Open.

If you see warning messages, you can ignore them by clicking OK.

Adding the mobile menu to your page

In the Mu_Resp_Menus.muse file, there are a series of pages. On each page is a version of a mobile menu. If you were to preview this site in a browser or within Muse Preview mode, you could preview each. For the purposes of this book, you will use the menu called "01 ham push."

Note: If you don't see that page name, you can open the "Mu_Resp_Menus.muse" site file in the Lessons > Lesson10 folder.

This menu is intended for use on smaller screens, so you will copy the menu from Mu_Resp_Menus.muse then paste it on the Home-master page in the CoffeeShop site at a smaller screen size. The existing menu will also need to be hidden.

1 With the Mu_Resp_Menus.muse site file open in Muse and Plan mode showing, double-click the "01 ham push" page thumbnail to open the page.

2 Position the pointer over the gray area at the top of the page. When the word "Accordion" appears next to the pointer in a tooltip, click to select the mobile menu.

▶ **Tip:** To see how the menu is built, check out the video titled "Mobile Menu Creation" that is a part of the Web Edition. For more information, see the "Web Edition" section of Getting Started at the beginning of the book.

The menu is inside of an Accordion widget. An Accordion widget has a trigger (called a "label"), and a target (called the "content area"), similar to a Composition widget. The label is the gray bar across the top with the X on the right end. The mobile menu is in the content area. When you click (tap) the label, the content area slides open, revealing the menu.

3 Choose Edit > Copy.

You can close the Mu_Resp_Menus.muse site if you would like since you won't be needing it again. I closed the site file without saving.

4 Click the Home-master tab at the top of the Document window to return to that page, if necessary.

Now you need to view the page at a smaller screen size, hide the existing menu, and paste the new one in.

5 Click in the breakpoint at 550 pixels to preview the page at that width.

6 With the Selection tool selected, click to select the menu already on the page. Choose Object > Hide In Breakpoint.

The mobile menu you will paste from the Mu_Resp_Menus.muse file already has a menu in place. Also, if you place the menu currently on the page in the mobile menu, eventually it will be hidden on the other breakpoints, so you won't have a menu at larger screen sizes.

▶ **Tip:** The icons ✕ and ☰ you will see in the mobile menu are background images in the different states of the Accordion widget label.

7 Choose Edit > Paste In Place.

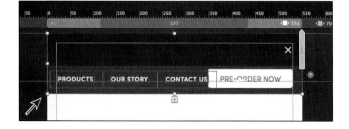

Did you remember layers? In this case, when you selected the menu in the header the Header layer became selected. When you pasted the mobile menu it was put on the selected layer (Header). Second, did you see the command Edit > Paste And Create Breakpoints? That command can be very useful if copying content from one page to another (in the same site or different sites). Any breakpoints associated with the content are also copied into the page.

8 Choose Object > Send To Back so the menu is behind the logo.

9 Choose Object > Hide In Other Breakpoints and leave the content selected.

When working with fluid width pages and breakpoints, ensuring that this type of content only shows in the breakpoints you need is important. Otherwise, in the case of this mobile menu, it would be showing on the desktop size screen.

10 Choose File > Save Site.

Making menu changes

With the mobile menu in place, you will need to make some changes to it. For instance, the menu you just pasted is a "manual" menu, which means it does not reflect the pages in your site.

1 Click twice on the PRE-ORDER NOW button to select it. Press Backspace or Delete to delete the button.

● **Note:** The figure shows the PRE-ORDER NOW button selected, right before deleting it.

2 Click to select the menu. Click the blue options button to show the Options menu. Choose Top Level Pages from the Menu Type menu, that way the menu shows the pages in your site. Choose Uniform Size from the Item Size Menu.

3 With the menu still selected, drag the right, middle bounding point to the right to make the menu wider. Stop when you see a Width value of *approximately* 300 pixels in the measurement label next to the pointer.

4 Drag the menu into the horizontal center of the content area (an arrow is pointing to the center in the following figure).

● **Note:** In this case, choosing None from the Resize menu means the menu will not change width on different screen sizes.

5 Choose None from the Resize menu in the Control panel, so it stays the same width. Click the center box (⊡) in the Pin option (called Pin To Center) in the Control panel.

● **Note:** When you preview the site at a smaller screen size, when the mobile menu shows, you'll notice that the menu item states don't match the appearance of the menu you first added to the pages back in Lesson 3. Feel free to edit the appearance of the menu item states in the States panel right now.

6 With the menu still selected, click one of the menu items to select it. Change the Font to Lucida Sans in the Text panel, so it more closely matches the original menu you created.

7 Choose Edit > Deselect All.

Editing the appearance of the mobile menu

Next, you'll make some changes to the general appearance of the Accordion widget that the menu is in.

1   Position the pointer anywhere over the gray area of the menu area. When you see the word "Accordion" next to the pointer, click to select it. Position the pointer in the gray area in the top half of the mobile menu. When you see the word "Label," click.

 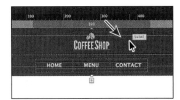 

The background color of the menu area will change. This represents the "Normal" state of the Label in the Accordion widget.

2   Change the Fill color to the Black swatch in the Control panel.

3   Click the Normal link on the left end of the Control panel to reveal the States panel. Select the Active link.

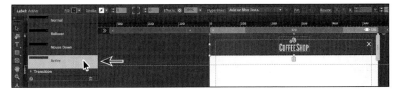

4   Change the Fill color to the FooterStroke swatch in the Control panel. Press the Escape key to hide the Color Picker, if necessary.

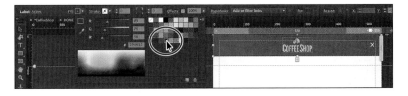

▶ **Tip:** You can also add a transition to the normal and active states in the States panel so that the color will fade between the states when a user clicks on the label of the Accordion widget.

5   Click the brown Label area at the top of the accordion to show the menu. Position the pointer over the area that the menu is in and click once to select it.

6 Click the Active link in the upper-left corner of the Control panel to show the States panel again. Select the Normal state and change the Fill color to the FooterStroke swatch in the Control panel.

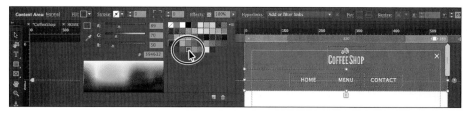

7 Click the Normal link in the upper-left corner of the Control panel. In the States panel that appears, click each of the remaining states (Rollover, Mouse Down, and Active) to ensure that they all look like the Normal state.

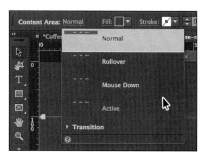

● **Note:** However you leave the mobile menu (opened or closed) is how users will first see it.

8 Click the brown Label area at the top of the accordion to hide the menu.

9 Choose File > Save Site.

10 Choose File > Preview Site In Browser.

● **Note:** You may see a warning dialog box discussing fonts. Click OK.

11 In your default browser, drag the corner or edge of the browser window to make the browser narrower (if viewing on desktop). You will see the mobile menu appear at a small enough browser window width.

● **Note:** If you visit the MENU or CONTACT pages, you will see the transparent black bar behind the new mobile menu. As a bit of practice, you can hide it. Open the Internal-master page in Muse. Create a breakpoint at 550 pixels and hide the transparent black bar in that breakpoint *only*.

12 Close the browser and return to Muse.

13 Close all open files except for the CoffeeShop.muse site file in Plan mode.

Review questions

1 How can you embed HTML content in your pages?

2 What content can be saved in a library in the CC Libraries panel?

3 Describe how to add a graphic to a library in the CC Libraries panel?

4 What advantages are there in saving content in the CC Libraries panel?

5 What is a Muse widget?

Review answers

1 You can insert HTML source code generated by a third-party website by copying the source code from the original website, choosing Object > Insert HTML, pasting the code into the dialog box that appears, and clicking OK. You can also paste the HTML content directly into a page in Design mode.

2 In Adobe Muse, you can save colors and graphics in a library in the CC Libraries panel.

3 You can drag artwork into the CC Libraries panel or select artwork and click the Add Graphic button () at the bottom of the CC Libraries panel. The assets you store as a graphic in a Creative Cloud Library retain their original form, whether that's text, raster or vector.

4 Creative Cloud Libraries are an easy way to create and share stored content such as graphics, colors, Adobe Stock assets, Creative Cloud Market assets, and more within sites in Muse or between Adobe Muse, Adobe Photoshop CC, Adobe Illustrator CC, Adobe InDesign CC, and certain Adobe mobile apps. If you place graphics in Muse saved in a Creative Cloud Library from Illustrator or Photoshop, for instance, and the original asset is modified, Adobe Muse indicates that you need to synchronize the outdated assets.

5 Muse widgets can be stored in the Library panel (Window > Library) and are used as a way to extend Muse and add other functionality. From the Library panel, you can access a growing library of widgets found on the Adobe Muse Widget Directory website (http://resources.muse.adobe.com/collections/widgets). On that site, you can search for, discover, and download libraries to use within your Muse projects.

11 PUBLISHING AND EXPORTING YOUR SITE

Lesson overview

In this lesson, you'll learn how to:

- Exclude pages from export

- Publish your site as a temporary site

- Publish changes

- Upgrade a temporary site to a paid site

- Publish your site to a host of your choice

- Export your site as HTML

- Collect Assets

- Work with In-Browser Editing

This lesson takes approximately 25 minutes to complete. To download the project files for this lesson, log in or set up an account at peachpit.com. Enter the book's ISBN (9780134547275) or go directly to the book's product page to register. Once on the book's page, click the Register Your Product link. The book will show up in your list of registered products along with a link to the book's bonus content. Click the link to access the lesson files for the book. Store the files on your computer in a convenient location, as described in the "Getting Started" section of this book. Your Account page is also where you'll find any updates to the chapters or to the lesson files. If you are starting from scratch in this lesson, use the method described in the "Jumpstart" section in "Getting Started."

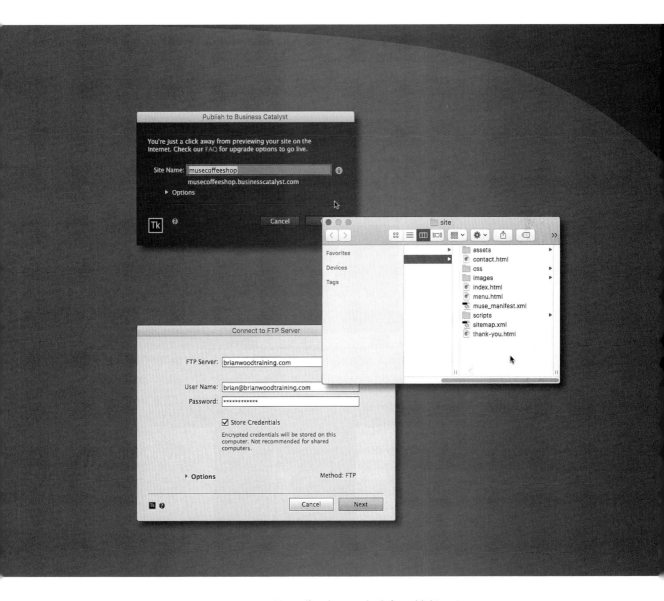

Muse offers three methods for publishing site
content: You can publish directly from Muse to
Adobe web hosting, publish to a third-party host,
or choose File > Export As HTML to create a local
copy of all the files for your website.

Understanding Adobe Muse publishing

Note: If you are starting from scratch using the Jumpstart method described in the "Jumpstart" section of "Getting Started," your workspace may look different from the figures you see in this lesson.

After you've finished designing your site, the next step is to publish the site or export the site content. If you want to publish the site for the world to see, you can publish directly to Adobe web hosting or to your own hosting provider from within Muse. If you plan on uploading the site to your host using a different FTP client, you want to keep a local copy of the site files, or you want to get the optimized content like images that Muse generates, you can choose File > Export As HTML.

Using any of these methods, Muse will generate HTML files, CSS, related script files, images, and other content necessary to make the site work in a browser. All of the .psd and .ai files in your Muse site will also be converted at this point to the best web format, depending on the image content. If you added alternate layouts to your site (you didn't need to since this was a fluid width layout, aka responsive web design, those will also be published or exported.

Excluding pages from export

When you publish your site or export it as HTML, Muse exports all of the pages in your site map, including those that you've excluded from the navigation like the EVENT page in the CoffeeShop.muse site. If you are experimenting with a design, have a page containing an old product, or have an outdated sales page, you may not want to export that page. To hold back pages that aren't necessary, you can exclude them from export, specifying them either from Plan or Design mode. If you stop a page from exporting, none of the assets unique to that page export either. Assets, such as images, which are common to the excluded page and other necessary pages, do export.

Note: If you have not already downloaded the project files for this lesson to your computer from your Account page, make sure to do so now. See "Getting Started" at the beginning of the book.

Although clearing your site map of extraneous pages as you work is the best practice, excluding pages at the end of the design process is simple and effective.

Note: You need to be careful when choosing which pages to exclude from export. Suppose you choose not to export a page that appears in a Menu widget. The text label displaying the excluded page's name will still appear in the dynamically generated menu item (the default setting) when the site is exported, but the page will not exist, so the link will be broken.

Next, you'll exclude the EVENT page from exporting when the site is published or exported, since it's not ready yet.

1 With the CoffeeShop.muse site open and Plan mode showing, right-click the
   EVENT page thumbnail and choose Export Page to deselect the option.

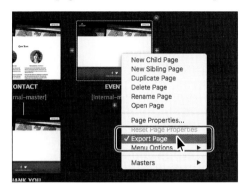

   When a check mark appears to the left of the Export Page command, the page
   will export when you either publish by choosing File > Upload To FTP Host
   or File > Publish To Business Catalyst, or export when you choose the File >
   Export As HTML command. The page thumbnail appears to be dimmed when
   it no longer will export with the rest of the site content.

2 Choose File > Save Site.

Publishing your site

With Muse, you can create and publish an unlimited number of temporary sites
using Adobe web hosting. Each temporary site you create is active for 30 days
and has a temporary URL, for example, http://my_site.businesscatalyst.com.
The "my_site" part of the URL is something you can customize. The site is live
on the web and can be visited via a web browser using the supplied URL, even
on different devices.

Publishing temporary sites is an easy way to upload in-progress sites to share
with your clients or to review the live sites in a browser and test them on various
screens and devices before showing them to your clients. As you work with your
clients through the design and approval process, you can choose either to update
the existing temporary site or to publish new temporary sites to compare several
iterations. Some clients prefer to visit links to preview several different designs at
once, so they can view them side by side during the approval process.

Tip: If a temporary
site you are designing
expires, you can
extend it by simply
opening the .muse file
and publishing the
site again. Using this
strategy, you can keep
working on a site and
incorporating client
feedback until the site
design is complete.

Publishing a temporary site

Next, you'll publish the CoffeeShop.muse site as a temporary site. Later, if you wish to continue hosting on Adobe hosting servers, a temporary site can be upgraded to a paid hosting site on Adobe hosting servers as well. Whether or not you are ultimately planning on hosting the site using Adobe web hosting, you can publish the site temporarily and test the site for free.

Note: You will most likely see that there are several missing assets. In the real world, you would click Cancel and fix this in the Assets panel. In this case, the missing assets are coming from the mobile menu widget, so for this instance, simply click OK.

1   With the CoffeeShop.muse site still open, choose File > Publish To Business Catalyst. If there are any missing fonts or issues with assets, a dialog box will appear indicating that you should fix the issue before proceeding. Click OK.

2   Click Next in the Connecting To Typekit dialog box.

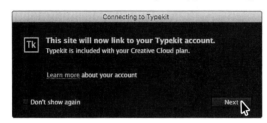

This dialog box indicates that the site uses Typekit fonts and the site will link to your Typekit account, which is included in your Creative Cloud subscription.

Tip: In the Publish To Business Catalyst dialog box, click the FAQ link to learn more about the publishing process.

3   In the Publish To Business Catalyst dialog box, enter a site name and leave the Publish To Business Catalyst dialog box open. You could type **Muse Coffee Shop**, and the suggested URL beneath the field will look something like "musecoffeeshop05.businesscatalyst.com." The 05 (or other number) indicates that the URL you entered was already taken by someone else.

Note: The site URL field in the Options section automatically removes any special characters and spaces that you enter in the Site Name field. It creates a suggested URL that will be used to access the live temporary site. You can edit the contents of the URL field to change the automatically generated URL, if desired.

When you publish this site as a temporary site for testing, the name you choose will be a part of the initial URL. Muse checks the starting part of the address ("musecoffeeshop," in this instance) to determine if it's valid (it doesn't contain unsupported characters, for instance) *and* if it's available. If the name is not available, the field will update with an alternate suggestion. You do not have to use that suggestion if you prefer to change the site name to another name that is not yet taken. This will be the temporary address at which you can view the site in a browser or send to your clients for reviewing the site. You can change the address to something permanent later if you upgrade the site to a paid site or use one of the hosting credits that are included with your Creative Cloud subscription.

4 Click the word Options to reveal more options and set the following:

- Publish To: **New Site** (the default setting)
- URL: Leave the URL unless you want to change it
- Data Center: **Automatic** (the default setting. This sets the location where the site will be hosted.)

Note: If your client lives in a different country, you can choose the Data Center closest to your client's location. The site will load and perform best in the location that corresponds with the Data Center you select. So if your client is viewing the site in Australia, you can choose the Australia Data Center option to ensure that the site looks best to them, even if you are located in the United States.

5 Click OK.

For each page, Muse now generates the HTML files, CSS, related script files, images, and other content that is necessary to make the site work in a browser. That content is then uploaded to the Adobe web hosting servers. Muse also converts any .psd and .ai files in your site to the best web format, depending on the image content. This may take a little while. When Muse completes its work, the temporary site is published to an Adobe hosting server. The updated site will also open in the default browser, unless there are publishing issues, such as a missing file.

Note: You may see a warning dialog box about a failure to generate the code. This could be due to missing Typekit fonts. Try opening the pages of the site in Muse before you publish.

6 Close the browser and go back to Muse, if necessary.

In the Publish To Business Catalyst dialog box, you'll see possible next steps like adding In-Browser Editing Users or assigning a custom domain name. Both of those actions will take you to an Admin Console for your newly published site in your default browser.

7 Click OK in the Publish To Business Catalyst dialog box to close it.

Now that the site has been published, you can share the domain name (mine is musecoffeeshop.businesscatalyst.com) with your clients to review by simply emailing them the domain name. A notification message is also sent to the email address associated with Publish With Account found in Muse preferences. The email message tells the recipient that a temporary website has been created and includes the URL and instructions for taking the site live.

After publishing your temporary site, you may forget the URL for the site. The following method is an easy way to help you remember the site domain name.

8 Click the Publish link in the upper-right corner of the Application window or choose File > Publish To Business Catalyst. If an Information dialog box appears, click OK to dismiss it.

9 Click Next in the Connecting To Typekit dialog box, if it appears.

10 Click the URL link (musecoffeeshop.businesscatalyst.com/index.html for me) to open the default browser on your machine and view the live site. You could also use a mobile device and type the URL in the device browser to view the site.

● **Note:** If you are working on a shared workstation with another person, you can change the publish account associated with Muse. Choose Adobe Muse CC > Preferences (Edit > Preferences), and select Switch Accounts from the Publish With Account menu. This will allow you to enter the username and password of an existing Adobe ID. Using this strategy, you can each use your own preferences. Whenever you sign into Muse on the computer, your preferences will be preserved.

11 Close the browser and return to Muse.

12 In the Publish To Business Catalyst dialog box click Cancel.

If you were to click OK, any changes you made to the site would be published.

Making changes and publishing again

After you publish your site, you can make changes in Muse, and then upload any changes you make, which overwrites existing files on the host server with the new content. In this exercise, you'll make a change to the CONTACT page in your site and publish the changed content.

1 In Plan mode, double-click the CONTACT page thumbnail to open that page in Design mode.

2 Choose View > Fit Page In Window, if necessary.

3 Click the breakpoint at 1200 to ensure that the page is previewing at that width.

4 Select the Text tool (**T**) and select the heading text "Our Team." Change the heading to **The CoffeeShop Team**.

▶ **Tip:** You could also copy and paste the "The CoffeeShop Team" heading and create another heading above the form. Maybe changing the text in the copy to "Contact Us." Just remember, whenever you add new content to a page, you need to preview the page in different screen sizes.

This simple text change will be mirrored in all of the breakpoints. You should probably drag the scrubber to preview the page at smaller screen sizes to make sure the text still fits horizontally and doesn't wrap.

5 Choose File > Save Site.

6 Click the Publish link in the upper-right corner of the Application window. If you see a warning dialog click OK.

7 If you see the Connecting To Typekit dialog box, click Next.

8 In the Publish To Business Catalyst dialog box, click the word Options. Notice that the Publish To menu currently shows the URL of the temporary site (musecoffeeshop.businesscatalyst.com in my case). That information is saved with the Muse file.

▶ **Tip:** You could also choose File > Publish To Business Catalyst or press Command+Option+P (Ctrl+Alt+P).

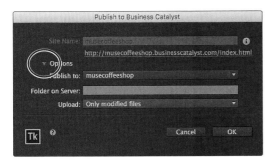

9 Click the Publish To menu. You can publish the site to a new site (to experiment with a new design without affecting the original testing site), or you could associate the files with another published site by selecting that site in the menu. Any other Muse sites that you have previously published are listed in the Publish To menu. You can overwrite them with the current file, *but choose carefully*! If you make a mistake, you'll have to open the other site's .muse file and publish it again to restore an existing site.

10 Click away from the Publish To menu without making a change, *within the Publish To Business Catalyst dialog box*, to hide the menu.

Notice in the Publish menu that there is now a Folder On Server option beneath the Publish To option. The Folder On Server option allows you to publish the site content to a subdirectory on the hosting server. This can be very useful for site content organization, for creating another section of your site from content in another .muse site file, or for creating a microsite for an event that has a URL named something like "mysite.com/conference."

You need to specify a folder name, and if the folder does not exist on the server, it will be created by Muse during the publish process. This is a more advanced option and will not be used by everyone.

11 Click the Upload menu to see that you can choose to upload all of the files or only those that have been modified. The default option of Only Modified Files is preferred if you are making changes.

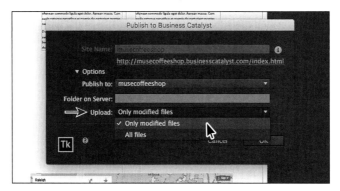

Publishing only the modified files will most certainly be faster because only the files that have been changed will be uploaded to the server. If you find that there are issues with the site, someone has made changes using In-Browser Editing that you want to overwrite (which you'll learn about later in this lesson), or you just want to upload all of the site content again, you would choose All Files from the Upload menu.

12 Click OK to publish just the modified files. The updated site will open in the default browser, unless there are publishing issues, such as a missing file.

13 Close the browser and return to Muse. In Muse, click OK to close the Publish To Business Catalyst dialog box.

By default, Muse publishes only the content in your site that has been changed. In this case, it publishes the CONTACT HTML page and any other files necessary, such as CSS and related scripts. If you add a new image or other asset, that new asset is converted to a web format, if necessary, and uploaded along with the page, replacing just those files on the server. If you select All Files in the Upload menu, Muse publishes all of the site content and replaces the files currently on the server.

14 Close the CONTACT page to return to Plan mode.

Upgrade a temporary site to a paid site ▇◀

To learn how to upgrade your temporary site to a paid site with Adobe hosting, check out the video titled "Upgrade a Temporary Site to a Paid Site" that is a part of the Web Edition. For more information, see the "Web Edition" section of Getting Started at the beginning of the book.

Uploading your site to a third-party host

With Adobe Muse, you can also upload a site you create in Muse to a third-party hosting service by choosing File > Upload To FTP Host. Before proceeding with this command to publish your site to a host of your choice, you need to have a hosting account set up with that host. After you create a hosting account, the host should supply you with information necessary to upload to its servers, such as a domain name (URL), FTP Host address, username, and password.

Next, you'll explore the process for uploading to a third-party host.

1 With your CoffeeShop.muse site file open in Muse, choose File > Upload To FTP Host. If you see a warning dialog box click OK.

2 Click Next in the Connecting To Typekit dialog box, if necessary.

> **Note:** You will need to set up a hosting account with a third-party hosting service before proceeding.

Note: If you click "Options," there a few more options you can set, such as different methods of FTP (SFTP, for instance), and mode. Leave these options alone unless you know that they need to be changed.

3 In the Connect To FTP Server dialog box, enter the required information and ensure that Store Credentials is selected to save the FTP information with the site.

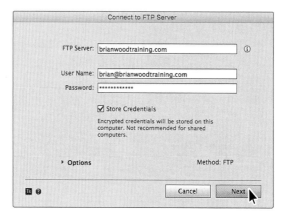

Tip: If your site has more than one URL associated with it, such as websitename.biz and websitename.com, you can click the plus (+) to the right of the Site URL to add any additional URLs.

Note: If you didn't select Store Credentials, a warning dialog box may appear.

If you are not sure of the FTP host, host directory, and login credentials required to access your hosting account, contact your hosting provider. In many cases, your provider sends the information via an email message when you first sign up. You also don't need to save the FTP credentials with Muse, but if you don't, Muse won't be able to automatically check for changes made using In-Browser Editing whenever a site file is open.

4 Click Next in the Connect To FTP Server dialog box.

5 In the Upload To FTP Host dialog box that appears after the FTP information is verified, enter the Site URL if it is not correct. The site URL is required because it is used to generate a sitemap.xml file. A site map represents the hierarchical structure of a web site and can be used for SEO (Search Engine Optimization) by some search engines.

You can publish to a specific folder on the server using the Folder On Server option. This can be a great way to publish a site or section of a site to a subfolder of the main site. Suppose that the main site URL is "mysite.com." If you publish a new Muse site (for instance) to a folder on the server (subfolder) and name that subfolder "clients," the URL for the new site would be "mysite.com/clients." That Muse site could be a microsite, such as an event site, that has a URL like mysite.com/conference2017. Publishing to a Host Directory can also be useful for organizing your site content and can have potential SEO benefits.

6 In the Upload To FTP Host dialog box, leave the Folder On Server field blank (unless you determine that you need one), and choose All Files from the Upload menu. I added a folder name. Click OK.

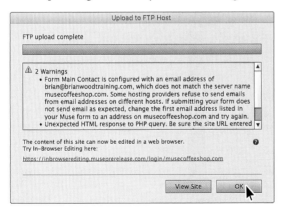

Note: In the figure a folder name was added.

If you entered a domain name that cannot be verified in regards to whether it's associated with the FTP server and folder, a warning dialog box will appear. If the warning dialog does appear, either click Fix and enter the correct domain or click Ignore and know that forms you create may not work properly and the sitemap.xml file that is generated may not help with SEO (Search Engine Optimization); however, the site files will be uploaded to the server, and the site will work.

Note: If you enter a folder name in the Upload To FTP Host dialog box and the folder doesn't exist, a dialog box will appear called FTP – Create Folder, indicating that the folder was not found and will be created at the root level of the server.

7   After uploading, the Upload To FTP Host dialog box will show any issues that Muse ran across when generating and uploading the files.

Pay attention to the warnings because they can impact the appearance and functionality of your site. You can click View Site to open the site in the browser. Know that Muse will attempt to launch the domain name you entered when uploading the site to your web hosting account.

8   Click OK in the Upload To FTP Host dialog box to close it.

If you stored the credentials when you first uploaded the site, once you upload to a 3rd party host, you can simply choose File > Upload To FTP Host or click the Publish button in the upper-right corner of the Application window. This uploads any changes without having to re-enter the FTP info for the hosting account.

Exporting your site as HTML

If you simply want to access the site code generated by Muse to edit in another application, such as Adobe Dreamweaver (which is not recommended, but your experience may vary depending on the site's layout and content), or you want to export a folder of conveniently sliced and optimized image files to use for other web purposes (newsletters, social media site updates, email signatures, mobile apps, and more), you can export the site as HTML. When you export, Muse generates the HTML, CSS, JavaScript, and web-friendly image files necessary to run the site.

Next, you'll export the CoffeeShop.muse site as HTML.

1   With the CoffeeShop.muse site open, choose File > Export As HTML. If you see a warning dialog click OK.

2   Click Next in the Connecting To Typekit dialog box, if necessary.

● **Note:** If you don't have a domain name for the site, you can enter a placeholder domain name. Know that the resulting sitemap.xml file should be discarded rather than uploaded if you do that.

3   In the Export As HTML dialog box, enter a domain name for the site. This URL is used in the sitemap.xml file that is generated for the site when it is exported.

4   Click the Location folder icon. In the dialog box that opens, create a new folder on your Desktop or choose an existing folder and then click Choose. Click OK.

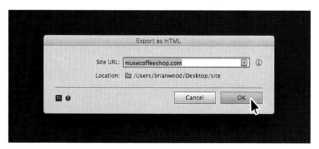

● **Note:** You may see a warning dialog box about a failure to generate the code. This could be due to missing Typekit fonts. Try opening the pages of the site in Muse before you export.

5   After Muse finishes exporting the site, the local site will most likely open in your default browser. Close the browser and return to Muse.

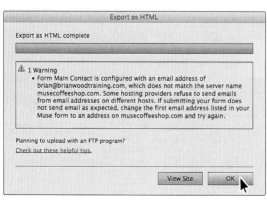

In the Export As HTML dialog box, you may see warnings. Pay attention to these warnings because they may affect the appearance and/or functionality of the site. Also, when you export HTML from Muse, the files that Muse generates cannot be opened in Muse. In other words, if you make any changes to the site in Muse, you will need to re-export the HTML and then re-upload the entire folder of site files to the host server (if you did that already).

6 Go to the folder on your desktop into which you exported the site content to see what Muse created.

7 Return to Muse and click OK to close the dialog box.

Collecting assets

In Muse you can also gather all original linked assets of your site so you can move a project, if necessary. The Collect All Assets command, found in the Assets panel (Window > Assets), copies all of the assets used in a site to a single location on your computer.

Next, you'll collect all of the assets used on the CoffeeShop.muse site.

1 With the CoffeeShop.muse site still open, and Plan mode showing, double-click the HOME page thumbnail to open it in Design mode.

2 Open the Assets panel (Window > Assets). Click the Collect All Assets button (⊞) at the bottom of the Assets panel. In the dialog box that appears, create a new folder on your Desktop or choose an existing folder and then click Choose.

The linked assets are copied and placed in the folder you chose. A Collection Summary dialog box will appear giving you a count of all assets collected. If any files were missing, they will not be collected. There may be a disparity in

▶ **Tip:** You can also collect specific assets you select in the Assets panel by right-clicking one of the selected assets and choosing either "Collect Asset" with one asset selected or "Collect Selected Assets" with more than one asset selected.

the number of files actually collected and the number of total files available. The backtotop_button.psd file is a single PSD, but appears more than once in the Assets panel because it is a button with states.

3 Click OK in the Collection Summary dialog box to close it.

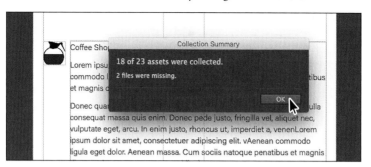

4 Go to the folder on your desktop that contains the assets that you collected to see what Muse created.

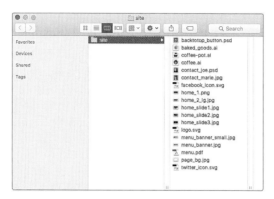

5 Return to Muse. Choose File > Close Site unless you plan on continuing to the In-Browser Editing section next (video).

There you have it. You did it! You just created a responsive website using Adobe Muse. Is there more you can (and possibly want) to add to your site? I'm sure. This book was meant to lay the groundwork for you to explore further. I'll leave it up to you to push your creative boundaries!

Work with In-Browser Editing ◼◀

To learn about In-Browser Editing, check out the video titled "In-Browser Editing" that is a part of the Web Edition. For more information, see the "Web Edition" section of Getting Started at the beginning of the book.

Review questions

1 Describe the benefits of excluding pages from exporting.

2 Using the Muse workspace, where can you publish your site to?

3 What does the term "temporary site" mean?

4 Name a reason why you might export as HTML.

5 What is collected when you run the Collect Assets command?

Review answers

1 Excluding pages from exporting in Muse will not publish or export the designated pages or the content that is unique to excluded pages (image files, etc.). This is useful when you're designing test pages or to hide pages that contain a product you are no longer selling, for instance.

2 From within Muse, you can publish to either Adobe web hosting by choosing File > Publish To Business Catalyst or by clicking the arrow to the right of the Publish link in the upper-right corner of the Application window and choosing Business Catalyst. You can also publish the site to a third-party host of your choice by choosing File > Upload To FTP Host or by clicking the arrow to the right of the Publish link in the upper-right corner of the Application window and choosing FTP Host.

3 A temporary site is a site published from Muse using the Publish command (File > Publish To Business Catalyst) or by clicking the arrow to the right of the Publish link in the upper-right corner of the Application window and choosing Business Catalyst. It has a temporary URL (musecoffeeshop.businesscatalyst.com, for instance).

4 You might export as HTML if you plan on using a third-party hosting provider and you want to upload the site using your favorite FTP client. You can also export a site to repurpose the web optimized image files for social network sites, email newsletter campaigns, mobile applications, and more.

5 When you choose to collect assets in the Assets panel, any linked assets that are not missing for the current site are copied and the copies are placed in a folder you choose. You can collect all assets by clicking the Collect All Assets button (⊞) at the bottom of the Assets panel or select specific assets and right-click on one of them in the Assets panel to collect those selected assets.

INDEX

A

AATCs (Adobe Authorized Training Centers), 7
About this book, 1–7, 159
Accordion widgets, 165, 256, 318, 321
Active state, 83, 229–230
Adaptive (alternate) layouts, 158, 186
Add Or Filter Links menu, 220–221, 223–224, 236–237
Adobe Animate CC file (.oam), 151–153
Adobe Creative Cloud Learn, 7
Adobe Forums, 7
Adobe Illustrator (.ai) files, 127–129, 133–134
Alignment, 103
Alt fonts, 97
Alternate (adaptive) layouts, 158, 186
Alternative text, adding to images, 154
Anchor button, 243–244
Anchors, 242, 243–244
Angle, in Shadow effect, 216
Animate CC (.oam) file, Adobe, 151–153
Application bar, Design mode, 15
Application frame (Mac OS), 18
Aqua gap measurements, Smart Guides, 177, 277
Arranging content, 208–209
Assets panel, 21
Automatic Size, gradients, 205

B

Background images, 61–62, 207, 210–212
Basic Slideshow widget, 290–298
Bevel effects, 213
Blank layout, 160
Blank Slideshow widget, 290
Blur, in Shadow effect, 216

Bold attribute, text link styles, 229
Borders, 200–203, 250
Bottom of Browser guide, 57–58
Bottom of Page guide, 57
Breakpoint bar, 15, 18–20, 161–164
Breakpoint Properties dialog box, 163–164, 172, 176, 284
Breakpoints, 18–20, 161–163, 171–186
Brightness, 195, 197–198, 201
Browser(s), 10, 18–20, 29–30
Bulleted lists, 105–106, 119–120
Button widgets, 257
Buttons, 160, 232–242

C

Capitalization, editing paragraph styles, 111
Case of text, 105, 240
Character styles, 115–118
Child pages, 37, 40–43, 77
CMYK (Cyan, Magenta, Yellow, Black), print design, 12
Collect All Assets command, 337–338
Color
  background image, 206–208, 210–212
  editing page appearance, 62–63
  editing strokes, 200–203
  gradients, 203–205
  sampling, 198–199
  saving to CC Libraries, 305–306
  Shadow effect, 216
  swatch, 195, 197–199
  text, 80, 105
  text link styles, 229
  working with, 194–195
Color fill, 195–196, 203–205, 215
Color Picker, 195–198, 200–204
Column guides, 57

Columns, 34, 36, 160
Composition widgets
  across screen sizes, 270–271
  inserting/editing, 258–259
  responsive behavior of, 256
  working with target containers, 266–269
  working with triggers, 260–266
Connect To FTP Server dialog box, 334
Connecting To Typekit dialog box, 328, 330, 331, 333, 336
Constrain Width And Height Proportionally button, 133
Contact form widgets. *See* Form widgets
CONTACT page, 38–40, 68
Content
  adjusting opacity of, 214–215
  applying from one master page to another, 70
  arranging on page, 208–209
  assigning to footer, 206
  creating/sharing. *See* Creative Cloud Libraries
  footer, 190–193
  grouping/locking, 141–142
  inline, 140
  layout of, 165–170
  rotating, 143–144
  rounding corners on, 213–214
  for smaller screens, 160
  using layers for, 71–74
  wireframing web workflow, 11
  wrapping text around, 139–141
Content Grabber, 138
Content tab, Site Properties, 36, 228
Control panel, 17–18
Copy/Paste
  anchors, 243
  images, 128–129, 131, 206
  text, 118